The U.S.S.R. after 50 Years

Promise and Reality

The U.S.S.R. after 50 Years

RANDOLPH L. BRAHAM

SAMUEL HENDEL

WILLIAM M. MANDEL

ALFRED G. MEYER

Promise and Reality

WRIGHT MILLER

URI RA'ANAN

FREDERICK L. SCHUMAN

PETER WILES

BERTRAM D. WOLFE

Edited by Samuel Hendel
and Randolph L. Braham

THE CITY COLLEGE OF THE CITY UNIVERSITY OF NEW YORK

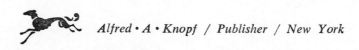 *Alfred · A · Knopf* / *Publisher* / *New York*

Preface

Envisioned by some as the dawn of a new, ideal era and identified by others as the beginning of an all-pervasive and destructive despotism, the Bolshevik Revolution undoubtedly is a major landmark in the history of mankind. The Revolution and the social experiments undertaken in its wake have continued to fascinate both partisans and opponents of the Soviet regime.

Those fired by the idealism of the Marxist vision believed that it would usher in a new, socialist system which, based on the common ownership of the means of production and concerned with the satisfaction of needs rather than the pursuit of profit, would bring an end to the evils inherent in and engendered by an acquisitive and exploitive capitalist society. They further envisioned that after a protracted period of time, in the course of which there would be a growth of productive forces, elimination of class conflict, and education of the people in communal living, a higher, communist phase—a stateless, classless society—would emerge. Such a society, built upon voluntary cooperation and eschewing all organized force, would lend dignity to human labor, allow for the full development of the individual, provide true freedom, and proclaim the principle of genuine equality: "From each according to his ability, to each according to his needs."

While exuberant expectations have been marred by the realities of Soviet life, it cannot be denied that in half a century the Soviet Union has been transformed—at a rate rarely matched in history—from a relatively backward, illiterate and predominantly agricultural country into one of the two most powerful industrial nations in the world. This achievement, to be sure, in the judgment of many scholars, has been attained at a tremendous human and material cost. In the words of one socialist but anti-Bolshevik philosopher, Morris Raphael Cohen, "the program of civil war, dictatorship and the illiberal or fanatically intolerant spirit" ushered in by the Bolshevik Revolution was bound to

v

bring and brought "more miseries than those that the Communists seek to remove."

Now fifty years after the Revolution—one of the most world-shaking in the annals of human history and pregnant with continuing consequences for mankind—it is appropriate to consider and evaluate the promise and the reality; the achievements, failures and challenges of the Soviet system, particularly in light of the Marxist vision that influenced and inspired it. This is the purpose of our book. In the attempt to achieve this purpose, we present essays by distinguished Sovietologists dealing with the fifty-year period of Soviet development and experience. Inevitably, while there is considerable agreement among them, or some of them, on many aspects of Soviet society and Soviet policy, there are some sharply divergent evaluations and opinions. This is especially true of two particularly controversial sections, "Reflections on the Soviet System" and "The U.S.S.R. in World Affairs," for each of which two contributions were specifically invited.

In general, this volume is an attempt to present in broad perspective a picture of the fascinating, if often chaotic, development of the U.S.S.R. It is hoped that it will prove of interest not only to specialists in Soviet affairs and to the college community generally but also to readers with little experience in the esoterics of Marxism-Leninism and little previous knowledge of the Soviet Union.

We are, of course, tremendously indebted to the authors who, drawing on their accumulation of many years of close study of the U.S.S.R., have contributed their knowledge and insight to this volume. We owe thanks, too, to the representatives of Alfred A. Knopf with whom it was a pleasure to work: to Dr. Clifford Mortimer Crist for first suggesting the project and stimulating our interest in it; to Miss Anne D. Murphy for her clarity of mind and judgment, which proved helpful at every stage and in every phase of our undertaking; and to Mrs. Eve Shapinsky for her painstaking supervision of the complicated task of editing the manuscript. Finally, we are grateful to our wives—Clara Hendel and Elizabeth Braham—for their understanding and encouragement.

Samuel Hendel

New York, N. Y., June 1967   Randolph L. Braham

Contents

The U.S.S.R. after 50 Years

Promise and Reality

I

The U.S.S.R. after Fifty Years:
An Overview

by SAMUEL HENDEL

Writing of governments in general more than two thousand years ago, Aristotle maintained that in the preceding millennia, institutions, "if they were good, would certainly not have been unknown; for almost everything has been found out." He urged, accordingly, that the wisdom of the ages not be lightly discarded. The bolshevik revolution, basing itself on the philosophy of Marx and Lenin, however, proceeded on the assumption that—technical advances apart—very little indeed of the old political, social, and economic order was worth preserving.

After a lapse of fifty years, it is appropriate to ask: What is the nature of Soviet society today? To what extent does it correspond to the image of Marx and Lenin? What have been its successes and failures? What are its future prospects?

With regard to the essential nature of the Soviet system, many Western scholars purport to find the key to understanding in one or another theory. Thus, to cite only a few examples, Edward Hallett

3

Carr suggests that, speaking broadly, the greater the lapse of time from the bolshevik revolution, the more decisively do the forces of tradition and continuity reassert themselves against those of revolution and change. Isaac Deutscher, on the other hand, insists that Marxism has entered into the very core of national consciousness and, whatever its mutations, remains the mainstream of Soviet thought, which is bound to have an increasingly important impact in the years to come. For Daniel Bell, contrariwise, Marxism has been exhausted, lost its truth and power to persuade. The true nature of the Soviet system, W. W. Rostow affirms, is the maintenance and extension of the power of its elite, which exercises its dictatorship over the majority to serve its own interests. As for the future, against Deutscher's insistence that the processes of change cannot be halted or aborted (except temporarily) short of the realization of a democratic socialist society truly in the image of Marx, Leonard Schapiro, for one, suggests that increasing benevolence may make the basically despotic system more acceptable and thus more durable.

These varying conceptions simply illustrate the difficulty involved in any attempt to explain the Soviet system, or project its future, by reference to any single and central principle. In my view, any such attempt inevitably takes inadequate account of the complexity of Soviet society and the limitations of human knowledge, and thus is bound to suffer from the fallacy of simplism. The better part of wisdom, it seems to me, lies in the recognition that the Union of Soviet Socialist Republics is a complex interpenetration and amalgam of many forces, which include Marxist ideology, the compulsions of the practical and expedient, the quest by Soviet leaders for personal and national power, the persistence and continuity of the old Russian conditions, traditions, and mores, and the recalcitrance of the human condition. It is, in short, a unique historical phenomenon, at one and the same time, in significant respects, Marxist, non-Marxist, and anti-Marxist—and, as such, it defies monistic interpretation and characterization. What is more, the Soviet system, in fifty years of history, has to its credit some truly noteworthy accomplishments and successes and, at the same time, has been responsible for some great failures and near disasters.

These statements are made not to create some artificial or mechanical balance but because they correspond to the reality that neither Soviet apologists, in some respects, nor many Western Soviet critics, in others, are prepared to recognize or accept. In support of these propositions, it will be useful to begin with a brief description of the historical background.

Setting and Historical Background

The U.S.S.R. had an estimated population of 234 million on January 1, 1967. In 1959, according to the official census, its population was 208.8 million—of whom 55 percent were women and 45 percent men. The disproportion is largely attributed to the massive loss of male lives during World War II.

The U.S.S.R. covers an area of over 8.5 million square miles, extending across one sixth of the surface of the globe, and is more than twice the size of the second largest country, China. Its land, which runs to some 800 miles north of the Arctic Circle, stretches south to the borders of China, Afghanistan, and Iran, and west from the Pacific Ocean to the Baltic and Black seas. In general, the country lies so far north that Yalta, at the southern tip of the Crimea, is approximately the same latitude as southern Minnesota.

With much of its territory a vast plain lacking natural frontiers —its borders add up to a length of well over 30,000 miles—Russian history for centuries was an almost continuous series of wars of invasion and expansion. As consequences, as V. O. Klyuchevsky wrote, "The state swelled and the people grew thin"; and serfdom at a time when it was already being abolished in western Europe continued to develop in Russia, so that the country could be organized to meet the exigent demands of war and each village be held communally responsible for money and men.

The Russian czar was an autocrat of unlimited power long after a series of checks upon absolutism had developed in western Europe. No representative national assembly met in Russia between the seventeenth and twentieth centuries. The Revolution of 1905 led to the promulgation of a constitution and provision for a Duma, or elected National Assembly, which convened in 1906; but the Duma was reconstituted and made less representative soon after the revolutionary tide had ebbed. Even so, when it raised some serious and embarrassing questions, it was suddenly and arbitrarily prorogued.

The church and the nobility with rare exceptions were docile or willing instruments in the hands of the czar. No czar went to Canossa to kneel in the snow and beg forgiveness of a Russian pope. No Russian ruler yielded the effective authority that English monarchs were compelled to grant in Magna Carta, the Bill of Rights, and Petition of Rights. The Renaissance, the Reformation, the English, French, and American revolutions, each in its own way affirming the dignity and worth of the individual with vast consequences for Western society, had little contemporary impact upon Russia. Illiteracy, superstition, and monarchical cruelty or obtuseness in unparalleled degree characterized old Russia.

The Russian people, to be sure, had gained some experience in a form of self-government through the *mir,* or village commune, an institution of peculiarly Slavic origin, in existence from at least the sixteenth century. Operating through a village assembly and elected officials, the *mir* had considerable authority over the peasant household and was responsible for manpower, taxes, the uses, allotment, and repartitioning of lands, and the admission of new members.

Similarly *Zemstvos,* first established in 1864, served as elected district and provincial councils, agencies of local self-government, with the obligation to keep roads and bridges in repair, look after primary education and sanitary affairs, and take measures against threat of famine. However, fearing that even such limited authority posed a threat to autocratic power, imperial officials in 1890 curtailed the role and activity of the *Zemstvos.*

Also constituting a challenge to autocracy and contributing to the enlightenment of the Russian people were the amazing creative awakening and ferment in the nineteenth century that produced such great poets as Pushkin and Lermontov, such extraordinary novelists as Tolstoi, Dostoevski, Turgenev, and Gogol, a host of remarkable musicians, artists, scientists, historians, and, not least, a radical intelligentsia, many of whom contributed to and inspired— and some of whom lived to witness—the March and November revolutions of 1917.[1]

---

[1] On January 26, 1918, the Gregorian calendar was adopted to begin with February 1, 1918, which was designated as February 14. As a consequence, the anniversaries of the February and October revolutions fall in March and November.

Notwithstanding these moderating forces, in the beginning of the twentieth century Russia was steeped in backwardness and autocracy; it was a semi-Asiatic and barbaric despotism (to use a favorite phrase of Lenin's) that proclaimed the monarch as an unlimited autocrat obedience to whom was ordained by God himself. The Russian people were in large measure lacking in literacy, understanding, or appreciation of free elections, parliamentary institutions, and civil liberties. In 1917, as such "fortress of reaction," as Engels had called it, Russia certainly was infertile soil for the establishment of a political democracy. In this connection Harold J. Laski wisely wrote, "A people, as every profound revolution has gone to show, must grow into the use of political freedom. It cannot plunge into its full employment directly after a long immersion, amid manifold disasters, in a semi-barbaric and wholly reactionary despotism." Similarly, in the early years of the twentieth century, as an overwhelmingly agricultural country without a highly developed industrial base and a mature and powerful proletariat, Russia was unripe for a *socialist* revolution. And for many years Lenin shared this view, believing as the Marxists generally did, that Russia would first have to go through a phase of further capitalist development producing "the gravediggers" of capitalism before it would be prepared for proletarian revolution and socialism.

However, the fundamental and historic backwardness and inequities of Russia's political, economic, and social structures and, more immediately, the privations of war, the inequalities of burdens, the incompetency and corruption of the imperial court, military inefficiency, and widespread agitation culminated in March 1917 in the collapse of czardom. And, in the months that followed, the failure of the Provisional Government, an essentially broad coalition, to assuage the land hunger of the peasants and end a war, so stained with imperialist purposes and Russian blood, created the massive dissatisfaction and disaffection that made possible the bolshevik seizure of power in November 1917 and the establishment of a so-called dictatorship of the proletariat that made the transition toward the building of a socialist state.

The Soviet Political System

According to Marx and Engels, the destruction of capitalism would bring about the dictatorship of the proletariat—that is, "the proletariat organized as the ruling class"—and "establish democracy." This, explained Lenin, while involving suppression of the bourgeoisie would at the same time lead to "an immense expansion of democracy" for the proletariat, that is to say, "democracy for the vast majority of the people." All officials without exception would be subject to election and recall. And from the time of its taking power, the proletarian state, as an instrumentality of force in the hands of the vast majority directed against a small minority, would begin to wither away until, after a protracted period of time, there would exist only a stateless, classless society.

More specifically, the dictatorship of the proletariat, as Lenin, the Bolsheviks, and Marxists generally conceived of it *before* the bolshevik seizure of power in November 1917, would have permitted all leftist parties to compete for the support of the masses. No Marxist then thought of the dictatorship of the proletariat as equivalent to the dictatorship of one party and certainly not of any one group within a party. It is true that Lenin, with specific regard to Russia, "amid the gloom of autocracy," opposed the use of broad principles of democracy in the organization of the Russian socialist party in the *preparation and making* of the Revolution. But for many years he was convinced that Russia, as a backward, agricultural country, *after* the Revolution, would be ready only for a bourgeois, capitalist phase of development and probably would be governed by a coalition of parties, representing the proletariat, peasantry, and sections of the bourgeoisie. Lenin, for example, had rejected the Parvus-Trotsky formula, which had called for a minority dictatorship of the proletariat in Russia. While after April 1917 he came closer to accepting this formula, the fact is that even the revolutionary seizure of power in November 1917 was in the name of the Soviet in which several parties were represented.

Under Lenin, however, in the years that followed, the Bolsheviks suppressed all other working class and peasant as well as bourgeois parties and their press and, in addition, outlawed all organized "factions" within the Communist Party itself. Lenin, to be sure, had proposed or agreed to these measures in the face of war, civil war, intervention, and desperate economic circumstances. And while he lived, he and his ideas were openly criticized and attacked at Party congresses and conferences; on occasions, he was even outvoted.

In any event, whatever the explanation, the dictatorship of the proletariat became under Lenin the dictatorship of the Communist Party and at times of the Politburo, a small group of Party leaders, while under Stalin it degenerated from a dictatorship of a small group of Party leaders into as thoroughgoing a dictatorship of one man as modern history has offered. While circumstances and conditions may explain, if they do not justify, the concentration of power in Lenin's day, there is no similar explanation or justification for Stalin's dictatorship.

Soviet Socialist "Democracy"

In 1936, at the very apogee of Stalin's power, the present Soviet constitution was adopted and proclaimed by him to be "the only thoroughly democratic constitution in the world"; as one Soviet writer put it, "a million times more democratic than that of the most democratic bourgeois republic." The Soviet people, asserted Khrushchev, "are the freest of the free in the world," and this view continues to be echoed by Soviet leaders and writers to this day.

The whole question of Soviet "democracy" might perhaps be dismissed with the statement that these affirmations rest on a particular definition and that the U.S.S.R. is free to define democracy any way it pleases. But it is not a question of semantics. The concept of democracy corresponds to one of the deepest and noblest aspirations of mankind and has great attraction and appeal throughout the world. It is well to consider, therefore, whether the Russian claim can be supported by any meaningful, reasonable, and consistent definition of democracy—non-Marxist or Marxist.

To begin with, no honest observer would seriously maintain that Soviet practice conforms to the criteria suggested in the West, for example, by Ernest Barker, one of Britain's leading political philosophers, who wrote in *Principles of Social and Political Theory* that democracy is not a solution, but a way of seeking solutions—not a form of State devoted to this or that particular end (whether of private enterprise or public management), but a form of State devoted, whatever its end may be, to the single means and method of determining that end. The core of democracy is choice, and not something chosen; choice among a number of ideas, and choice, too, of the scheme on which those ideas are eventually composed. . . .

And, to make those choices meaningful, as Professor Robert M. MacIver has insisted, it is a necessary condition of democracy that opposing doctrines remain free to express themselves, to seek converts, to form organizations, and so to compete for success before the bar of public opinion.

If these "Western" standards are not those of the Soviet Union, what then are the bases upon which the claim of the Soviet regime to democracy is made to rest? Allegedly of particular importance are the guarantees (in Article 125) of the Soviet constitution of freedom of speech, press, assembly, and street processions and demonstrations with the proviso that these rights are "ensured" by placing at the disposal of the working people printing presses and other material requisites for their exercise.

But the fact is that the very provision granting these rights imposes the limitation that they must be exercised "in conformity with the interests of the working people, and in order to strengthen the socialist system," judgments resting, of course, not with the proletariat or with the people themselves but with the Party or, more accurately, with the Party leaders.

Even before these constitutional guarantees of freedom of speech and related freedoms were adopted, *Pravda,* on June 2, 1936, warned that:

> He who makes it his task to unsettle the socialist structure, to undermine socialist ownership . . . is an enemy of the people. He gets not a scrap of paper, he does not set foot over the threshold of the printing press, to realize his base designs. He gets no hall, no room, no cover to inject poison by word of mouth.

And, of course, the Party continues to exercise pervasive control over press, radio, television, and other media of information and influence within the U.S.S.R.

A second basis upon which the U.S.S.R. predicates its claim

to democracy is the widespread participation of its people not only in formal state elections but in the running of factories, farms, and enterprises. Soviet writers have boasted that their turnout at the polls is much higher than in any other nonsocialist country and that their representatives can "in all justice be called the elect of the people, because all the electors, with scarcely any exception, vote for them."

Now it must be conceded that on what Sir John Maynard years ago called "the lower planes of public affairs" there is a "kind of democracy which is altogether *sui generis*" in the sense that factories, farms, and enterprises are run under the continual criticism of workers who freely express opinions and make suggestions. What is more, workers' dwellings are managed by committees chosen by and responsible to them. And it is true that on occasion the Party invites widespread public discussion of policies under consideration. Recent cases in point were the national debate over a new family law and new model rules for collective farms. But to suppose that this enables the Soviet people to change its governors without force or the violation of law is plainly untrue. Furthermore, there is a clear and vital distinction between general freedom of criticism and of choice, on the one hand, and public discussion of policies selected, submitted, delimited, and ultimately decided from above, on the other.

As for almost unanimous approval of the single slate of candidates offered to the Soviet voters, these "ritualistic exercises in unanimity," as they were called by a largely friendly observer of the Soviet scene, must inherently be viewed with suspicion. But, how is it possible, Soviet writer V. Denisov asks, "to force the people of a huge multi-national state to vote against their own will and interests, when there is universal and equal suffrage by secret ballot (whose existence none deny)?" "The question alone," he maintains, "demonstrates the absurdity of such allegations."

It may be asked in turn, how it is possible to explain that in the 1938 election to the republican Supreme Soviet, 99.8 percent of the Volga Germans went to the polls, of whom 99.7 percent voted for the official list of candidates, while three years later the entire population was accused of harboring "tens of thousands of deviationists and spies" and deported en masse for disloyalty? How explain, in general, that although in the course of World War II seven nationalities were deported en masse for disloyalty their votes in favor of the official list in the elections to the Supreme Soviet in 1937 were stated to have been well in excess of 90 percent?

Nor is the further argument of Soviet writers that "the genuine freedom of Soviet elections consists first and foremost in the fact that candidates are nominated by the workers themselves, from among themselves" any more persuasive. It is true that Article 141 of the Soviet constitution vests the right to nominate candidates for all soviets in "public organizations and societies of the working people: Communist Party organizations, trade unions, cooperatives, youth organizations and cultural societies." However, while in theory this makes possible a number of candidates, in all elections thus far held to the Supreme Soviet (including 1966) the name of only one candidate has appeared on the ballot in each constituency. What is critical, therefore, is obviously the process of elimination of nominees. And this process designed to assure "dependable" candidates, it is clear, is carried on by and through the Communist Party, which is declared by the constitution (Article 126) to be "the leading core of all organizations of the working people, both public and state," and "the vanguard of the working class."

The leadership of the Communist Party, in turn, although theoretically constituted on the basis of free elections in ascending hierarchies, in fact represented at the height of Stalin's power a virtual dictatorship of one man, and in more recent times continues to reflect a marked concentration of power. With rare exceptions, since Lenin's death the leaders at the top of the hierarchy have been able to control and limit the discussion of policy at all lower levels and in all media, and determine or control the selection of personnel for all important positions. There is a vast difference, as Plekhanov once pointed out, between the dictatorship of the proletariat and of a group.

Another basis upon which the U.S.S.R. claim to democracy is advanced is that under the leadership of the Communist Party it has, in fundamental and far-reaching respects, served the interests and advanced the well-being of the Soviet peoples. By turning the means of production into the property of the people, by destroying exploitation, by eliminating poverty and unemployment, the Soviet peoples, it is maintained, have achieved *real* freedom. In this view, the existence of a democracy is determined, as G. F. Aleksandrov wrote, "by the substance of the policy pursued by the state, by whether this or that policy is carried out in the interests of the people, in the interests of its overwhelming majority, or in the interests of its minority."

It cannot be gainsaid that, under the domination of the Communist Party, the U.S.S.R. has made great advances in industrialization, in education, in cultural areas, and in the eradication of many forms of discrimination and inequality characteristic of the czarist period. Concomitantly, great hardships and burdens were imposed upon the Soviet people, particularly in the process of rapid industrialization and collectivization. But important as the benefits conferred and hardships imposed are for other purposes, they have little or no relevance to the existence or nonexistence of *political* democracy in the Soviet Union. The essence of democracy, in any meaningful sense, must surely lie in self-government rather than in service to the interests of the people (although it is of course probably true that in the long run self-government alone will provide good government). If democracy does not involve self-government then the term not only loses all connection with its historic connotations but may be reduced to a manifest absurdity to describe the most thoroughgoing dictatorship provided only that it is benevolent or enlightened (or, perhaps, only claims to be so). What is more, to deny or denigrate self-government as the essence of democracy, would be, as has been shown, to do violence not only to conceptions of capitalist democracy but to *Marxist* conceptions of socialist democracy as well.

But we are told that because of the "great concord" of the Soviet peoples and the absence of hostile or antagonistic classes there is no need for Western indicia of self-government since "there are no grounds for the existence of several parties, and therefore for the existence of freedom of such parties in the U.S.S.R." "The Party and the people in our country are as one," said Khrushchev, "so why do the Soviet people need other parties? Or are they to be created especially for the people in capitalist countries who are not satisfied with the socialist system?" The Soviet people, Soviet writer D. Zemlyansky tells us, "are all united in a common purpose: the construction of a happy classless society, communism."

It is revealing, when some measure of opposition or dissent is permitted to find expression in the U.S.S.R., how quickly the notion of a "great concord" is dispelled. But even assuming the absence of antagonistic classes in the U.S.S.R. and a great concord on Marxist *ends,* is it really possible to argue in light of the known facts of Soviet history that at all times the Soviet people were agreed on *means?* Were all "as one" on the tempo of industrialization, on "socialism in one country," on aid to World Revolution, on the Nazi-Soviet pact, on the dissolution of the Comintern, and on official attitudes toward religion, art, and literature? Did (and do) good socialists disagree among themselves about these and myriad other questions—especially in light of occasional sudden and drastic shifts of policy—without finding any legal means to express dissent, except on those occasions when invited from above? The answers to these questions are in part given by the *official* denunciation of the wanton purges of the 1930s based, concededly, in good part on nothing more than honest disagreement with Stalin.

It remains to deal with the most recent conception of socialist democracy in the U.S.S.R. According to the New Program of the Communist Party, adopted in October 1961 (only the third formal program in the history of the Party), the U.S.S.R., which "arose as a state of the dictatorship of the proletariat, has in the new, present stage turned into a state of the entire people, an agency expressing the interests and will of the people as a whole." This development, it is maintained, involves a comprehensive extension and perfection of socialist democracy, including active participation of all citizens in the administration of the state and management of the economy. And, it is contemplated, "as socialist democracy develops further, the agencies of state power will gradually be transformed into agencies of public self-government."

Parenthetically, in relation to the question of the continuity of Marxist theory in Soviet practice, it must be said that the whole conception of "a state of the entire people" is alien to Marxism and quite possibly anti-Marxist. In the Marxist view, the state arose with the rise of antagonistic classes and is *necessarily* an organ of domination and oppression of one class by another; the existence of the state, to cite a passage from Engels quoted approvingly by Lenin, "is tantamount to an acknowledgment that the given society has become entangled in an insoluble contradiction within itself, and it has broken into irreconcilable antagonisms, of which it is power-less to rid itself." With the disappearance of classes, Engels added, the state too will inevitably disappear. The integral connection between the existence of the state *and* antagonistic classes was proclaimed in the second program of the Communist Party, adopted in 1919, as follows:

> In contrast to bourgeois democracy, which concealed the class character of the state, the Soviet authority openly acknowledges that every state must inevitably bear a class character until the division of society into classes has been abolished and all government disappears.

Now, it is officially maintained, as we have seen, that there are no longer hostile or antagonistic classes in the U.S.S.R. Why then the state? The Soviet Union has explained the failure of the state to wither away by the fact that it continues to live in a predominantly nonsocialist and, to a marked extent, hostile world. However, whatever the objective necessity for the U.S.S.R., in the absence of class conflict, to maintain its panoply of state power, its continuance is clearly inconsistent with basic Marxist theory and assumptions.

In any event, it is abundantly manifest that "the state of the entire people" is not intended to interfere with the hegemony, power, and control of the Communist Party. The New Party Program, which proclaimed this stage, added that it "is characterized by a further *rise in the role and importance of the Communist Party* as the leading and guiding force of Soviet society." (Italics in original.) And that such role is not to be limited to criminal, parasitic, and procapitalistic elements is evidenced, to cite an important example, by continuing close control (despite some relaxation) over the press and the arts. Speaking to the twenty-third Party Congress in 1966, Brezhnev went to special pains to assert that the Party is "unswervingly guided by the principle of party-mindedness in art, a class approach in the evaluation of everything that is done in the field of culture." This insistence sounded the keynote for the Fourth National Congress of Soviet Writers held in May 1967 which was dominated by the Party. The Congress, for example, ignored Alexander Solzhenitsyn's appeal to adopt a resolution which would release publishing houses from the obligation to obtain authorization for the publication of *every* printed word of fiction; an obligation which he characterized as a "yoke" that gives "people who are unversed in literature arbitrary control over writers."

And it is clear that there is no intention to allow open, public presentation of opposing positions nor factional organization within the Party. Khrushchev, on his ouster in 1964, for example, was afforded no opportunity to reply to his denunciation in *Pravda* for "harebrained scheming, immature conclusions, hasty decisions, actions divorced from reality, bragging, phrase-mongering, and commandism." Of course, this was no worse than the fate meted out by Khrushchev to the so-called Anti-Party group in 1957, which included Malenkov, Molotov, and Kaganovich, who were subjected to even worse vilification without opportunity to respond.

The Widening Scope of Controversy

On the other hand, since the death of Stalin in March 1953, it cannot be doubted that there have been some highly significant changes in the U.S.S.R. that, while they do not amount to a thoroughgoing democratization of Soviet society, do represent a substantial liberalization and widening of the scope of permissible controversy and dissent. These changes are reflected in virtually every facet of Soviet life including the economy, law, science, literature, and art. Proposals for reform of economic practices and procedures have been widely reported in the West so I shall cite only some other illustrations.

With respect to the Soviet legal system, for example, despite the reimposition of harsh criminal penalties in 1961 and 1962 for serious economic offenses, there has been a far-reaching and genuine liberalization of both substantive and procedural law including the elimination of the use of terror in legal guise, and of punishment by analogy, that is, by reference to a law proscribing a similar act; curbs on the powers of the security police, on the uses of confession testimony, and on searches and seizure; and some extension of the right to counsel prior to trial.

In scientific discussions the president of the Soviet Academy of Sciences, M. V. Keldysh, has condemned "the monopoly position" of T. D. Lysenko and his followers who with Party support for a long time dominated Soviet genetic investigation and imposed their views with great damage to scientific inquiry. So also Soviet physicist Peter Kapitsa took to task some Soviet philosophers who "dogmatically applying the method of dialectics proved that the theory of relativity was without foundation" and rejected cybernetics as a "reactionary pseudo-science."

Expression of literary ferment, to refer to only a few dramatic illustrations, is to be found in the publication *within the U.S.S.R.* of the memoirs of Ilya Ehrenburg, which revealed that although many had known of Stalin's abuses they had seen no alternative but to remain silent and live "with clenched teeth"; Alexander Solzhenitsyn's *One Day in the Life of Ivan Denisovitch,* an understated and thus all the more powerful story of life in a Soviet concentration camp; Viktor Nekrasov's *On Both Sides of the Ocean* and *A Month in France,* unusually balanced accounts of his visits to Italy, the United States, and France; and, not least, the poetry of the outspoken and courageous anti-Stalinists typified by Yevgeny Yevtushenko's "Stalin's Heirs," with its appeal

> To double
> To triple,
> The guard . . .
> So that Stalin may not rise,
> And, with Stalin,
> The past . . .
>
> Here
> I mean by the past
> The ignoring of the people's welfare
> The calumnies
> The arrests of the innocent.[2]

It is true that in the years after Stalin's death there have been some swings of the pendulum involving greater restraint (as well as latitude), of which the Sinyavsky-Daniel trial is a case in point, and that the Party retains its hegemony and the legal basis with which to curb dissent. It is still a crime, according to Soviet law, to carry on "agitation or propaganda" with the object of undermining or weakening state power or to disseminate or even possess materials of such defamatory nature. But the fact remains that without resort to mass police terror it may be possible to limit or curb but it will not be possible to destroy the new community of liberal writers and artists and widespread intellectual ferment in the Soviet

[2] Yevgeny Yevtushenko, "Stalin's Heirs." Translation from *The Current Digest of the Soviet Press* (October 31, 1962), published weekly at Columbia University by the Joint Committee on Slavic Studies, appointed by the American Council of Learned Societies and the Social Science Research Council. Copyright © 1962 (Vol. XIV, No. 40), the Joint Committee on Slavic Studies. Reprinted by permission.

Union. And reinstitution of systematic and pervasive terror, to assure the virtually total outward conformity and uniformity that marked long periods of Communist Party rule, seems to me extremely unlikely for a variety of reasons.

The Soviet people know the massive, wanton, and often senseless cruelty that so poignantly affected so many of their lives, and are likely to resist its recurrence. What is more, they—and particularly the youth among them—have breathed some of the intoxicating air of greater freedom and developed expectations of greater benefits (material, cultural, and political) that they will not willingly forego. In an important sense, too, the leadership has staked its own future, against internal and external pressures, on its anti-Stalinist position. And apart from concern with self-preservation, no doubt many of the new leaders recoil from the reimposition of the rule of terror as a matter of principle but, in any event, as inexpedient if the creative energies and initiative of the Soviet people are to be fully released.

Then, too, while the Soviet leaders may be unimpressed with appeals for greater freedom from cold-war and ideological opponents, they must concern themselves with the opinion of neutrals and, even more assuredly, with that of allied communist parties. A striking illustration is the late Italian communist leader Palmiro Togliatti's call, published in September 1964 (in the U.S.S.R. as well as abroad), for "open debates on current problems" and for greater attention to overcoming the "restrictions and suppressions of democratic and personal freedom introduced by Stalin." Subsequently, in October 1964, the summary dismissal of Khrushchev from all positions of Party leadership evoked the comment from Togliatti's successor, Luigi Longo, that "The manner in which this change in the summit of the Soviet party and state occurred leaves us preoccupied and critical." Similar concern was expressed by Party leaders in France, Hungary, and Poland.

It is I believe true, too, that the leadership that came to power with the ouster of Khrushchev shares power *collectively* to an extent largely unparalleled in Soviet history. It is possible, of course, that in this instance, as in the past, collective leadership will prove only to have been a brief prelude to the emergence of a single peerless *Vozhd*; but it appears to me dubious that in the foreseeable and predictable future—barring a great catastrophe—any one man could arrogate to himself the plenitude of power of a Stalin or even of a Khrushchev. For one thing, each ouster, with its revelation of prior abuses, makes it more difficult to cloak a new leader with the necessary charisma and mantle of infallibility. For another, any attempt at organized and massive terror of the kind on which Stalin relied to curb all opposition, real, potential, and imagined, would undoubtedly meet with great resistance.

In all these circumstances, I conclude that while it is incorrect to suggest that political democracy in any thoroughgoing sense (Western or Marxist) exists in the U.S.S.R., a return to a prototype of Stalinist totalitarianism and terror seems to be excluded. What is more, at and near the top of the Party, governmental and other hierarchies, there has been some diffusion of power and responsibility; and, at lower levels, increased participation and activity by the Soviet people in public affairs. In general, as Professor Frederick C. Barghoorn has written, "there has recently been an encouraging revival of rational and empirical thinking in many fields," and there has developed "the rudiments of a free, critical public opinion," which, though shackled, is "almost unimaginable when measured by the Stalinist yardstick." The U.S.S.R. continues to retain and foster slogans and appeals toward a more far-reaching and more genuine socialist democracy. This affords basis for hope that in the coming years the Soviet people will imbue the slogans and appeals with greater substance and reality.

The Structure and Content
of Soviet Intra-national Relations

One of the proudest boasts of the U.S.S.R. is that "it has solved the nationality problem—completely and finally." While this is unquestionably a gross exaggeration, the U.S.S.R. must be credited with great achievements in the educational, cultural, and economic development of its far-flung areas of mixed populations and national minorities—estimated as 194 distinguishable races, nationalities, and tribes in the 1926 census and as 126 in the 1959 census—who speak some 125 different languages or dialects and adhere to 40 different religions.

It must be remembered that czarist governments, in good

part, had attempted to deal with national minorities by a policy of repression and forcible Russification. The written use of non-Russian languages was discouraged and sometimes forbidden. Outlying areas were left undeveloped and largely treated as fit only for exploitation; their populations were frequently steeped in ignorance and superstition. Czarist officials often thought it expedient to sow hatred and discord among them and at times even to organize or condone pogroms against particular minorities.

Appraisal of contemporary Soviet policies and practices affecting national minorities, in my judgment, must proceed from a recognition of this background and from two standpoints, political and non-political.

Federalism and Political Equality

In formal structure, the U.S.S.R. is declared by its constitution to be "a federal state, formed on the basis of a voluntary union of equal Soviet Socialist Republics," of which there are fifteen. The national legislature, the Supreme Soviet, "the highest organ of state power," is a bicameral body "with equal rights" for the two houses consisting of "The Soviet of the Union," to which delegates are elected throughout the U.S.S.R. purely on a population basis, and "The Soviet of Nationalities," with a specified number of deputies from each Union Republic, Autonomous Republic, Autonomous Region, and National Area.

Soviet writers, in maintaining that a genuine and advanced type of federalism prevails in the U.S.S.R., emphasize the coordinate legislative power of the Soviet of Nationalities and point out, as did A. Denisov and M. Kirichenko in *Soviet State Law,* published in 1960, that the Soviet republics enjoy "the right of nations to self-determination including the right to secession and the formation of independent states."

In reality, since the Communist Party throughout the U.S.S.R., in both theory and practice, is a highly centralized body that, as early as the Second Party Congress in 1903, strongly repudiated the federal principle of organization (rejecting autonomy for any national group), and is the source of all important legislation, "federalism," in the sense of political independence or autonomy, has been from beginning to end a pretense. The fact is that repeatedly over the years national boundaries have been altered (for example, the transfer of the Crimea from the Russian Soviet Federative Socialist Republic [R.S.F.S.R.] to the Ukraine in February 1954, and the absorption of the Karelo-Finnish Soviet Socialist Republic into the R.S.F.S.R. in July 1956), the division of powers has been modified, and whole populations have been uprooted, without resort to any "federal" procedure of decision-making.

As for the constitutional "right" of secession, it obviously has no meaning without the right of advocacy; and such advocacy has been considered a counterrevolutionary crime in the U.S.S.R. Many hundreds if not thousands of officials, teachers, and writers have been expelled from the Party or lost their positions, at the very least, and at worst have been imprisoned or executed on charges of bourgeois nationalism, a term of opprobrium automatically applicable to anyone seeking the separation of any nationality from the U.S.S.R.

On the other hand, however devoid of real content *political* federalism in fact is, it cannot and should not be denied that, in many important nonpolitical respects, Soviet treatment of its national minorities has been forward-looking and enlightened.

Federalism and Social Equality

Article 123 of the Soviet constitution provides that "Equality of rights of citizens of the U.S.S.R., irrespective of their nationality or race, in all spheres of economic, government, cultural, political, and other public activity, is an indefeasible law." It makes any restriction on such equality "as well as any advocacy of racial or national exclusiveness or hatred and contempt" punishable by law.

In support of these principles basic to Marxism and civilized society the Soviet Union, with an occasional glaring exception, has utilized its media of education and persuasion—schools, books, press, journals, radio, television, and mass organizations—to underscore the essential equality of all men and to undermine national and racial prejudice. Bigotry, to be sure, dies hard, and it would be fatuous to suppose that it no longer exists in the U.S.S.R.; but it cannot be denied that official policy vigorously combats it.

Additionally, apart from preaching equality, in practice, in certain basic areas of Soviet life, substantial equality of all peoples and races has been achieved. Literacy has been brought to all the nationalities of the U.S.S.R., including about fifty for whom a written language had first to be developed. Overall literacy was raised from 51 percent in 1926 (it was less than 30 percent at the end of the czarist period) to 98.5 percent in 1959 (when the last official census was taken). Particularly in the "backward" areas, the level of elementary, secondary, and higher education has been dramatically brought up. For example, in the territory of the five Central Asian republics, regarded as among the most backward under czarism, in 1914–1915 there were only 136,000 pupils in the elementary and secondary schools, an insignificant percentage of such pupils in the whole of Russia, but by 1955–1956 these schools had an enrollment of 3.59 million, a twenty-five-fold increase. This brought the total to about 13 percent of the whole, a figure corresponding to the area's proportionate population. And, whereas before the Revolution institutions of higher learning were virtually nonexistent in this area, by 1955 such institutions had an enrollment of 155,000 students, or about 9 percent of the total for the U.S.S.R. In 1914 there were only 400 students in the elementary-secondary schools in the whole of Tadzhikistan; in September 1965 the number had reached 535,000. Similarly, while in the prerevolutionary period the territory of present-day Uzbekistan had not a single institution of higher education, 154,000 students were enrolled in such institutions in September 1965.

The evidence also does show that, generally speaking, other educational and cultural facilities, including theaters, sport stadia, clubs, libraries, newspapers, journals, radio and television stations, have been provided on the basis of equality or relative equality. Similarly, medical attention has been made widely available throughout the U.S.S.R.; so that, for example, in 1961 in Turkmenia there were seventeen doctors per ten thousand population, well in excess of the number found in many parts of the United States.

In the process of industrialization and overall economic development, it appears to be true, too, that there has been little or no significant discrimination in favor of the Great Russian area. On the contrary, it is fair to say that the allocation of investment for economic development has often involved (because of initial backwardness) disproportionate benefits to the outlying regions; so that Armenia, for example, one of the least is now one of the most advanced economic areas in the U.S.S.R.

Now it is true that some imbalances favorable to the Russian Republic continue to exist. For example, in 1960 according to official Soviet figures there were nineteen college-trained specialists for every thousand inhabitants in the R.S.F.S.R. but only nine per thousand among the Kazakh, Kirghiz and Turkmen people and only eight among the Tadzhiks and Uzbeks. Similarly, official statistics reveal that in 1962 in the R.S.F.S.R. the output of electric power was over 2,000 kilowatt hours per inhabitant but only 513 among the Tadzhiks, 555 among the Byelorussians, and 598 among the Turkmen.

These continuing imbalances, however, while they appear to suggest some favoritism for the Russian Republic, may be explainable in good part by the inherent difficulties involved in massive equalization programs, and by legitimate concern for economic efficiency and defense needs that do require some concentration of resources and efforts.

In sum, speaking generally, the conclusion is warranted that the U.S.S.R. has afforded its minorities a large measure of equality of treatment in education, economic opportunity, cultural and social benefits—always, to be sure, within the context of and limitations imposed by the Soviet formula, "national in form, socialist in content."

The Special Case of the Jews

The Jews, like other officially recognized nationalities in the Soviet Union, for many years enjoyed cultural autonomy. In the 1930s and into the 1940s there were numerous Yiddish theaters, newspapers, and journals, several *thousand* writers, poets, and actors producing and performing in the Yiddish language, the largest network of Yiddish schools, and the only Jewish institution of higher learning in the world. In predominantly Jewish areas even some local soviets conducted their proceedings in Yiddish.

With the development of the campaign against "cosmopolitanism" in the late 1940s, virtually every distinctive institution and facility of Jewish cultural life was destroyed, and thousands of Jewish writers and actors were imprisoned (many of whom were subsequently executed). The campaign against the Jews culminated in the charge in January 1953 that a number of prominent Jewish doctors had been engaged in a plot to kill and had actually killed important Soviet leaders. (While some non-Jewish doctors were also named, emphasis was placed on the Jewish "conspirators.")

On the death of Stalin in March 1953 the Jewish doctors' plot was promptly and officially exposed as a fabrication from beginning to end. Nonetheless, very little indeed has been done to restore Jewish cultural institutions. And this continues to be true despite the fact that according to the 1959 official Soviet census, 2,268,000 persons declared themselves to be Jews, of whom 472,000 named Yiddish as their native tongue—which in the context of nationality development in the U.S.S.R. means for many, particularly of the older generation, their only spoken and written language.

The failure to restore Jewish cultural facilities has been the subject of severe criticism by many leading Communists throughout the world. To cite one example, in October 1964, the editor of *Political Affairs,* the theoretical journal of the Communist Party of the United States, while denying that official anti-Semitism exists in the Soviet Union, nevertheless pointed out that "the restoration of Yiddish cultural institutions admittedly falls considerably short of what existed prior to 1948." Specifically, he noted that

> the publication of books in Yiddish has so far been limited to a small number of volumes. There are no Yiddish newspapers other than the *Birobidjaner Shtern* [published in a very small edition and circulating locally in an area remote from the large centers of Jewish population]. Nor are there any Jewish newspapers in Russian or other languages. The state theater in Moscow, headed by Mikhoels, has not been restored. No schools or classes or even textbooks in the Yiddish language exist.

By way of contrast, it is noteworthy that the Volga Germans, removed en masse from the Soviet borderland in 1941, have nonetheless been accorded opportunities for a full cultural life in their native language. And consider that in 1963 alone Soviet presses produced 90 books for the Maris (1959 census population 504,000) and 117 for the Yakuts (population 236,000) in their own tongues. Parenthetically, Poland, another communist land, with no more than 25,000 Jews, has a daily newspaper published in Warsaw in Yiddish, a Yiddish theater, and a thriving Jewish cultural life.

In the face of these facts, it is clearly impossible to accept the official Soviet explanation (as many Communists outside the Soviet

Union have recognized and admitted) that the Jews have been linguistically and culturally assimilated and have no further need for separate institutions.

Egalitarianism in General

A fundamental, theoretical "end" of Marxism is the realization of a thoroughly egalitarian society. It was Marx's view that in the socialist phase, the economic system would provide payment to its workers "proportioned to the labor they supply," and equality would consist "in the fact that measurement is made with an equal standard, labor." But true equality would be achieved only in the higher, communist phase, "after the productive forces have also increased with the all-round development of the individual, and all the springs of cooperative wealth flow more abundantly." Then would the standard prevail, "From each according to his ability, to each according to his needs."

In the aftermath of the bolshevik revolution, and during the period of "war communism," equality to its uttermost limits was the order of the day. As David J. Dallin wrote, "Everything that stood in the way of equality was to be abolished, at once, completely: that was the spiritual crux of the November revolution and of the ideology of the early period of the Soviet regime." Workers' control of factories, division of the landlords' estates, equality in the distribution of food and housing, elimination of army ranks— all were instituted to destroy every vestige of the old inequality.

In this period wages too tended toward equality and by 1921 workers of widely varying qualifications, skill, or performance received nearly equal wages. But this equality, extorted from an economy of want and scarcity (a base that made a travesty of Marx's vision), had to be abandoned to restore the ravaged economy. Under the New Economic Policy (N.E.P.), traders and small entrepreneurs were invited back and peasants given the right to sell their products in the free market. The inevitable effect was marked differentiation in income. With the ebbing of revolutionary élan and under conditions of poverty, higher earnings provided the strongest incentive to more productive and skilled work for the working class as well. N.E.P. lasted until the introduction of the first Five Year Plan in 1929 under which by June 1931, Stalin was decrying "the consequences of wage equalization," which deprived unskilled workers of incentive to become skilled workers and led to heavy turnover in labor. "In order to put an end to this evil," he said, "we must abolish wage equalization and discard the old wage scales."

In typical fashion, Stalin sought to make a virtue of what may well have been a necessity; and, what is more, carried the inequalities far beyond the needs, or even utility, of the case. Accordingly, in 1934, Stalin characterized the views of those who "think that Socialism calls for equalization, for levelling the requirements and the individual lives of the members of society" as "petty-bourgeois views of our leftist blockheads." With regard to their "one time" attempt to organize industry to provide equal compensation for skilled and unskilled workers, he added, "You know what harm these infantile equalitarian exercises of our 'left' blockheads caused our industry."

More inequality became the fashion and the cry. As a consequence, the piecework wage became the prevailing system and gross disparities developed between the earnings of the skilled and the unskilled so that, as William Mandel points out, as early as 1927 "Soviet labor law provided seventeen wage gradations, with the highest paid eight times as much as the lowest." (This was accompanied by draconian measures of labor discipline.) And, in 1940, a decree was issued requiring payment of tuition fees for upper secondary and higher education.

In light of these developments, it was quite generally predicted in the West that egalitarianism had been permanently and irrevocably abandoned as a goal of Soviet policy. Typical was the statement of Arthur Koestler in 1942 that a survey of the trends in the U.S.S.R. "contradicts the alleged temporariness of these expedients and reveals a continuous and coherent movement in a direction opposed to fundamental principles of socialism."

But it is noteworthy that with postwar recovery and further progress in building a high industrial base, a number of measures were adopted to restore greater equality. These included currency devaluation (which had a particularly adverse effect on high-income groups who had to yield their old currency for the new in decreasing ratio, and on black marketers who, in addition, risked exposure), the ending of the tuition system (making education generally available to the talented, at all levels, without tuition fee), an increase in minimum wages and pensions, extension of the pension system to farm workers, special tax concessions for low-income groups, and reduction in the use of the piecework system—all of which have been of special and substantial benefit to those at the bottom of the economic scale. Labor benefited, too, from a shorter workweek, and reform and liberalization of the labor code.

It must be said with respect to the standard of living of the Soviet people, particularly since Stalin's death in 1953, that there has been a fairly steady improvement. According to the Soviet claim (which is probably exaggerated and so must be discounted but cannot be dismissed), in the past decade, the real income of its working people increased substantially; by the beginning of 1966 about half of the population had moved into new homes or improved their housing; public-fund expenditures encompassing costs of social insurance, pensions, stipends, vacation pay, education and medical services, sanitariums and rest-home facilities, and child care in kindergartens and nurseries increased from 15 billion to about 41.5 billion rubles (the ruble is officially valued at $1.11); and, whereas in 1939 about 16 million people had a higher or secondary school education, by 1964 there were more than 70 million, or four and a half times as many. And, according to Mark G. Field, an American specialist, in his *Soviet Socialized Medicine,* published in 1967, the U.S.S.R. has one of the highest, if not the highest doctor-patient ratios in the world—about 50 percent higher than the corresponding ratio in the United States.

The Soviet Economic System

At the outset, I pointed out that the U.S.S.R. is a unique historical phenomenon combining Marxist, non-Marxist, and anti-Marxist elements. So far as its political system goes, as I have attempted to show, its power base and institutional structures bear little resemblance to Marxist and early Leninist conceptions. (This has been true throughout although, as Alfred G. Meyer says, the dictatorship has been exercised with varying degrees of arbitrariness.)

I am persuaded, however, that the Soviet economic system, despite distortions that derive from its political structure and from what John Plamenatz has called the "premature" nature of a Marxist revolution in a backward country, is in a basic sense Marxist in conception and spirit. I regard this proposition as central to understanding, particularly in light of some recent notions in the West that the Soviet Union is abandoning socialism and substituting a "profit" system. I shall deal with it, therefore, before turning to a consideration of some recent Soviet economic developments and future prospects.[3]

The Influence of Marxism

In *The Communist Manifesto,* Marx and Engels wrote that "the distinguishing feature of communism" is "the abolition of bourgeois property," a system based on "class antagonism, or the exploitation of the many by the few," and added, "in this sense, the theory of the Communists may be summed up in a single sentence: Abolition of private property."

The Soviet constitution proclaims that "the economic foundation of the U.S.S.R. is the socialist system of economy and the socialist ownership of the instruments and means of production." It provides that "the economic life of the U.S.S.R. is determined by the state national-economic plan," and declares work to be "a duty and a matter of honor for every able-bodied citizen." While some provisions of the Soviet constitution are devoid of significance and others more honored in the breach than the observance, these institutions are so fundamentally rooted in the beliefs of the people including the leaders that, for the foreseeable future, they are as unlikely to be abolished as is the basic system of private property in the United States.

Now it is true that the ultimate end Marx had in mind was the full and free development and integration of man in society—"to end human alienation by changing the world," as Robert Tucker cogently put it—and it would be difficult to maintain that this objective has been approximated, let alone achieved, in the U.S.S.R. The fact however cannot be gainsaid that from a *Marxist* point of view the basis for the development of unalienated man was made to rest on

[3] For a fuller analysis of the influence of Marxist theory on Soviet practice, see this author's "The Soviet Union: The Search for Theory," in William G. Andrews, ed., *European Politics I: The Restless Search* (Princeton: Van Nostrand, 1966), pp. 216–240.

the abolition of private ownership, a centrally planned economy, and production for use instead of for profit—and insofar as the U.S.S.R. corresponds to this conception, as it surely does in substantial degree, it may be said in a real and meaningful sense to derive from Marxism.

It is also true that dictatorial controls in the U.S.S.R. mean that the Marxist scheme, particularly in its conception of socialist democracy, has not been realized. Undeniably, this lack of freedom in turn affects and limits the common ownership of property, but it does not negate it. Milovan Djilas, for example, goes too far when he maintains that in effect the communist political bureaucracy owns the nationalized property because it "uses, enjoys, and disposes" of it. While their controls give the bureaucrats important and special benefits, so long as marked fluidity prevails and national property may not be inherited, the privileges of the party leaders, as Molotov, Malenkov, and Khrushchev discovered, fall far short of ownership.

Not only does the fundamental organization of the economy reflect the Marxist scheme, but the strength of ideology is shown by frequently stubborn adherence to doctrine at the expense of rationality and efficiency. For example, planners in the U.S.S.R., basing themselves on Marx's proposition that only labor creates value, for a long time considered themselves ideologically debarred from imposing an interest charge for the use of capital. If used, it would have served as a means of efficient allocation and rationing of scarce capital. To be sure, the Russians succeeded in part in getting around this difficulty by using certain other devices, but these are not entirely satisfactory substitutes.

So also, recent steps to provide for interest on capital, a system of plant and individual "profit" incentive, a new pricing system to reflect more accurately labor and material costs and stimulate production of new items and improve quality, fines for delivery delays, and other techniques are designed to improve the planning system, not to replace it. In any event, ultimate intrusion of elements of rationality into the planned economy is akin to the fact that welfare-state measures are permitted to alter our free-enterprise system without destroying it. I, for one, see no reason to doubt the basic validity of Kosygin's statement with regard to the new economic techniques that "Our underlying principles are inviolate. There are no means of production in private hands. . . ."

Agriculture presents an even clearer and more dramatic example of the compulsion of theory. It must first be said that there are many explanations for the failure of the U.S.S.R. to achieve the repeatedly promised high level of agricultural production. These include the infertility of much Soviet land, inadequate rainfall, lack of mechanization, storage, and transport facilities, and heavy dependence on the labor of women and children—but surely a primary factor is the basic inadequacy of the present system of collectivization itself. It is not only tied up in the peasant's mind with bitter memories of forced collectivization but simply does not give him sufficient incentive to produce abundantly.

This failure is pointed up by the vitality of the dwarf private-farm sector. Although only 1.4 percent of the total agricultural land area and 3.3 percent of the total sown area in 1962, this sector contributes a heavily disproportionate share of the total output of many important foods such as fruits, vegetables, potatoes, meat, milk, and eggs. That year, according to official Soviet sources, the private sector accounted for about a third of gross agricultural output including 45 percent of total meat and milk production, 76 percent of eggs, 22 percent of wool, 70 percent of potatoes, 42 percent of vegetables, and 66 percent of fruit. By contrast, the results achieved in the public agricultural sector are incredibly low.

Soviet leaders have frequently admitted the comparative inefficiency of Soviet agriculture. Characteristically, Khrushchev commented in 1956 that "available data show that in our country considerably more labor is spent to produce a ton of milk or meat than in the United States," and in 1963, that Soviet agriculture involved uneconomic practices that would be "inconceivable to an American farmer." More recently, Brezhnev said that some Soviet collective farms have become virtually unmanageable.

Why then does the Soviet Union continue to adhere to the collective and state farm systems (with a preference for the latter as the more ideologically advanced)? Surely a primary consideration must be a deep and genuine commitment to Marxist theory. Socialized property, after all, was a basic Marxist goal, out of dedication to which the Soviet leaders became revolutionaries and languished in czarist prisons. And, whatever compromises may be dictated by practical exigencies today, it would not seem possible for any Soviet leader to dismantle or fundamentally alter the collectivist industrial and agricultural systems and restore private property and free enterprise.

Recent Economic Developments

Viewed historically, the rate of industrial development and overall economic growth of the U.S.S.R. has been quite phenomenal. In a rather short span of nonwar years, the Soviet Union rose from relative backwardness and underdevelopment to become the second most powerful industrial nation in the world. At the same time it must be recognized that this spectacular record of growth was achieved in good part at the expense of the consumer, whose preferences were not consulted and upon whom heavy sacrifices were imposed. The nature, significance, and impact of Soviet economic successes and failures are dealt with in detail in a number of essays in this volume. I shall limit myself largely, therefore, to recent economic developments and their implications.

It is undeniable that the past few years have seen a sharp decline in the Soviet Union's *rate* of economic growth. To understand what has happened, and why, the reader must bear with a few key statistics. According to official Soviet sources, in the basic area of industrial production, in which the U.S.S.R. consistently claimed growth by 10 to 20 percent in the late 1940s and the 1950s, the rate of increase reported was 9.1 percent in 1961, 9.7 percent in 1962, 8.5 percent in 1963, 7.1 percent in 1964, and precisely 8.6 percent in both 1965 and 1966. If we take account of other sectors of the Soviet economy, including agriculture, with its admittedly poor record in 1962 and 1963 and unimpressive record in 1965, and transmute the figures into terms of gross national product (G.N.P.) —a concept used in the West to cover the sum of *all* goods and services produced—the official Soviet claim suggests an average overall rate for the period of about 5 percent.

This figure, however, has been substantially discounted by many Western economists. In 1964 experts in the United States, in separate studies submitted to the Joint Economic Committee of Congress and the Central Intelligence Agency, estimated the Soviet Union's economic growth for 1962 and 1963 at less than 2.5 percent. In October 1965 Gardner Ackley, chairman of the American Council of Economic Advisers, reported that a State Department study had shown that, in general, the growth rate of Soviet national output had fallen one third during the past five years, from "a very impressive" 6.5 percent a year during the 1950s to an average of about 4.3 percent per year since 1960.

In any event, while there is a dispute among Western specialists as to the *extent* of the decline in the Soviet rate of growth—some question the low figures set in the cited reports—what is indisputable (and acknowledged by the U.S.S.R.) is that a sharp drop has in fact taken place. Why has this happened? The explanation is complex and it is possible to suggest here only in summary form some of the relevant factors. Furthermore, to judge their significance, it is necessary to distinguish between those difficulties which may be temporary and those which appear to be more deep-rooted and intractable.

A major element in the poor growth of the Soviet Union in recent years undoubtedly lies in the high priority given by the U.S.S.R. to its military and space programs, which have preempted a large share of the highly trained men, machinery, and materials that might otherwise have been devoted to modernizing industry and agriculture. Another factor has been the failure of agriculture, accounting for almost a third of Soviet G.N.P., to keep pace with industry. Part of the explanation for this lies in the disastrous weather conditions in major farm areas in the U.S.S.R. in some recent years. Beginning with 1959 the U.S.S.R. had only two good harvest years—1964 (which followed the extreme drought of 1963, the worst in three quarters of a century) and 1966 (which followed the relatively poor harvest of 1965). As a consequence, the U.S.S.R. had to buy millions of tons of grain abroad and slaughter 40 percent of its national stock of pigs, the number of which declined from 70 million in 1962 to 52.8 million in 1964. In 1965, the Soviet Union admitted that "plans for procurement of meat, milk, eggs, and wool" in 1964 "were not fulfilled." One Western specialist estimates that "the net agricultural product—a more meaningful measure than the gross product—showed in 1964 no more than a 5 percent increase over that of 1958, while the population grew 9.7 percent during the same period." The Soviet agricultural deficiency, in turn, concededly adversely affected the processed-food industry and related branches of light industry.

Looking ahead, it is obvious that a continued favorable turn in the weather will bring substantial gains in agricultural output. It is also probable that improvement will result from implementation of the plans outlined by Party leaders in March 1965 and subsequently. These provide for stable grain procurement and delivery prices, a substantial increase in prices to be paid by the state for planned agricultural purchases, a considerable increase in state investments in agriculture, strengthening of the authority of local agricultural specialists, and cancellation of the debts of many of the weak *kolkhozes*. Nonetheless, a serious question remains as to whether the persistently poor performance of the agricultural sector—which employs about 40 percent of the Soviet labor force to produce the food and fiber to meet the needs of the Soviet people, while the 8 percent employed in agriculture in the United States oversupplies the American people—can be drastically improved within the framework of the present collective-farm system.

Other factors retarding the growth rate of the Soviet economy are due to the shift in investment emphasis from heavy industry, raw materials, and power supply into agriculture, chemical technology, and service and consumer areas. These have already led and may continue to lead to a decline in the productivity (growth intensity) of investment. "It was easier," one analyst commented, "to build more and more steel mills and cement plants and hydroelectric dams than it is to build chemical plants and diversified consumer goods."

Another cardinal difficulty derives from the very nature of a centrally planned and directed economy, which threatens to drown Soviet planners in a paper ocean. With the inherent complexity of planning the production of literally millions of items in their multiple interrelationship, the use of computers and other advanced instruments and techniques may be expected to mitigate, but not to eliminate, the difficulty.

Other defects of the Soviet system of planning, at least as heretofore practiced and applied, have been the failure to use adequate devices to set reasonable limits on the amount of capital that enterprises will seek to employ, the inefficient dispersal of capital investments, the lack of a price system that properly measures the real cost of resources, the chronic understatement of production goals to enhance improperly enterprise profit and bonuses, and the pressure to meet set quotas at the expense of quality, diversity, and technical advances. It remains to be seen whether the proposals of some leading Soviet economists for a variety of techniques to improve Soviet economic performance, which were tested in some instances and are supposed to be gradually introduced, will be extensively adopted and, if so, prove practical within the framework of a centrally planned and governed economy.

To conclude our discussion at this point would be to give a partial and one-sided view of Soviet reality. Its centrally planned economy also has certain strengths and advantages. To begin with, it now seems to be firmly established that the Soviet institutional arrangements are such that its system is not subject to severe depressions or recessions. (It can no longer be argued, as it once was, that this would prove true only in the period of initial and rapid industrialization.) Related is the fact that, notwithstanding the inefficiency and waste involved in central planning and in the actual distribution and application of resources, the U.S.S.R. does employ the resources it has developed to full or nearly full capacity. It would be unthinkable, in short, for the U.S.S.R. to have the capacity to produce, let us say, 90 million metric tons of steel and in the presence of continuing social need produce only half that amount. Even in agriculture—where the Soviet failure in light of the input of effort has been egregious—a centrally planned economy makes possible extensive and systematic mechanization. It is true, too, that the nature of that system discourages expenditures for the production of socially useless, or even harmful, products and services. It must be said, finally, that while the rate of economic growth in general has slowed down in recent years in the U.S.S.R. as compared with the trend in the 1950s and the performance of countries like Japan and West Germany for a number of years in the post-war period, the Soviet Union continued throughout to make progress that, by generally prevailing international standards, is quite respectable.

The New Five Year Plan

All of the factors just mentioned are pertinent to an evaluation of the prospects of the new Soviet Five Year Plan, adopted by the Twenty-third Party Congress in 1966.

First, let us take a look at the plan's promises and prognoses. It envisages increases in the five-year period 1966–1970 of approximately 40 percent in national income; 30 percent in real per capita income; 50 percent in industrial output; 25 percent in farm output (predicated in part on extraordinarily large capital investment); 30 percent in housing construction; and 40 percent in the sale of consumer goods of improved quality and variety, including a rise in production of refrigerators from 1.7 to 5.5 million, of TV sets from 3.7 to 7.6 million, and of automobiles from 201,200 to 750,000.

In addition, the plan anticipates institution of monthly guaranteed remuneration for collective farmers corresponding to the level of wages paid to state farm workers; a number of wage increases and a further narrowing of the disparity between high and low incomes generally; a rise in minimum old-age pensions for workers and farmers; marked improvement in the population's diet and increased access to fabrics, clothing, and knitted goods; substantial increase in educational opportunities at all levels; and marked improvement of medical services including a 2.68 million increase in hospital beds.

Several comments are in order. It is noteworthy that the new plan sets goals that are substantially below those projected by Nikita Khrushchev for 1970 at the Twenty-second Party Congress in 1961. Nor does the new plan assert that the Soviet economy will catch up with (let alone surpass) that of the United States by 1970—a claim repeatedly put forth by Khrushchev. Furthermore, if the goals of the new plan for 1966–1970 are contrasted with actual achievements in the preceding five years, it must be said that they appear fairly moderate. Specifically, the planned increase in national income of 40 percent, industrial production of 50 percent, and agricultural output (in comparison with *average* annual output in the preceding five years) of 25 percent compares with actual increases for 1961–1965 in these categories of 35 percent, 50 percent, and 10 percent respectively. Finally, the fact is that the plan reveals more concern for consumer interests and desires than has characterized Soviet economic planning for several decades.

However in light of continued emphasis on heavy industry and space expenditures, the deficiencies of collectivized agriculture, imbalances of the Soviet economy, chronic shortages, broken promises, and Soviet international obligations, it is not improbable that the U.S.S.R. will fail to meet some of its goals in the time set. But it would be well to recognize that by Soviet standards the goals are fairly modest and realistic and hence appear to be largely realizable.

The long-range implications of these varied considerations are difficult to project. There is every reason to believe that, notwithstanding its problems, the Soviet economy, barring war or major catastrophe, will continue to grow systematically and steadily and make substantial progress toward the realization of its economic and welfare goals. By contrast, there is no assurance of similar regular and consistent growth with respect to the American economy, whose performance, viewed historically, has been much more erratic and cyclical. And this remains a problem although, in light of the knowledge and experience gained in the past several decades, a serious depression in the United States would seem to be excluded and our needs, in important respects, are quite different. For the U.S.S.R., for example, a substantial increase in agricultural production is vital; but we have no need to increase our already ample food supply for internal consumption. Also, as a society of relative scarcity, the Soviet Union must still concern itself greatly with quantity; we, on the other hand, can afford to concern ourselves more with quality (and, increasingly, it is hoped, will concern ourselves with equality).

Finally, it is worth emphasizing that while economic factors are vital to any evaluation, particularly of a society in the stage of overcoming backwardness, as Karl Kautsky pointed out, in the final analysis "it is not technical and economic innovations but the human aspects of a society that matter."

Some Conclusions

The conclusions of this essay will not appeal to those who are attracted to tidy and simplistic explanations. In my opinion the Soviet record is a mixed one of successes and failures, of hopes realized and hopes shattered. And, specifically with respect to the continuing importance of Marxism, that record clearly demonstrates that certain of its doctrines, in the hands of the Soviet leaders, have been attenuated, perverted, deferred, and, in some instances, discarded. Soviet "democracy," for example, bears no relation to its Marxist conception. And the failure of the Soviet state to wither away, in the face of the claim that the U.S.S.R. has already achieved socialism and a classless society, however justified or rationalized, is nonetheless in conflict with Marxist theory.

On the other hand, it is demonstrable that some Marxist doctrines have to an important extent influenced and shaped decisions of the Soviet leaders. This has been true with respect to the fundamental nature of the economy grounded upon the principle of collective ownership and control. And, however tarnished the record in some respects, it seems to me undeniable that Marxist theory has had and continues to have a significant impact in underscoring the essential equality of all races and peoples. Finally, while the motivations for social welfare in the U.S.S.R. are varied and complex, I think it is reasonable to conclude that the egalitarianism suggested in Marx's vision of a socialist society—a vision in which the Soviet leaders, like the Soviet people, have been educated and reared—played and continues to play an important part.

To say, as Irving Kristol has said, that "Marxism as an intellectual system and a *Weltanschauung* is dead" and that what alone survives are "movements and governments which use the tatters of its ideology as a justification for autocratic rule" or to maintain, as W. W. Rostow has done, that Soviet leaders are concerned with the welfare of the Soviet people only or mainly as a reflex to their power goals is, in my judgment, to be guilty of oversimplification; as guilty as those in the U.S.S.R. who wrote in the New Party Program (1961) that a "bourgeois republic, however democratic" inevitably constitutes "a machine for the exploitation and suppression of the vast majority of the working people by a handful of capitalists."

In general, the demise of Marxist ideology, like Mark Twain's comment on the report of his death, has been greatly exaggerated; and there may be more than a little truth to Clark Kissinger's comment that "When they [the old left] proclaim the end of ideology, it's like an old man proclaiming the end of sex. Because he doesn't feel it any more, he thinks it's disappeared."

Similarly, to conceive of Marxist ideology as a species of opium with which the Soviet leaders lull the people while taking care never to inhale themselves is, as R. N. Carew Hunt has wisely said, "to attribute to them an ability to dissociate themselves from the logic of their system—an ability which it is unlikely they possess."

So, also, to maintain that because departures from Marxism have been far-reaching in some areas, Marxism cannot possibly have *any* continuing impact or significance, is to insist upon the absolute indivisibility of Marxist doctrine—a test we would be unable to apply to other doctrines. By so rigorous a standard, it would be impossible to explain the coexistence of democracy and slavery in the United States for nearly a hundred years, or the coexistence of Christianity (and other religions) and un-Christian-like tyranny for nearly two thousand years.

Even in the areas where distortion or perversion of Marxism has manifestly taken place, it is revealing to observe how "old truths" persist so that a measure of relaxation promptly brings people to the fore who seek to restore Marx's true meaning and purpose. Typical is that group of intellectuals in the U.S.S.R. today whose attitude is perhaps best (or at least most overtly) expressed by Yevtushenko who cautioned that "those who speak in the name of Communism but in reality pervert its meaning are among its most dangerous enemies, perhaps even more dangerous than its enemies in the West," and by Boris Slutsky who wrote:

> Time to bring the dreams to pass.
> Yes, with neither doubt nor hesitation—
> To get to work and bring the dreams to pass.[4]

It is one thing, however, to recognize the continuing importance of the revolutionary dynamic; it is quite another to predict the future configuration of Soviet society or specifically to maintain that relaxation of the dictatorship in the U.S.S.R. cannot and will not be halted or aborted short of realization of a democratic socialist society truly in the image of Marx. Such a far-reaching projection belongs in the realm of prophecy that this writer, mindful of J. B. Bury's pungent comment that "it is the function of history to belie prophets," will not essay.

[4] Boris Slutsky, "Time to Bring the Dreams to Pass." Translation from *The Current Digest of the Soviet Press* (December 26, 1962), published weekly at Columbia University by the Joint Committee on Slavic Studies, appointed by the American Council of Learned Societies and the Social Science Research Council. Copyright © 1962 (Vol. XIV, No. 48), the Joint Committee on Slavic Studies. Reprinted by permission.

II

The Soviet Political System

by ALFRED G. MEYER

I

A. C. H. C. de Tocqueville had it easier than we. Like us, he represented a political tradition that had been challenged by a revolutionary new order established half a century before. Like us, he wished to study this new political system and assess its strengths and weaknesses, its achievements and failures. Unlike us, however, he had infinitely greater opportunities for using his eyes and ears for the extensive survey he wished to make. Moreover, there was no cold war raging then to inflame the passions and blind the eyes. To be sure, democracy was as frightening a bogey in 1831 as communism is in 1967; and there was an ideological barrier, a modicum of reserve if not suspicion putting the young aristocrat on guard against the revolutionary experiment in the New World. Yet this latent hostility pales in comparison with the antagonism between the Western de Tocquevilles of today and the more recent revolutionary experiment in the U.S.S.R. After all, his own country had made its experiments with revolutionary democracy at the same time as the

New World, and was soon to make others, whereas the Western world today, facing the communist world, still has its *ancien régime*. For this reason alone, the ideological gulf appears deeper.

This gulf opens at the very moment we begin to assess the development and achievements of the Soviet political system in the first half-century of its existence. Our first impulse might be to go back to the birth of the system and examine the expectations with which it came into life. Already at this point, ideological differences appear, because different people expressed divergent expectations. In the Western world, and among Russian counterrevolutionaries, the political leaders were nearly unanimous at first in predicting the early collapse of the bolshevik regime. They did not credit the bolshevik leadership with sufficient political skill to maintain themselves in power or to create any orderly governmental machinery; nor did they believe a socialist or communist social order capable of functioning. The pervasiveness and strength of these views in the first years after the October Revolution deserves to be remembered. Indeed, thirty years after the bolshevik seizure of power, assumptions of this sort still formed the basis for the judgment of George Kennan and others, who argued that the Soviet regime was by its nature incapable of satisfying a sufficient number of citizens, hence unable to acquire stability or legitimacy.

Only seemingly in contrast with such pessimistic (or, from the point of view of Western observers, optimistic) appraisals of the system's staying power are views that prevailed among Western scholars in the first ten years after World War II, the formative years of American Sovietology. During that period, most writers seemed to take it for granted that the Soviet political system was innately incapable of changing. More specifically, those of its features deemed most obnoxious (individual dictatorship, terror, total indoctrination and thought control, as well as economic austerity) were regarded as essential elements of "totalitarianism" without which the entire system would disintegrate. Indeed, the basic lack of legitimacy, stability, and viability of the regime, it was argued, made "totalitarianism" and its syndrome of negative features inevitable. Thus the two seemingly opposite hypotheses—instability and inability to change—were linked to each other.

Prognoses of this kind are now being reviewed by our Western de Tocquevilles, who today tend to smile at the earlier expectations engendered by the October Revolution. They do have the satisfaction to know that the people on the other side were equally hasty in predicting the results of communist rule. What the bolshevik leaders expected at the time of the October Revolution is well known. Lenin and his party comrades predicted the immediate establishment of a socialist society managed in democratic fashion by the masses of the citizens themselves. It would be a society of equals, without classes or a strict division of labor, and without exploitation. Such a polity would no longer require institutions of coercion or a complex administrative machinery; they would disappear together with oppressive kinship rules, moral codes, false ideologies, internecine competition between individuals, and other concomitants of class-torn societies. The speedy development of this new society, the Bolsheviks argued, was guaranteed by the impending spread of communism over all or most of the civilized world.

Obviously, this extension of communist rule has not taken place; and, equally clearly, the Soviet political system of 1967 corresponds to the expectations of its founders as little as it does to the prognoses of their enemies. The task remains of defining what in fact it has been and now is, and in what fields of endeavor it has succeeded or failed.

Let me begin by challenging the reader with an exaggeration: to define the Soviet system as it has existed in the past five decades is impossible because it has changed so often and so thoroughly. In other words, there is no such thing as The Soviet Political System; there is only a succession of systems sharply differing from each other in purpose, structure, and functioning.

Having overstated my case, I hasten to point to a number of continuities in the entire history of the Soviet Union. Except in periods of total revolutionary change, there are some elements of political systems that are fundamentally "given," that change slowly or not at all—the geographic and demographic base, the social structure, the political culture. Still, one might argue that one of the persistent traits of Soviet politics is the attempt of the rulers to wreak change in this very substructure. Some scholars think of communist rule as self-perpetuating revolution. The very factors we see as given, factors underlying not only the entire Soviet history, but also linking the Soviet system to its czarist predecessor, are among the factors that communism seeks to change. Communist political systems would thus come close to the dialectical model combining perpetual self-destruction with self-perpetuation or, more aptly, perpetual self-renewal, with stress on the newness.

There are, however, continuities of a less substructural kind, perpetual traits present in all phases of the Soviet regime. To support my claim that there has been a succession of different political systems since the October Revolution, I would have to convince my readers that these are merely *formal,* hence illusory, continuities, which obscure the succession of several different systems.

One could argue, for instance, that the Soviet political system from its beginning to our day has been governed by the same Party. Therefore, the political leadership that came to power in 1917 has managed to perpetuate itself more successfully than most other contemporary elites. Moreover, the position their Party has occupied within the political structure of the country, the functions it has served within the system, the methods it has applied, the goals that have guided it, the world outlook its leaders have professed—all these central features, one might claim, have remained constant. My view is that the external forms have remained relatively constant, but the actual political relationships have been extremely variable. The self-perpetuation of the Communist Party as the sovereign elite conceals the fundamental transformations that have occurred in the Party—the several shifts in the character of its membership; the repeated and thorough turnover of leaders, obscured though it is by the longevity and staying power of selected personalities; the subtle but by no means negligible changes in its relation to the political system as a whole. The continuity in ideological heritage can be dismissed as purely formal, because, despite the perennial use of identical words, both the content and the functions of "Marxism-Leninism" within the Soviet political system have changed repeatedly and thoroughly. Robert V. Daniels has aptly referred to these shifts as ideological vector changes. Again, the persistence of dictatorship and paternalism, the perennial readiness of Soviet rulers to use violence, their ever-present fear of spontaneous activity—in short, the persistent authoritarianism of Soviet government—should not prevent us from seeing the countervailing tendencies that have made themselves felt, with varying strength, in different periods. I have in mind the preoccupation of the communist leadership with methods of rational management, with the establishment of stable structures and orderly routines and indeed the rule of law. Dictatorship may have persisted, but it has been exercised with varying degrees of arbitrariness. Similarly, the social base of the dictatorship has been in flux, as the class structure of Soviet society was subjected to violent shocks and revolutionary changes, only to show recurrent tendencies to settle in a fixed mold. There have been significant changes in the degree and manner of citizens' participation in government, in the material benefits the system granted them, in popular attitudes toward the entire system, and many other crucial variables. In short, by concentrating on the persistence of dictatorship, we neglect the changing nature, intensity, aims, and effects of this dictatorship and of the entire system. Perhaps many of us tend to forget how prevalent dictatorship is among political systems, and how rare and vulnerable are the polities that have managed to dispense with it. Because of this prevalence of authoritarianism, it is necessary to differentiate between its many forms.

The reason for the changeability of the Soviet system (or for its succession of stages) might be presented in several ways. Earlier, I alluded to the built-in urge for perpetual revolution. This urge can be explained as a function of an interplay between the various "input" forces impinging on Soviet politics—changing elite goals, conflicting priorities among such goals, changes in the political culture of the masses, challenges coming in from the outside world—or one could show that in the first half-century of the Soviet system these and other inputs have never been in a stable equilibrium. Another explanation (possibly no more than a rephrasing of what was just said) could be sought in the technological revolution of our century, which has a tendency to impose permanent instability on the entire society and thus to make any political system obsolete as soon as it has established itself, precisely because technological change upsets the balance of societal forces of which the political system is a function.

One can, of course, conceive of political systems that restructure themselves in response to such substructural changes, in the manner of self-regulating automatic machines. Karl Deutsch, in his *The Nerves of Government* has made this one of the salient features in his model of a well-functioning political system. But 120 years earlier Karl Marx already argued that the ideal democratic constitution would be such a self-regulator; and his self-professed adherents in the U.S.S.R. argue that their political order is in fact such a self-adjusting democracy. Were this correct, my assertion that since 1917 we have witnessed a succession of political systems would have to be rejected. Instead, we would have observed one marvelously designed system changing itself in response to changes in circumstances.

I do not mean to get bogged down in scholastic arguments. But I do wish to make clear why I am not ready to accept such a view. The reason is that, in my opinion, it gives a false image of spontaneous, smooth, and effective self-adjustment; it presents a picture of a political machinery so finely devised that it does in fact regulate itself. In reality, the Soviet system has shown little talent for smooth self-regulation. On the contrary, it has manifested recurrent tendencies toward institutional, procedural, and ideological rigidity and conservatism, in short, toward self-entrenchment. To use another Marxian concept: the superstructure has again and again assumed a dynamic of its own; it has lagged behind substructural developments and become dysfunctional to the social system. Major adjustments therefore had to be made in near-revolutionary (or near-counterrevolutionary) fashion. They have usually been violent, and they could be accomplished only because at the top of the system a powerful dictatorship or oligarchy was operating with few restraints. Today, the checks or arbitrariness, hence on permanent revolution, are getting stronger; and perhaps the Soviet political system is entering a phase during which self-regulating adjustments or grand restructuring by dictatorial fiat become more difficult. In any event, neither the past nor the present Soviet political system can be described as the marvelous self-regulating machinery that it proclaims to be. Instead, every readjustment has been a major crisis.

One final explanation of the instability of the system is a reference to its revolutionary origins. As Crane Brinton has shown, the process of great revolutions takes on a morphology incorporating a number of typical phases. One need not accept the pattern he has outlined in order to apply this insight to the Russian Revolution of 1917; and one then discerns distinct stages of Soviet political development. At each stage, the society faced challenges specific to that stage and responded to them with an equally specific political system. At the same time, each of these successive political systems had to deal with ever recurrent problems—challenges to which every

Russian ruler, or every modern state, or any political system whatever, must respond. In order to justify my viewpoint about a succession of political systems, I would have to show that each of the
Soviet regimes tackled these persistent tasks in its own specific
fashion. Within the space allotted here, I will probably not be able
to give more than hints and scattered examples.

II

Let me begin with a brief description of the successive political
systems. The first, in existence from 1917 to the end of 1920, is
aptly called War Communism. Its chief problem undoubtedly was
to maintain the newly established communist rule against seemingly
overwhelming challenges and, by destroying the challengers, to
institutionalize itself. Its principal methods of government were
destructive: military operations against foreign and domestic troops;
the destruction of all rival political parties; the abolition of established property relations; and serious attempts to do away with the
entire framework of entrenched institutions, including the family,
the churches, laws and courts, money, and moral codes. From the
ruins of the old order, the Communists assumed, a new system
would rise at once, conforming to the more utopian hopes of Marx
and his bolshevik followers. We have sketched the outlines of
this utopia in the beginnings of this chapter. In retrospect, one
must point out that the new rulers had totally inadequate notions
about how to implement such a program or about the difficulties
standing in the way of its spontaneous emergence. The communist
leadership at the time was so constituted, however, that it could not
sufficiently become aware of this inadequacy. And when the masses
of the citizens wanted to act out their own utopian expectations,
the regime restrained them forcibly.

As a result, War Communism was characterized by the sharpest
possible tension between intentions and capabilities, between expectations and potentialities, from the points of view of both the
elite and the masses. Such tension is not conducive to the formation
of a viable political system, because effective and reasonably stable
institutions can develop only where the ruling elite and the people
have a fairly realistic conception of the resources at their disposal

and, on that basis, work out policies, programs, aspirations, and expectations.

At the same time, in the years 1917–1921, there were no resources for orderly government of any kind in Russia, nor was there any elite or counterelite that could have found or created them. The old system had disintegrated. The economy was ruined. The population was bitterly divided, so that civil war was inevitable; the people were in a destructive mood. The mass of the citizens, moreover, was illiterate and lacked almost all traditions of self-government. To the extent self-government operated, it had a divisive, anarchic effect. In short, it would have been impossible to create a stable political system. Hence the only elite that could have managed to impose any semblance of order was one out of tune with reality. Only utopians and fanatics could have had the recklessness or courage to go on governing. Realists would have despaired. Precisely because the Bolsheviks had expectations ludicrously out of tune with reality did they hold the system together.

If, indeed, one can speak of a system at all. Even though some basic institutions were established, Soviet politics during the civil war was primarily chaos, improvisation, and a succession of dire emergencies. It was rule by sheer force—government by pointing the loaded pistol. Such a nonsystem could maintain itself only because of the war and the resulting militarization of all politics. Once the civil war was over, it was scrapped just before it was threatening to collapse entirely.

The second Soviet political system (1921–1927) was in many essentials the reverse of the first. I am tempted to sum it up by stating that it sought to make do with the society that had emerged from the civil war. This society included the numerically overwhelming class of economically independent peasants owning small plots of land; these peasants the regime sought to use by making it profitable for them to farm their plots. The regime furthermore endeavored to make use of all members of the prerevolutionary professional elite still remaining in the country. It even utilized institutions copied from the capitalist world. Such institutions as civil law and a stable currency, to mention only two, had to be reintroduced, having been abolished or left to disappear by the first Soviet political system. The entire policy of making do with social and cultural forces available was symbolized by the slogan of "peaceful coexistence." Although it was meant to express the aims of Soviet foreign policy, it can be applied to domestic policies just as well.

The first system had lived on dreams. In the second, the dreams were shelved for the time being. The first had been revolutionary; the second was one of retreat and retrenchment. The first had been destructive; the second was interested in reconstruction of what had existed before. Beyond this, it sought to improve these residues of the past: to make the economy more efficient, to make the peasants literate, to teach former professional revolutionaries how to function as effective administrators. Socialism was to be achieved, according to Party doctrine at the time, by the wise utilization and improvement of the things czarism and capitalism had left.

For the Communist Party, the second Soviet political system was an interregnum during which neither leadership nor long-range policy was well defined. Hence both were the subject of controversy. Lenin, who had created both the first and the second Soviet system, did not survive the formation of the second one for very long. His illness and death plunged the U.S.S.R. into a succession crisis lasting until the end of the second phase. At the same time, his passing became the occasion for a significant transformation of the Party membership, through the admission of large numbers of new applicants.

The leadership was divided in groping for definitions of problems and policies. In the administration of virtually all social endeavors, it collaborated with the intellectual holdovers from czarism. It showed grudging toleration for heterogeneity and noncommunist subcultures in its policies toward the peasants, toward trade unions, toward national minorities, private traders, and foreign capitalist concessionaires. The Party showed this tolerance probably because the system as a whole was too weak to fight these undesired elements. The entire political system was a holding action—an attempt to maintain Party supremacy within an unfavorable political culture, so as to preserve the power conferred on the Party by the Revolution and the civil war. The entire functioning of the system was related to this uneasy balance between the Party and the hostile society it sought to contain. While engaged in this holding action, however, the Party repaired its unity and built up its political strength. Hence a remade Party emerged at the end of this second Soviet political system.

Once it had gathered strength and unity, the Communist Party destroyed the second political system it had created. It launched a new revolution designed to eliminate the various subcultures the previous system had tolerated and integrated, and on whose participation and cooperation it had depended. Again, therefore, the new order was in some crucial aspects a reversal of the preceding one. This is true not only of the underlying social structure, but also of the functioning of the system. The second Soviet political system had been founded on an attitude of compromise, retrenchment, and grudging compromise. The third was militant in its outlook and violent in its methods. It resembled the first phase more than the second.

It did so not only in its destructiveness and violence, but also in its constructive efforts. Whereas the second system had sought to improve existing resources, the third attempted to construct an entirely new economy and polity, one that, this time, would surely transform the country into a socialist one. The methods it employed for this, too, were similar to those of the first phase: industrialization took the form of a reckless crash program. It was undertaken with sovereign disregard for the difficulties, hence quite irrationally, and was carried out in a euphoric spirit of storming the heavens, quite in contrast to the sense of boredom, futility, if not despair, prevalent in the Party during the preceding system.

System No. 2 had begun modestly and almost inadvertently: a single concession to the peasants had necessitated, as if on afterthought, a thorough restructuring of the social and political order. Similarly, the crash program of industrialization led to a restructuring of Soviet politics so thorough that an entire new system emerged in the late 1930s. Because this system was created and operated by Joseph Stalin, it may appropriately be called the Stalinist political system.

The Stalinist system was built around industrialization as a long-range undertaking, to which all the resources of the society should be devoted. It might therefore be defined as the institutionalization of the crash program. A crash program is an effort in which the style is determined by impatience and a sense of dire urgency. It operates by commandeering resources and deploying them by command, emphasizing rapid expansion rather than balance, quantity rather than quality, quick results rather than smooth operations.

The difference between a crash program and a more deliberate or "rational" effort can be symbolized by an example from engineering. Before building a dam across a river, those in charge of the construction project, ideally, should study the geomorphology of the dam site, together with pertinent data about such things as water flow, annual rainfall, ice formation, maximum and minimum temperatures, soils, rocks, and other geological facts. By complicated calculations, the engineer can then determine the necessary strength, curvature, height, and other features of the dam. But he can also dispense with such calculations, either in impatience or because of lack of skilled personnel, and simply start to pour concrete as high and as thick as his budget will allow. If the budget is skimpy, as it is likely to be in an economy where scarcity reigns, he will sacrifice all refinements for the purpose of sinking the biggest and strongest possible slab of rock into the river gorge. The method is crude, but it works. And the U.S.S.R. under Stalin not only built dams in this fashion but, figuratively speaking, its entire economy.

The third Soviet political system (1928 to the mid-1930s), in mobilizing the citizens for the construction effort, had relied primarily on command, violence, and revolutionary enthusiasm. Under Stalinism, much of the enthusiasm had waned. Violence and command, meanwhile, had lost their sporadic character and turned into routines and institutions. They were supplemented by a system of positive incentives, through managed inequality, and a concerted effort of education and indoctrination. The Stalinist regime endeavored not only to create a new technical-managerial elite; it also sought to reeducate the entire population for life in the machine age and for accepting the Stalinist system as legitimate.

Stalinism, then, was a period of system-building on a grand scale. All previous Soviet systems either were oriented to destructive tasks or appear, in retrospect, to have been false starts, interregnums, or breathers between revolutions. The system emerging under Stalin had greater permanency. Or so it seemed to Western social scientists, who until recently tended to assume that under Stalin the Soviet political system emerged in its permanent form.

The beginnings of the Stalinist system took on the character of yet another bloody revolution—the Great Purge of the late 1930s, which almost completely destroyed the previous political elite. This removal of Lenin's comrades-in-arms was accompanied by a re-definition of the ruling ideology so thorough that we must see it as a radical change in contents. Furthermore, the basic institutional structure of the country underwent significant change: the sovereignty of the Communist Party gave way to the sovereignty of Stalin and his personal secretariat. The Party, in declining, became merely one of the dictator's instruments of rule, on an equal footing, so to speak, with the police. Rapid sociological change, typical of industrializa-tion and urbanization processes everywhere, resulted from the eco-nomic growth the system promoted. This change included the emer-gence of a new pattern of social stratification, or class structure, together with an ideology designed both to conceal and to justify it. It was accompanied by changes in family life, religious habits, and the ethnic distribution of the population, as well as by deep changes in the educational profile of the population. In short, Stalinism created Soviet society as we know it today. It did so, again, by command, formulated at times by whim or by rule of thumb, backed up by a harsh system of sanctions and sharply differentiated re-wards, and complemented by indoctrination designed to restructure the citizens' personalities. In seeking to educate a "new Soviet man," the Stalinist system attempted to create a civic culture of obedience, collectivism, and statism. The people were to endure hardships cheer-fully while denying their existence, toil joyously for the common good, and heartily agree with every pronouncement of the dictator.

Let me exaggerate once again. Every Soviet political system destroyed itself by its success. Each rendered itself superfluous and jeopardized its own existence by solving some major problem or problems confronting it; precisely for the solution of those problems it functioned and structured itself.

The first system successfully utilized the utopian anarchism of workers, poor peasants, and national minorities for destructive tasks and almost succumbed to this destructiveness.

The second system successfully utilized classes and cultures antagonistic to communism to such an extent that it perceived these classes and cultures as a threat. At the same time, one might argue that their usefulness had been exhausted toward the end of the second system.

The third system once again made use of revolutionary urges in the party and the population, only to perceive them as dangers once the drive for industrialization was well under way and the classes deemed hostile had been destroyed. Hence the revolutionary ideology was changed to an ideology of collective entrepreneurship, and the sovereign party, with its old personnel, was superseded by a ruthless, single-minded entrepreneur who fashioned a primitive command system for the task of building the industrial society.

This crude, primitive, but effective Stalinist system, once again, became obsolete because of its success. Having built an industrial society, it was poorly equipped by its own structure and operating methods to maintain, manage, and improve this society. Erected around a crash program of system-building, the political machinery of the Soviet Union was unsuited for the orderly routines necessary for system-management.

Soviet society has become complex and heterogeneous. Its components have become increasingly interdependent. Hence it is a society in need of ever more sensitive, sophisticated, and difficult coordination. A congeries of interests has developed, which must be balanced and aggregated to ensure the continued functioning of the system. This need for balance and smooth functioning has tended to overshadow the urge for rapid growth.

In short, the Soviet political system must find structures and methods designed to accommodate it to heterogeneity and interest conflict. This means that terror has become dysfunctional, and so has the overwhelming emphasis Stalinism gave to command and centralized control. The society simply has become too complex to be run from one central control post or by one strongman. Similarly, the ideological dogma can no longer reign sovereign over all thought processes. Total indoctrination has become a hindrance to the smooth functioning of a modern industrial society. And if some of the functions that the indoctrination process served must still be served, then indoctrination has to be replaced by other processes, just as an increase in rewards may be a substitute for, indeed an improvement over, the use of terror—an improvement, that is, from the point of view of the political elite: when available, rewards may be more effective than terror in strengthening a system's legitimacy and authority.

The political developments that have been going on in the

Soviet Union since Stalin's death (1953) are, in my opinion, attempts of the system thus to restructure itself. In recent years, I
have compared this process to analogous transformations in American corporations, namely, to the shift from centralized authoritarian
companies run or command by single-minded, unsophisticated entrepreneurs like John D. Rockefeller or Henry Ford (the Stalins of
American industry) to streamlined, decentralized organizations managed by smooth, rational, urbane manipulators like Alfred Sloan
or Robert McNamara. If we wanted to use the language of Pareto,
we could also describe this process as the replacement of lions by
foxes.

When foxes oust the lions or merely supersede them, far more
is involved, of course, than merely a subtle change in the character
of the elite. Even if we stay within the conceptual framework of
Paretan elitism, it would be clear that foxes require different structures from lions, and that their method of government will be
different. However gradual it be, the replacement of lions by foxes
is a systemic change; it implies the replacement of an entire political
system by another. That, too, can be a gradual process, of course.
One might add to this that, perhaps, lions (at least human ones)
are apt to coalesce into tighter oligarchies, whereas foxes split up
into smaller packs. Hence the victory of the latter over the former
is likely also to promote the emergence of counterelites.

The systemic change we are witnessing at the present time
seems to include some of the following transformations. First, there
may be a subtle shift from personal dictatorship to institutional or
bureaucratic authority. The indications of this are weak and inconclusive; and built-in urges toward personal dictatorship may reassert
themselves repeatedly, or even win out. Since the precise flow of
authority at the very tip of the Soviet power pyramid is unknown
to us, we can do little more than remain alert to the possibility.

A broader restructuring of authority concerns the function of
the top leadership within the entire political system, regardless of
whether we see this leadership embodied in a single person, a small
group, or the entire top personnel of the Communist Party. Under
Stalin, the top leadership was in full command. It ruled as sov-
ereignly as an absolute prince. Stalin, his lieutenants, and his Party,
were the architects of the system and indeed of the entire social
structure. They created and abolished institutions as if at will.

Today, such sovereign rule has become more difficult, though not entirely impossible. Strongly entrenched social forces have been created by the Stalinist system, with which his successors have to reckon, and which no longer are subject to such easy tinkering. Hence the relationship between the society and the political leadership is changing. Instead of being able to create and undo, political authority may be shifting to the role of interest aggregator, of arbiter between conflicting groups in society. It will have to respond to pressures from below rather than putting society under pressure. Society is beginning to "determine" the state. The base is beginning to assert an influence over the superstructure.

In order to bring out another facet of this development, let me point out that this growing influence of society over the state must bring with it the institutionalization of conflict within the political system. Previous Soviet political systems, with the exception of the second, made no allowance for conflict. Where it did arise, it was either open class warfare or disagreement among the top leadership, the legitimacy of which was not acknowledged. Both kinds of conflict arose over the most fundamental questions; the very nature of the system depended on how these conflicts would be resolved. In other words, from the point of view of the system they were life-or-death conflicts. Hence they decided over life and death also for the individuals participating and the classes involved.

The post-Stalinist system now developing, however, may be able to routinize and institutionalize conflict precisely because it is now over managerial problems rather than problems of system-building. It is therefore likely also to be less deadly for the losers. The succession crises since the execution of Beria and his police chiefs have demonstrated this. Indeed, deadly conflict would endanger the system now emerging far more than its predecessors: while heterogeneity induces conflicts, the heterogeneous society is more vulnerable to basic and violent conflicts. We may have here something on the societal level analogous to a phenomenon Freud observed in the individual: the higher the civilization, the greater the need for sublimation.

Incidentally, the growing freedom of discussion (which is not identical with freedom of speech) fits in with this increasing assertion of the divergent forces present in the society Stalin created. Here, too, the political system is likely to be forced in the direction of greater openness and accommodation, that is, toward the institutionalization of debate, dissent, toward the discussion of topics hitherto protected by taboos, and a growing readiness to learn techniques and concepts from Western societies.

III

The Soviet political system, in its various stages of development, is worth studying carefully, not so much because the U.S.S.R. is a major world power, although that should not be disregarded, but because it has contributed novel institutions and patterns of government of considerable influence in the contemporary world of politics.

Many Western scholars have dwelled on the novelty of the Soviet system. Most have symbolized it by asserting that the total political experience of the Russian Revolution has led to the development of an entirely new form of government called "totalitarianism." That term has been defined in various ways, but most writers might agree that it had best be regarded as a syndrome of institutions and operating characteristics. We shall discuss some of these below, but also dwell on novel features not usually included in the "totalitarian" syndrome.

First, however, I should like to return to the novelty of the entire Soviet political experience. I prefer to express it by a definition of the Soviet political system so broad that it subsumes most of this experience. This, then, is my definition: The Soviet Union is a political system governed by Communists, that is, by an elite that feels the need to legitimize all its activities by referring to the writings of Marx and Lenin. This elite is preoccupied with the task of industrialization and modernization and seeks to solve it by applying bureaucratic methods of management to the entire social system. It has, on the whole, been successful in this task, having transformed the Soviet Union into a major industrial power. With this success, the Soviet political system has established itself as a successful alternative to the social and political systems of western Europe and North America.

Several features of this successful alternative must be considered important contributions to modern political experience. One of them is the attempt to plan and manage an entire economy on a national scale. Even the inefficiencies, mistakes, and failures accompanying this effort have been instructive, and mankind might benefit from the lessons that can be learned by studying it.

Of equal interest has been the development of a political system operating with only one party. One might well argue that the one-party system was invented or pioneered by the Soviet Union, although political scientists from Alabama, Vermont, or Kansas might claim this honor for their own home state. In any event, it has been an exceedingly important invention: even though the one-party system might be on the decline in the Deep South and the Yankee North, it seems to be very much in the ascendancy in many parts of the globe today. The number of functions served by the party in such systems is great and varied. Single parties therefore have been forced to become vast, complex, and highly differentiated political machines —governments within the government. Fifty years of experience with single-party government in a succession of divergent systems have provided students of modern politics important material for the comparative study of one-party systems that has not yet been analyzed sufficiently.

Another major contribution Soviet rule has made consists in its several attempts, some successful, others unsuccessful, to draw the masses of the citizens into active participation in public affairs, to mobilize them for productive work as well as civic activities. The need for this attempt is implicit in Lenin's views concerning the organization of the single party. In its organization and functioning, it was to combine leaders and masses, authority and democracy, discipline and freedom. Consequently, every Soviet system has experimented with institutions designed to promote mass participation in many fields of endeavor. The nature of such institutions and their relation to the total system has varied greatly from one phase of Soviet rule to the other.

This change in nature and function can be seen when studying Soviet labor unions, for instance. But it is best illustrated, perhaps, by the institution that has lent its name to the U.S.S.R.—the soviet. In 1917, as in 1905, socialists hailed soviets as a novel form of democracy, more direct, more representative, more responsive to public opinion, than any previous democratic institution. And, fifty years ago, the creators of the bolshevik state similarly claimed that a republic of soviets was a novel form of democracy preferable to any previous ones.

Soviets, indeed, originated as institutions of self-government created by the people in times of revolutionary anarchy. In the brief periods during which they functioned more or less spontaneously, they faithfully expressed the rebellious spirit of the poor, for whom they spoke. They enabled people from among the lowest classes to participate in political activity, people who as a rule had not taken part in public life before. The hostility of the soviets, as institutions, to restrictive organization and procedures, their deliberately undefined structure and resistance to institutionalization—these features made the soviets sensitive to the moods of the masses and effective indicators of the anarchic spirit that always accompanies the overthrow of a tyrannical regime. Soviets are institutions of the revolution. More specifically, they symbolize the socialist revolution, because they express the yearning not only for freedom and self-government, but also the spirit of collectivism.

But the same qualities make them unstable and disorderly. Hence to function within a reasonably settled political system (as, for instance, the second Soviet political system), they had to be drained of the anarchic spirit that had created them in the first place. One might describe the process accomplishing this as the taming of the soviets by the Communist Party. In subtle fashion, the Party managed to transform them into administrative organs responsive to the Party leaders rather than to the masses. The soviets lost the sovereignty within the political system that they had possessed for but a fleeting moment (and still have, on paper); they turned into executive agencies. Their representative function was severely diluted. Their decisions were now dictated by the Party; their role within the political system became perfunctory.

Still, in the last decade, we have witnessed a certain reversal of this trend. Since Stalin's death, the leaders of the U.S.S.R. have made persistent efforts to draw larger and larger numbers of citizens into participation in public affairs and in this to widen somewhat the range of discretion that the citizens might wield in such matters. The benefits accruing to the system from wider and more autonomous participation are the mobilization of talent, the tapping of citizens' initiative in matters that might otherwise bog down in bureaucratic routines; they include the ability to spot potential leaders and to give civic-minded activists a sense of participation, hence a stake in the system. They also may include an improvement in the

Party's ability to supervise and control the lives of the citizens. In general, citizens' participation forges needed links between the government and the people.

I said above that the Soviet system might be defined as an application of bureaucratic methods of management to a crash program of modernization. Mass participation, at first glance, seems to contradict the emphasis on command, hierarchy, and manipulation, implied by the use of the term "bureaucracy." Participation fits in, however, when we see it as managed participation. Using soviets, trade unions, many other "mass organization" and peer groups to make a thoroughly bureaucratic system function is a technique that the Soviet political system at the moment is in the process of perfecting. I am tempted to assert that the ideal toward which the system seems to be striving deserves the label "participative bureaucracy." I am inclined to define this as bureaucracy tempered, and made more tolerable, by extensive participation on the part of the administered. Or, in a rather more cynical mood (after attending yet another futile committee meeting), I might be tempted to define it as a system that adds the burdens of participation to the curse of authoritarianism. Whatever the mood participative bureaucracy engenders in us, it may well become a predominant type of political system in our century.

Consequently, we must acknowledge the pioneering nature of the Soviet system in developing a nationwide system of participative bureaucracy. And we must continue to observe the specific manner in which such a system provides for continued social mobility, for a rise in the general welfare, and for a host of other tokens of effectiveness.

At the same time, we must realize that there are problems that the Soviet political systems of the past have not managed to solve. Put more strongly: the Soviet political experience includes a number of conspicuous failures.

One such failure is the inability of all Soviet systems, so far, to establish orderly routines for replacing the top-ranking leader when his place becomes vacant. Hence every such vacancy leads to a crisis. The reason for this recurrence of succession crises is the discrepancy between the formal structure and the actual authority relations in the U.S.S.R. Formally, the system clings to the fiction of collective authority derived from the people or the Party members. It does not provide for the institution of a chief executive or Party leader. In actual fact, there has almost always been one man recognized as the nation's political leader and top authority. Since neither the constitution nor the Communist Party bylaws recognizes such a position, it must be filled by informal political maneuvers that may vary from one crisis to the next.

Another shortcoming of the political system, through all its transformation, has been the difficulty involved in finding a permanent structure suitable for it. To express this differently: the Soviet government has continually organized and reorganized itself. Its leaders have developed some basic principles for such an organizing effort, but some of these principles are in conflict with each other; and the system has not come up with any way out of the resulting dilemmas. Thus there is a nagging urge to find an overall structure (writers in the eighteenth century would have said, a constitution) ideally suited for a system trying to cope with a wide variety of specific problems; there is the perpetual urge to improve on the organization of the system; and no amount of tinkering ever satisfies for long.

The Soviet system shares this worrisome preoccupation with organizational forms and principles with all modern bureaucracies. It shares with them also a number of recurrent pathological features, which are so familiar to all students of bureaucratic management that I need not discuss them in detail.[1]

Further, Soviet political systems, especially the more recent ones, have had difficulty in living with the ideological heritage of Marxism-Leninism, on which nonetheless they depend for a variety of reasons. In other words, Soviet political systems live under an ideological tension resulting from the strain between the need for flexible, realistic self-orientation in a changing world, on the one hand, and a deep psychological and political commitment to a rather rigidly formulated dogma, on the other.[2] It would, of course, be an error to assume that similar strains do not beset other contemporary political systems as well.

[1] For elaboration, see my recent book, *The Soviet Political System* (New York: Random House, 1965), esp. pp. 205–243.

[2] I have tried to elaborate on this problem in "The Functions of Ideology in the Soviet Political System," *Soviet Studies*, XVII, 3 (January 1966), 273–285. See also the various comments on my article in subsequent issues of the same journal.

In a large number of problems, the Soviet political record is spotty or inconclusive, despite fifty years of experimentation. One such problem is that of forging the many varied national cultures of the U.S.S.R. into one homogeneous Soviet nation without lapsing into colonialism or other oppressive patterns. So far, no policy pursued in this field has been entirely successful, and even Soviet spokesmen today concede that national differences will continue to strain the political system for some time to come. Similarly, the Soviet system has not yet found a satisfactory method of integrating the peasantry into the fabric of Soviet society. The image of modernization prevalent in the Communist Party includes a strong urban and industrial bias. In the *ideal* communist society there is no room for peasants. Soviet ideology expresses this by saying that communism will wipe out the difference between city and country. Yet almost half of the Soviet population still lives on the land. The peasant way of life—traditional, anarchic, in some sense antisocial or at least antisocialist—still is strong. Mere destructiveness or violence, if applied too long, would be self-defeating. Without going into detail, I think I can assert that all the measures the Party has taken to integrate the peasants into the Soviet economic and political systems have been compromises satisfying neither the peasants nor the communist leadership.

Perennial strain has been present also in the relationship between the political elite and the professional elite of engineers, managers, scientists, and other experts in many fields. The strain reflects the mutual dependence of these elites on each other and their mutual antagonism and suspicion. Again, this ambivalent relationship is reflected in the institutions set up to regulate it. Here, too, none of the interests concerned is fully satisfied with the existing structures and practices.

Of course, if there were no unsolved problems, there would be no need for a political system at all.

IV

The study of the Soviet political system is as old as the Russian Revolution itself. Our ability to understand and analyze this New World of the twentieth century has improved considerably since

1917, even though we may not yet be able to do for the U.S.S.R. what de Tocqueville did for our own polity. On the fiftieth anniversary of the October Revolution, it may be proper to express the hope that the Soviet Union become as accessible to counterrevolutionary scholars as the United States was to the French aristocrat, and that the observers we will send to the shores of that new New World have the wisdom, the compassion, and the methodological sophistication of our predecessor. We all may still have a long way to go.

III

The Pursuit of Affluence:
The Economic Record

by PETER WILES

What you are thunders so loud that I cannot
hear what you say.
                                        —EMERSON.

"Socialism" and "Communism"

When the Communists seized power in November 1917 their long-term economic aims differed greatly from those they envisaged for the short and medium terms. This essay tries to show how their achievements so far fit either set of aims.

The short- and medium-term aims were "tactical" and did not on the whole rank as holy writ. They referred to the so-called building of socialism. It is mostly the long-term, or "strategic," aims that are enshrined irrevocably and explicitly in the writings of Marx and Engels. Thus there *was*—and is—a Marxist blueprint for postrevolutionary society. The Western belief that this is not so —a belief shared even by many scholars who should know better—

only rests upon the absence of a foreordained *path to* that society. Marx and Engels did indeed draw, in innumerable scattered passages, a consistent picture of the end stage of society. Its principle difference from the immediate aftermath of the Revolution was defined by Marx himself in his *Critique of the Gotha Program*. It lay in the nature of the economic incentive: instead of the principle of payment by results, common to both capitalism and socialism (to each according to his labor), men would work for the joy of the thing, in a total welfare state (to each according to his need). There would be no wages, and indeed no money—but to all this we return below.

In the first six months after the revolution Lenin neglected these ultimate aims and practiced a moderate economic policy very like the New Economic Policy or N.E.P. (1921–1928). Then the civil war began, and his attention was diverted to the front. Second-rank Party leaders, under the specious cover of the necessities of a war economy, tried to bring about a direct leap into Full Communism, which is what we shall call the end stage here. The capitalist and Czarist counterrevolutionaries were beaten, but the people rose in protest against their new bolshevik masters (the Kronstadt revolt, April 1921), mainly because of their extreme discontent with the economic system, which was a total failure. Lenin forced his colleagues to return to the original, more moderate policy, now called the N.E.P. The economic policy of the civil war period was subsequently written off as "War Communism"—though while it was official it had borne no such name and was not excused as a wartime necessity. It had indeed been very similar to the official long-term goals.

So in 1921 the Bolsheviks finally settled down to the long pull their aims evidently entailed. Abandoning no point of Full Communism, they merely postponed it to an indefinite future and elaborated a set of short- and medium-term goals that they came to call "socialism." These included:

(i) The means of production must be socialized, that is, brought under the direct ownership and control of the workers' state. And not, be it noted, by any old state. Ownership or control by a bourgeois state is not socialism at all, but "state capitalism." This is not wholly unprogressive, but it is no substitute for the proletarian revolution, and it does not in any way obviate its necessity. As to the form of this socialization, the "state" must eventually yield to "society," that is, planning must become persuasive, not coercive, and will involve the whole population in active consent (which is the Soviet definition of democracy).

(ii) Objects of consumption are not on the whole to be socialized, though there is a strong prejudice against large private objects of consumption like cars and town houses. Such things belong, of course, with great private wealth, whereas under socialism all substantial advances in consumption shall be as collective as possible. Thus townspeople shall live in high apartment blocks and use public transport; a laundry in the basement of a big building is fine but a private washing machine rather bad; collective tours good but private travel questionable.

(iii) In the special case of agriculture the millions of small traditionally minded peasants will not immediately accept state control. They must therefore be persuaded to pool their work and property locally, in small voluntary cooperative farms.

(iv) Artisan production and petty trade shall also be cooperatized.

(v) The national plan shall embrace not only long-term investment but also every detail of current operation. It will dictate wholly, by central command, the operation of socialized enterprises (i); it will strongly influence the actions of cooperative enterprises (iii); and it will work on private individuals as consumers, small farmers and workers by ordinary market means. For this latter end, and for the purpose of inter-enterprises accounting money shall be retained.

(vi) Incomes shall vary only as much as base unregenerate human nature requires for minimal incentives. All shall work at things defined as useful by the state. This will be easy, since it is the workers' own state.

(vii) No income shall be drawn from ownership of the means of production, except in a very modified sense by peasants. These must, if private, enjoy in essence management, not property rights, and over holdings of approximately equal worth. If cooperatized, they will enjoy no unearned income at all, except in the (mostly unrecognized, but very important) sense that a fortunately placed collective farm is more productive, or has lower transport costs, than a less fortunate one. No one shall employ the labor of another, since that would be exploitation.

(viii) As to sheer productivity, the socialist society must catch up and surpass the United States. And, in view of the deepening crisis of capitalism, this will not be difficult. The socialist society shall thus become the most prosperous society in the world.

The Quantitative Performance of the Economy

It is, of course, the Soviet success in attaining these "socialist" goals that must mainly interest us. We must not think of them as having been worked out at once, or set out in any brief single document. In particular the N.E.P. was characterized neither by collectivization (iii) nor by central planning (v). Nearly every leader wanted both, but both smacked too much of the system that had led to Kronstadt. It is Stalin's chief claim to fame that he introduced both, thereby ending the N.E.P. and beginning the present (nameless) period in 1928. This was the U.S.S.R.'s so-called second revolution, a greater and a bloodier one than that of 1917. But for all the importance of the first seven goals the really crucial one is clearly (viii): that of raising productivity and the standard of living, and surpassing the United States. We must remember, however, that if to the average American intellectual and to the average man in the United States or the Soviet Union this question seems most important, it is not necessarily so to a Communist or indeed to any kind of socialist. Questions of income distribution, property ownership, and planning may easily take precedence in his view. But item (viii) merits pride of place and a long section to itself, and one that must be crudely statistical. I make, then, no apology for imposing long rows of figures upon the reader, for there is no other conceivable answer to the question, how have they fulfilled their productive aims?

A word, first, about the quality of these data. The compilation and interpretation of such figures demands sophistication, courage, and literalness of mind. I have endeavored to supply all three qualities. As to "literalness of mind," many statistics float about the world without reference to the authority from which they are derived; here each single source is given in the *SEDEIS* bulletin[1] from which these data are taken. Often, too, definitions are unspecified: gross national product or net national product? land within farm boundaries or land under cultivation? wage rates or total earnings?

[1] *Analyse et prévision, SEDEIS* (Paris, September 1966).

prewar or postwar territory? It is not pedantry, but the mere desire to be meaningful at all, that has led to the proliferation of detail on these points.

Statistical courage is merely the preference for probability over omission. The publication of any numerical data about the economy of any country is an act of courage—the possibilities of error are enormous in the best-regulated societies. Thus our figures here will err because: the lower levels of Czarist society were illiterate; Czarist and Soviet society are alike very corrupt; there is great pressure on Soviet enterprises to falsify; the Czarist and Soviet governments have misrepresented the data coming up to them in order to present a more favorable picture; the governments have actually falsified the data.

But mere error creates mere uncertainty; it is biased error that threatens us with seriously wrong results. Of the above factors, the first two presumably cause no bias. It is natural to suppose that the third gives an upward bias to the Soviet results, but this is not certain. For if it is best to claim plan-fulfillment when one has in fact fallen short of it, and so get the considerable plan-fulfillment bonus, it is foolish to admit that one has overfulfilled the plan; since that leads the central planners to set a still more ambitious target next year, which may prove impossible to reach. Thus agricultural enterprises probably overreport, since they regularly underfulfill their plans; while industrial, construction, and transport enterprises may under- and overreport equally often, since they quite often overfulfill their plans and so have occasion to worry that next year's plan may be too high. Serious agricultural falsification at a low level, and always in an upward direction, has gone on into the 1960s. The Western sources used here represent the best that can be done with this, the most intractable source of bias. It is not a very good best.

Government falsification is very rare so far as is known. Perhaps the only serious instance is the official index of the volume of construction, 1928–1940—which is alleged to be in constant prices but is in fact in current ones. Misrepresentation is much commoner. The Czarist government overstated the growth of its budget revenues by including the total expenditures and revenues of its railroads, the Soviet government failed to warn readers when in 1932 it substituted the crop on the root for the (much smaller) crop in the barn, and so on. I am reasonably confident that all serious government misrepresentation and falsification have been extruded from the figures in the Appendix. This problem is of course by no means unknown among noncommunist governments: we may take as one simple instance the British government's manipulation of the cost-of-living index during World War II. But certainly among stable and well-organized governments the Soviet bears the palm for such practices.

How sophisticated is the treatment of the data? This is a matter of the formulae chosen, for which the reader is referred to pp. 91–94 in the Appendix at the end of the chapter.

What, then, are the broad results of sheer production performance in various fields? The all-too-often quoted success of industry in the late Czarist period must be seen in context (Tables 1–5, pp. 95–98). It was not exceptional by the standards of modern underdeveloped countries, nor by the standards of the then most progressive countries, and it depended very heavily on capital imports. It was also not enough to raise the whole national income at a rate worthy of note. Nevertheless there was substantial advance, and the Russia that Lenin took over was not grossly underdeveloped by the standards of 1913 or indeed of 1966. War, civil war, and so-called War Communism brought Soviet Russia to famine and industrial collapse. Then American aid and the repudiation of foreign debt set the economy on its feet, and the New Economic Policy saw a rapid expansion to a point about the level of 1913. Even so, toward the end of the N.E.P. agriculture began to level off: the rich peasants were unwilling to invest much under a communist government, and there were objective difficulties in the poverty of the soil and climatic conditions, which have dogged the U.S.S.R. ever since. Nevertheless industrial growth remained very high—higher than in the first Five Year Plan.

Then collectivization and the first Five Year Plan dealt this moderate prosperity a terrible blow. Living standards fell in town and country. The manufacture of consumer goods utterly failed to live up to its promises, while artisan production was nearly abolished. Livestock was slaughtered wholesale, and if this were to be duly accounted for there may have been no growth at all of national income in 1929–1931. The ground however was laid for future successes because construction and heavy industry grew much more rapidly than under the N.E.P. Building on this, in 1932–1937 growth was impressive indeed. Consumption rose sharply in all departments, agriculture recovered, the foreign debt was paid off. Poorer harvests and the Great Purge reduced the increase until 1940.

Recovery from the war was complete by 1950. Stalin's later years registered successes everywhere but in agriculture. They even included the building up of gold, nonferrous metal, and grain stocks, a steady rise in consumption and a remarkable fall in retail prices; but some of this must be written down to "foreign aid"—that is, the exploitation of his new satellites. No subsequent ruler has shown such a performance, except for Khrushchev's golden years in agriculture, 1954–1958. Even these years were bought at a tremendous cost in the inputs of industry and direct labor, costs which have subsequently grown still further. But from 1958 everything tapered off, in particular agriculture. If in 1950–1958 Soviet overall growth was still a wonder of the world, it is now merely a creditable also-ran in the international stakes.

So much for straight growth. As to the absolute levels obtained (Table 4), in 1955 the average Soviet citizen enjoyed about one third of an American's income, whereas in 1913 he had about one ninth. These interspatial comparisons raise the same statistical problems as intertemporal comparisons. For these problems the reader is referred to the Appendix.

It is in any case evident that the goal of overtaking the United States was an extremely ambitious one. So it involves no contradiction to say that enormous strides have been made toward it but that it remains very far from achievement. In nearly all peacetime years the U.S.S.R. has outgrown the United States, so that the goal *must* ultimately be achieved unless the relation between the growth rates ultimately changes. But the last war was a terrible setback. Moreover, many other countries continue to grow faster again, as is shown in Table 5.

In connection with the goal of "catching up and surpassing" the West, the behavior of the predestined capitalist victims has been wholly unforeseen and unorthodox. This is an essential part of the answer to the question, how far have the Soviets achieved this aim? Lenin held contemporary imperialism to be the last stage of capitalism, but colonial liberation has not hurt the advanced capitalist countries—nor indeed did all of them have colonies even then. Domestically, again, state capitalism—the ownership of the means of production by the bourgeois state—was supposed to be part of this last stage of a sick imperialist economy. But in fact if Western nationalization has turned out less than brilliantly, it has at least not proved to be the last stage of anything. Moreover it has had concomitants: exchange controls, tariffs, subsidies, and the French indicative planning. The positive role of these measures is somewhat clearer, though not above controversy. Still less controversial, and still more perplexing to Marxists, has been the near-abolition of unemployment by the Keynesian economics. *The General Theory of Employment, Interest and Money,* published in 1936, was directly irrelevant to Soviet-type economies, and indeed largely to underdeveloped countries. But its effect on developed capitalism has been electric; its implementation destroyed the Marxist hope of an automatic capitalist collapse, and changed the face of the world. Neither Marx nor Stalin dreamed of a capitalism that might, in good years and favored countries, actually outgrow socialism. For instance in the year of the very bad Soviet harvest, 1963, not merely the Japanese but even the sluggish American economy outgrew the Soviet.

Within this picture of general success and agricultural failure, what has succeeded particularly well for the Soviet Union? In terms of sheer output the answer is clear: space, armaments, heavy industry excluding chemicals, education, medicine, and research. This list makes clear how thorough and farsighted—and also how bellicose—the Soviet government has been. It also casts doubt on the widespread belief that this type of economy cannot produce sophisticated hardware; for what in all the industrial world is more sophisticated than an H-bomb or a Sputnik?

But productive success is also a matter of cost, and of the ultimate utility of the thing produced. We have no statistics for the specific costs of these developments. All enterprise is clumsy and wasteful in the Soviet economy, but doubtless the priority enterprises are less so. It is not the economist's function to speak of the utility to state and Party of space travel and arms. The writer can, however, record a personal conviction that there has been overinvestment in heavy industry and engineering education. Engineers have been produced where, even before decentralization, accountants and economists would have done better; and machinery has often been installed only to stand idle. In particular, there has been a snobbish insistence on the most complex and up-to-date machines when simpler and cheaper ones would have sufficed.

Again the Marxist prejudice against "unproductive" labor has led to gross underinvestment in certain services. True, not all services: education (especially technical), medicine, and research have been pushed ahead as strongly as heavy industry. But housing and retail trade have been kept far behind, and so even has been the transportation of goods, which cannot be called "unproductive" even in Marxist theory. In fact, however, it is grossly wasteful of consumer goods not to retail them properly, and an adequate urban house-building program, financed by economic rents, would have satisfied consumers out of given resources far more than the great expansion of manufactured goods in the stores.

Soviet success can scarcely be attributed to the Soviet system of particular priorities. It is due to the ruthless mobilization of people and capital, and the elimination of restrictive practices, vested interests, and other such barriers.

The Planning Hierarchy

Quantitative performance apart, the other goals enumerated in the first section are more simply dealt with.

Of all the communist goals, only (i), nationalization, really worked out even approximately as expected; but even that only in the limited sense that private property in the means of production is abolished. The problems of control over the new public property have never been solved, and administration continues to be in flux.

So nationalization is virtually complete. The collective farms and a minuscule private sector survive, but both are shrinking (Table 3). Here we should pause to note the difference in philosophy and (unspoken) constitutional theory between the communist and the Western concepts. In Western theory the state is never all in all, and nationalization, while it weakens capitalism, should not strengthen any new master. Therefore the industry's or firm's new manager is not an organic part of the government, but an independent public trustee. In communist theory—outside Yugoslavia—the new proletarian state smashes the old bourgeois one and seizes everything; so it is natural for the peak economic ministers to sit in the cabinet, as does the sole Western exception to the trusteeship principle, the postmaster general (whose position is historically derived from the king, not the state, so that he much predates all talk of socialism and trusteeship, and is simply one of the king's ministers). It is only with the onset of Full Communism that, as the state begins to wither away, the economic machine shows independence of it. Trusteeship is not a communist concept, but it would not be wholly misleading to describe the planning organ under Full Communism as a trustee—albeit it is to be single, not multiple, and its system of central commands continues. The state, then, is the political organ of coercion—army, police, law courts—alone.

In Khrushchev's period of rule, when the Party was supposed to be dominant, it was indeed suggested that the state was withering away. The principal practical effect of this was in the sphere of justice, where the lawyers saw such informal "popular" competitors grow up as the "comradely courts." But also in the economy Khrushchev made a revolutionary move, which was *ex post facto* represented as a partial "withering away": he substituted some one hundred special territorially defined administrations, each with its headquarters in a specific district, for the thirty old production-branch ministries. Thus, where an authority in Moscow had previously planned and operated all ferrous metallurgy, including the plant in Kiev, now an authority in Kiev planned and operated all plants in Kiev, including the steel mill.

These new authorities (*Sovnarkhozy*) have been much misunderstood. They were not officially supposed to represent decentralization, and, if that word is to be understood as greater rights for enterprises or an approach to a market economy, they did not. Again if the central power is defined as the central planning organ (the *Gosplan*) alone, the reform actually strengthened it, for many functions previously entrusted to ministries could not be performed by the *Sovnarkhozy*, but had to be loaded on to the *Gosplan*. Thus the *Sovnarkhozy* had nothing at all to do with the new market socialism, or with increased rationality. They constituted decentralization only in two senses. First, in a purely geographical way they removed a large number of planning officials from Moscow. This was politically important to Khrushchev, who found senior state officials overweening. Second, top local officials were better placed to influence planning and to "interpret" regulations. Such people were the managers of the more prestigious enterprises in each *Sovnarkhoz,* and above all *the local Party boss,* whose area of rule was quite deliberately kept coincident with the boundary of the *Sovnarkhoz.* So instead of a distant and very senior official in Moscow (the minister), he faced rather more junior officials on the spot—who would also see things in local terms.

Thus it was not so much the approach of Full Communism that concerned Khrushchev here, as the *subordination of the state to the Party.* The *Sovnarkhozy* were merely his most spectacular effort in this direction. But always in one way or another he returned to this preoccupation: the managerial technocracy is getting too big for its boots; it is taking advantage of the increasing sophistication and complexity of productive techniques, of the social sciences, of communications, of the arts of government. If the pure Party apparatus is not alert and is not itself well trained and duly empowered, it will lose its *raison d'être* in the economy. Since military and cultural life are open to the same threat, communism as a whole may go under. Therefore pure Party people must be better trained, but still managerial and planning procedures must be kept simple enough for them to understand; and the state must be so structured—and indeed restructured many times over—that they can control it. To this we return below in our discussion of "The Doctrine on the Future."

The *Sovnarkhozy* proved, predictably, to be a very clumsy administrative device. They were enlarged at one point, and their number was thus halved, but they suffered at all times from a fundamental technical defect: it is grossly inefficient to think first of areas and only second of commodities. It came as no surprise when Khrushchev's successors abolished his invention, restoring the ministries (1965). With this, however, at least a psychological blow was dealt to the withering away of the state, and to the primacy of the Party.

The Rationality of Resource Allocation

The dream of a detailed central-command economy without money was set aside at the beginning of the N.E.P., but not abandoned. In 1928 it was resumed with the first Five Year Plan but with the following qualifications: First, wages were paid to individual workers, and differentiated according to their scarcity in the market or in order to induce them to move or acquire new skills. Workers were not, with many exceptions noted in the section titled "Labor," actually directed to jobs. Second, the consumer was charged money for all noncollective consumption goods, and he was not normally rationed or directed to consume certain things. On the contrary, the state varied its prices, and therefore its profit rate, to equate consumer demand with the very haphazard supplies it provided. Third, varying and complicated mixtures of market incentive and administrative command were used upon the collective farms.

The system has worked well to produce the grandiose output performance described above, but it has been most irrational and wasteful in detail. For most details are mere happenstance. There is no reason why a rational planner should prefer pins to needles, or diesel locomotives to diesel-electric ones. Such matters really are better decided by on-the-spot bargaining between those who need them and those who make them, with a genuine possibility of competition on both sides of the market. So the planners have simply stumbled ahead, choosing wrongly in order to choose at all. Such manifest and all-pervading minor waste too easily impresses the Western observer, even until recently the Western economist. He supposes that an economy of that kind cannot really exist at all, or cannot grow, or need not be taken seriously. But this is not so. The refutation is exceedingly simple and is known as the "toothbrushes-and-nailbrushes argument." The Soviet economy, the argument runs, always produces too many, say, toothbrushes and too few nail-brushes in view of consumer tastes and needs and in view of the total volume of resources allocated to consumption. Moreover, both kinds of brush are of low quality, and they are all colored, say, pink, which is depressing. At any given moment a Western economy will satisfy consumer demand for such brushes much more economically out of the same amount of resources. But the Western rates of growth are in fact slower, and quality does in fact improve in the U.S.S.R. and even variety increases. So in the end the Soviet consumer will be better supplied even with nailbrushes.

Furthermore, since it is most improbable that such waste as a proportion of total output has increased since the early 1930s, the figures of growth from that period on are unaffected. But this waste does affect international comparisons, at a moment of time, with less wasteful systems. The neglect of consumer's sovereignty, and indeed of all detailed rationality, is or was a root principle of Marxism. But these losses, and the essential arbitrariness of detailed decisions, irritate Soviet planners and managers. East Europeans, unappreciative of the toothbrushes-and-nailbrushes argument and brought up in the Western tradition of economics, which used to lay all too much stress on these problems, have played a great part in pointing up this wastefulness; even Western economists' criticisms have taken their toll. Perhaps most important of all has been Stalin's death and the increased freedom to criticize.

But *are* other systems less wasteful? In the days of gross cyclical unemployment the capitalist system was indeed much more wasteful. However, as we saw, this is over: in Europe since 1946 and in the United States since, perhaps, President Kennedy's Yale speech of June 11, 1962. As to unemployment due to overpopulation, this is permanent, not cyclical, and it is not characterized by unemployed capital assets, since a superfluity of labor force over fixed assets is precisely the meaning of the term. Such unemployment is the hereditary curse of many underdeveloped countries, and it also plagued the U.S.S.R. until recently: in and even out of collective farms many were only nominally employed. If the advanced capitalist countries have avoided this, it is historical chance and not to their credit.

The chief remaining waste of the capitalist system, without parallel in communism, is noninformative advertising. Since all advertising claims 2 to 3 percent of the national income, the noninformative—that is, purely persuasive and often misleading—kind might be guessed at 1 to 1.5 percent. It is extremely difficult to believe that in the U.S.S.R. the full-time central planners, plus their full- and part-time correspondents in enterprises, do not absorb far more than this. Unfortunately there are no exact data, and one can only rely on literary impressions, derived from such a complaint as this:

> The Likhachev automobile factory *annually* receives ball bearings from the GPZ factory *next door*. The documentation of this transaction weighs over 400 pounds and is handled by fourteen agencies. . . . The investment project for the Novo-Lipetsk steel mill comprises 91 volumes totalling 70,000 pages.[2]

Capital is not, of course, distributed by a stock exchange but by political and administrative lobbying. He would be a bold man who

[2] L. Smolinski in *Foreign Affairs,* July 1964.

asserted which process used up more labor. Finally, if the U.S.S.R. uses fewer people in retail trade, this is probably itself a waste. Retailing is not mainly an administrative function: it adds to the product the very considerable values of timeliness, convenience, and accessibility.

The result of all these defects has been, since about 1960, a ferment of criticism, leading to actual reform. All critics of the detailed-command economy have demanded more rational and less wasteful systems of allocation; better ways of satisfying the consumer out of given resources; and prices on land and capital in order to prevent their use in the wrong branches and with the wrong techniques. But from here on the critics have diverged. Some have wanted to continue centralization, but under the management of computers and linear programming. Others, wiser as to the actual capacities of administrators and indeed computers, have recommended decentralization and a partial return to the market.

The government has at length (1966) accepted that which is common among the critics. Capital and land will shortly have prices attached to them, in flat and open contradiction to Marx. For the rest the second group of critics has been followed. The great period of detailed central command is over, and with it a whole part of Marxist theory is discredited. Detailed decisions will be made in accordance with purchasers' orders, actual costs, and even competition; all of which is also in total, but less open, contradiction to Marx. This, furthermore, is no temporary retreat as during the N.E.P.; it is a permanent, though as yet not officially acknowledged, acceptance of the invalidity of a large part of Marxism. It is, therefore, a change not merely in the tactics but the strategy—perhaps the greatest such change.

The substitution of profit for central command is neither a straight reversion to capitalism, as some Western journalists have said, nor a pure and undefiled preservation of socialism, as Soviet propaganda claims. For profit is now not only the *criterion of choice,* but also the *incentive to action.* The manager is to get a bonus out of the profit he makes; but this bonus is private, so private profit is now a motive. Moreover, the decisions that lead to this profit will now be more the manager's own: he will not earn it by fulfilling a plan someone else made, like a pieceworker, but by doing what he thinks best, like a—what else can I write?—capitalist.

On the other hand, the Soviet manager will no more than before be able to *own* or *sell* a title to the profit. His products he will of course sell, but he will not "own" them, whatever that means: only a very small part of the profit will accrue to him. He will even be allowed—he is already—to dispose of the means of production, especially of old machinery, and count that toward profit. But that again is not "ownership." He owes his present title to *appointment,* and so will his successor. There will still be no private "equity" in the Soviet enterprise, and the right to exercise ultimate power, and receive residual profit, will continue to belong to the state. With the absence of equity goes a virtually complete exclusion of capital gains. The enterprise will, no doubt, be able to make very small capital gains by holding on to inventories, but even here central price control will damp fluctuations. There will, of course, be no stock exchange—since there are no shares.

Thus the undoubted existence of private profit and decentralized decisions still leaves us many miles from capitalism. For a real threat of renascent capitalism, see our discussion on pp. 82–83.

Agriculture

Agricultural production has indeed been less fully socialized, just as set out in the official intentions. If we distinguish strictly the state farm, the collective farm, and the various forms of private agriculture we arrive at the results of Table 3.

The state farm is unremarkable: it is simply a socialist agricultural factory. With rather surprising tact the Communists did not condemn all peasants straight away to state farms, but formed very few, supposing that these recalcitrant small capitalists would later *voluntarily* pool their property in collective farms. As it turned out in 1929–1930, the collective farms were so unpopular, and collectivization so involuntary, that it would have made no difference to form state farms anyway.

Apart from the civil war and the Great Purge there was no greater act of violence. Born in bloodshed, deportation, and hypocrisy, the collective farm has been a daily act of conquest over the peasantry ever since. It has worked very badly, as Table 2, Column 1, shows. So, for that matter, has the state farm. However in fairness we must point out that not many countries' agriculture is progressive. This can only be said of the high-capitalist, heavily subsidized agriculture of northwestern Europe, north America, and Australasia. By world standards the collective farm is not utterly despicable—merely a failure based on a crime. Tradition-minded, prone to religion, drink, unofficial holidays, and other vices, most peasants have simply not cooperated. The work of an agricultural laborer is always hard to supervise, and most collectivized peasants have made full use of this simple fact, stealing and shirking—except on their own plots. The continued reliance on various forms of private agriculture is, in ideological terms, a major scandal.

A less well known but equally scandalous matter is the stupendous investment of resources put into agriculture without return. Machines and industrial raw materials have been lavished upon the farmer; capital has been squeezed out of his meager income and capital has been poured out from the budget; land areas the size of a respectable European country have been raped; even now straight agricultural subsidies have raised their ugly heads—and all to no avail. It is true that in the end the Soviet people have not starved (except in 1932 and 1946); that when harvests have failed, resources have recently been found to buy what is needed abroad; that the national income as a whole has shot ahead; that India and Pakistan, Indonesia, and—in its own way—China have done worse. Nevertheless it is abundantly clear that an untrammeled capitalist agriculture would have been better (Table 6). Moreover, costs rise sharply year by year, and this is a very bad omen for the future. The U.S.S.R. has not escaped from the clutches of the Malthusian devil.

Full Communism has been pursued in this field too. In the early 1930s, after vain experimentations with cooperative ownership, Stalin found that he could not trust collective farmers with tractors. They sabotaged them regularly, since the propaganda for collectivization had presented to them the tractor as an essential part of the scheme. So Stalin "statified" the tractors, putting them into Machine-Tractor Stations (M.T.S.) that were government property. Thus arose the fantastic situation that most agricultural machinery was not under the control of the farmer. (Not all: milking machines, for instance, and a few trucks, were always collective-farm property.)

Such an intolerable confusion had to be resolved. First Khrushchev briefly experimented with subordinating the collective farms to the M.T.S. This was the ideologically right thing to do, since it subordinated cooperative property to state property and tended to the absorption of the collective farms into the state. But it did not work administratively, and in 1958 Khrushchev took the obvious way out and sold the tractors to the farms. It should be noted, however, that the tractors were not given. Collective farms are not part of the socialist state. Just as until recently the collective farmer benefited by virtually no state welfare services, but had to rely on his collective, so he had to pay the state for the tractors. Previously he paid the M.T.S. a fee for the work the tractor did. For that matter, the state used to levy a high turnover tax on gasoline and building materials sold to collective farms, but none on those sold to factories or state farms. The tractor sale raised urgently the ideological issues: what is to happen to cooperative property under Full Communism? Is not the conversion of state into cooperative property a long step backward?

To these questions both a doctrinal and a practical answer have been given. Ideologically, state property itself will cease to exist under Full Communism, since the state will of course wither away (it will be borne in mind that the state is strictly only the coercive part of the government). All property will be "general-social"; so why not in due time directly promote cooperative property to this status, without an intervening period of "statification"? In practice, however, the state farm has continued to enjoy economic privileges, including subsidies and better supplies of fertilizer—and of course its own tractors—from the very beginning. Nor has Khrushchev's ideological defense been universally accepted. So since 1958 there has been a concomitant "statification" of selected collective farms, with the results shown in Table 3.

It is important never to be automatically cynical about the U.S.S.R. It is quite true that the collective farm is a democratic organization, whose members must vote on their statification. It is true that such decentralized local democracy is quite unknown in the state sector, and forms no part of Full Communism, in which all "democracy" is concentrated in the central planning organ. It is true that many collective farms chosen for the privilege of conversion have been suburban ones, where the members could make fantastic profits from their private plots; so that they voted, in accepting the state farm setup with its smaller private plots, for their own impoverishment. But it is also true that collective-farm democracy is a mockery anyway. The chairman is in nearly 100 percent of cases a pure Party nominee, and the annual members' meeting a farce; so nothing is lost. But above all, many of the selected collective farms come from the other end of the scale: they are those with the least fertile land, and the most distant from towns (so the least able to profit from the free market). "Statification" renders a farm eligible, like any factory, for subsidy. It gives the peasant, now a worker, the right to a fixed wage, which the state must pay. It is thus a huge advantage to the poorest peasants.

Labor

The logic of War Communism, with its equal wages, its rationing, and its inclusion of the private household into the planned sector, required that labor be directed. Only Trotsky and a few supporters had the tactless courage to say so, though this was in fact often done. But such a system is highly unpopular among workers or, in Marxist terminology, makes far too great demands on their "socialist consciousness."

The N.E.P. brought the direction of labor to an end, and it has never formally returned on any scale, except during World War II. Differentiated wages and free choice of job have been the rule. But there have been very many exceptions, which are worth listing. They were all brought in after the rebirth of central planning, although in principle that system also attracts labor by free bargains at differentiated wages.

The first kind of exception is aimed at excessive labor turnover. Principally between 1930 and 1949, very many workers were legally frozen in the jobs they happened to be in. Others, guilty of flitting from job to job, were punished by publicity and deprivation of rights to welfare services. Labor exchanges were abolished in 1931, so that from that day to this all labor recruitment has been highly haphazard and ill-informed. Even today, when turnover is no higher than in Britain, the government has a strong prejudice against it. For a free labor market is a nuisance in fact and a disappointment in ideology. The very phrase "labor market" is never used. In a centralized socialist state, people *ought* not to be able to better themselves by individual career choice or job change. Only in 1965, against strong ideological opposition, did the labor exchange begin to creep back.

Then there is the direction of people with special skills. The old Czarist practice of telling the new graduate where his first job shall be has been continued. This now reaches from the trade school to the university, and it leads to a staggering volume of parental pressure and lobbying. As for a Communist Party member, at all ages he can be directed by the Party.

From time to time, again, youth is mobilized on that "compulsorily voluntary" basis that characterizes so much of communism. The labor for the virgin lands, and for the great Siberian industrialization campaign that followed it, was recruited in this way. Young workers, who are neither advanced school graduates nor Party members, are "persuaded" by the *Komsomol* (Young Communist League), especially at the moment of military demobilization. This accounts for the Komsomol's practical interest in—and indeed skepticism about—labor-market arrangements. The workers' factual freedom is shown by the fact that most of these young people drift back home rather quickly, and that Siberia and Central Asia as a whole have in recent years added to their population by natural increase alone.

"Compulsorily voluntary" labor is also very common on a minor scale, without geographical movement. Unpaid overtime, literally work after hours without pay, has occurred quite recently in so civilized a place as Leningrad. Schools are often emptied to help with the harvest, and people's leisure is planned in some detail (p. 85). But these things were far more characteristic of War Communism, and are more prevalent in modern China.

The collective farmer is not in theory a free laborer at all. Belonging to what is officially a separate class, he is the victim of class discrimination. He acquires membership of his farm either by having been originally collectivized or by birth. In the second instance there is a formal admission procedure when he grows up.

The farm occasionally also admits outsiders by this procedure, but it is rare, so a peasant cannot freely migrate from one farm to another. Indeed he cannot change his residence at all without permission, because of the *internal passport*.

This Czarist device, denounced by Lenin before the Revolution and abolished by him after it, was most certainly no part of the Bolsheviks' long- or short-term aims. But Stalin reestablished it in 1932, and not only for security reasons. For in an underdeveloped country with a free labor market there is always a tendency for surplus agricultural labor to crowd into towns more rapidly than jobs become available. In this way slum suburbs, "shantytowns" or "bidonvilles," arise and present an appalling problem of health and public order. So the worker receives a full-fledged internal passport, which enables him to go where he will provided he reports on arrival; for him the passport is a security check. But the peasant has no passport; merely an *ad hoc* travel document defining the purpose and length of his stay away from the village. Thus townward migration is controlled, and the peasant can only live where he is born.

Practice evidently diverges very much from theory. The drift from the land has recently been frighteningly big, and rural Party secretaries complain of it. Thus either they cannot control the issue of proper passports to peasants, or nonissuance is not in fact a bar. Again it is common to get the best of both worlds: drawing a worker's wage but retaining the peasant's private plot and house, and the nominal status of collective farmer that is their prerequisite.

The final form of labor direction is or was penal. Marxist penology has always laid great stress on the curative value of labor. All abuses apart, it is surely superior in this to Western penology, with its fear of undercutting trade unions and its tolerance of mere make-work. But under Stalin, from about the mid-1920s, the abuses bulked infinitely larger than the underlying intentions, and added up to a horror story only exceeded—though considerably exceeded—by the Nazis.

Stalin's "corrective" labor camps were the resultant of three forces: his system of government by terror, the old Marxist faith in cure by labor, and the rule that all establishments must balance their budgets without subsidy. This rule, upon which the N.E.P. was built, was extended to prisons in 1925. There is almost no evidence that people were sentenced in order to provide cheap labor, but every evidence that they were made to provide cheap labor because they had been sentenced. Numerical plans for arrests did exist—as they have in most police forces—but clearly had their sole origin in a security paranoia.

In formal accountancy many, perhaps most, of the "corrective" labor camps did indeed fulfill the injunction of 1925: the prisoners' labor paid for their own meager upkeep and for the guards as well. But the death rate and the wastage of skill were appalling. As irrational was the curious geographical fallacy that the frozen North *ought* to be exploited; free labor would require altogether too expensive inducements, so "corrective" labor, paid a sub-subsistence wage, must be directed there. There is of course no reason at all why any state should develop the whole of its territory: in this case neither strategic nor economic welfare called for the colonization of ice. The death of an able-bodied prisoner from cold is a heavy cost to the economy, shown in no ordinary accountancy. He could have been better employed further south.

The numerical extent of Stalin's forced-labor system is the subject of vehement controversy and no hard data exist. I incline personally to a guesstimate of 6 million such laborers at the end of the Great Purge, in January 1939. The figure must have been of the same order of magnitude when Stalin died in 1953. His successors rapidly ran it down, so that by 1956 most of Stalin's prisoners were freed, and replacements were few. We can now speak of a *semi*-terroristic government, imprisoning *some* but not many more people than a Western democracy, and applying to them, with what success we hardly know, the Marxist penology of reform through labor, in severe but no longer impossible climatic conditions.

Other forms of penal labor direction, very often confused with "corrective" labor behind barbed wire, are the two forms of *exile*. The more severe is deportation to a specific spot. This was the preferred fate for *kulaks,* and for the wives of Great Purge victims. Also most prisoners released after Stalin's death were "deported" to their previous place of imprisonment; that is, the barbed wire was removed and their wages went up. The less severe form is exclusion from certain places, for example, from major cities and frontier areas. Under Stalin the deported alone were probably equal in number to the "corrective" laborers.

Like so many other devices in this section, all three of these
penal devices are of Czarist origin.

Distribution, Consumption, and the Private Sector

Crafts and petty trade, private medicine, the letting of seaside
bedrooms, are too often neglected in a global view. Yet they are
of enormous psychological importance. If a Soviet citizen really
wants a suit properly cut, a *private* holiday, a stove repaired, he
can always get it at a price. Sometimes, as in the *kolkhoz* market
for food, this is strictly legal; sometimes, as when Western jazz
records are cut on stolen hospital X-ray plates, it is strictly illegal.
Often the transaction is merely "gray": thus it is quite legal to
build a private house, but obstructive officials must be bribed and
scarce materials stolen.

All this sort of thing has of course to disappear under Full
Communism. Sometimes it is tolerated, sometimes forbidden, occasionally even encouraged. Sometimes taxes are very high, as on
earnings from private medical practice; sometimes inexplicably low
—food sold on *kolkhoz* markets escapes the huge turnover tax
the state food shops must pay. A favorite method of control is to
herd such entrepreneurs into cooperatives, where they are more
easily supervised by state and Party.

Statistics are poor on these embarrassing subjects. But a fair
guess would be that since the Stalinist system settled down and
private agricultural plots were formally legalized (c. 1934), the
proportion of income earned and spent on the free markets, white,
gray, and black, has not changed. As this is written, black and gray
are yielding to white as regulations are relaxed. This phase may
not last, but it is clearly both synchronous and sympathetic with the
decentralization of the command economy, discussed above. If
eastern Europe is any guide, such private activity will now expand
very greatly.

Collectivized consumption is another ultimate aim, so thoroughly
unpopular that it has not been pushed very hard. Nevertheless if
we compare the proportions of collective to total consumption, the
U.S.S.R. is undoubtedly more "socialist" than Western countries.
In the following comparison, "collective" means "paid for out of
other sources than take-home pay," and "consumption" means all

expenditure other than defense and investment. The merely statistical comparison, however, does little justice to the quality of life. The specific things collectivized are: education—almost 100 percent; medicine—much private practice on the black market, and some legally permitted; child-minding—about a quarter of the children between two and five inclusive are in free kindergartens; holidays—mainly paid by enterprises, and the usual facilities are designed to exclude privacy.

There are also many things privately paid for but publicly provided. Notable among these are: transport—very few private cars, and next to no arrangements for them; but public passenger transport is not subsidized to such an excess that a New Yorker would be shocked; domestic services—washing machines, kitchens, and refrigerators tend to be communal, although a charge goes into the rent; housing itself—about two thirds of urban housing, and all housing on state farms, is publicly owned. In collective farms all housing is private.

The private consumer's durable goods have a specially contentious status. For what, in the end, is a rich socialist citizen supposed to look like? Can he seriously be imagined in a bus, on a guided tour? Can his wife seriously be deprived of *Vogue*? Will he have no country cottage of his own? Khrushchev, a very orthodox if very unintellectual Marxist, was probably the last leader to give the right primitive answers to these questions. Already Kosygin is increasing the number of private cars, which threatens an entire transformation of the Soviet landscape and society. It is difficult not to see the roots of capitalism here. Moreover many of these durables react back on actual production. For instance a private car is invaluable to a black marketeer.

For the rest, consumption is private, and products are bought for money in stores very much as under capitalism. The consumer spends his money as he pleases, in view of the prices and quantities of things available. He has thus *free choice,* but he is not *sovereign*. For as we saw above the planners usually fail to alter outputs as consumers' tastes and purchases alter. Their more normal reactions are to let queues develop, or to raise or lower prices. Only in the case of continuous overproduction at any price is the waste so gross and evident that the output plan is changed. But even here the system is very sluggish, and monumental pile-ups occur.

We have no serious statistical data for the distribution of income, except for a short period in the late 1920s and early 1930s. The matter is one of acute ideological embarrassment, since very plainly the Soviet government, remarkably successful in raising non-agricultural output, has utterly failed to distribute it equally. Or at least failed after the initial changes of the Revolution. We can say that the pre-1913 distribution was one of the most unequal that human history has known. No excesses of Stalinism were able to restore it. The bourgeoisie and aristocracy were liquidated in 1917–1918, and with them virtually all unearned income. Inequality of earned income among the workers also diminished sharply until the N.E.P. From then on it grew until the death of Stalin, and is now sensibly diminishing. Even so, inequality remains very great indeed. It is very shocking by Chinese standards, and quite shocking by Polish standards. But it is still low in comparison with capitalism. Under capitalism the few fantastically high salaries at the top and the comparatively many unemployed at the bottom render even the distribution of earned income more unequal; and then that of capital and unearned income is still more unequal.

Inequality among peasants was reduced by War Communism, but then grew again under the N.E.P. The liquidation of the *kulaks* was rapidly succeeded by the growth of a rural "aristocracy" of *kolkhoz* chairmen, agronomists, village soviet officials, accountants, and so forth. We may doubt whether even today the distribution of income among peasants is less unequal than in 1913. The same probably applies to the comparison between peasants and workers. The latter probably averaged twice as much (even considering the peasants' side incomes).

According to theory, under "socialism" the worker is supposed to have superlative labor morale. While he mainly works for pay, he must from time to time donate his labor. In part he does this by working overtime on his normal job at regular rates, or even for nothing. These practices were much commoner in the past than now—a remarkable case of backsliding from pristine ideals. But the schoolchild and the collective farmer still find it difficult to avoid miscellaneous unpaid public work—for example, the schools are emptied to help with a bad harvest, or collective farmers build public roads.

However, leisure and the uses of leisure are more important

for the future. In reducing the formal hours of work there has been very fair success. It is, for instance, little known that hours fell during the first Five Year Plan, that giddy period of storm and waste. The most accurate figures are on an annual basis allowing for holidays, overtime, and short time. In 1955 the average worker in manufacturing put in 2,185 hours a year, compared with 2,015 in the United States. He works still less today. In 1913 the average number of hours in a week without holidays was fifty-nine in Russia, forty-nine in the United States. Yet no Western worker would wish to work so few hours while his real wage was so low. If the tastes of the Soviet worker resemble those of an American, not a Tahitian, he is permitted to work too little.

But Soviet society shows many curious contradictions. This same worker or his wife must put in many hours standing in line at stores, or in unnecessarily slow transport and restaurant service. His actual leisure time is thus hardly as much as an American's. Moreover, he is under pressure to spend much of it collectively and constructively: learning something, administering something, or going off in a group to see something "worthwhile." This certainly reduces leisure's value to him personally, but when one looks at the uses of American leisure one wonders about the social cost of such vacuity in the United States. It does not require a puritan hostility to pleasure, or intellectual snobbery, to be pessimistic about future generations in a society where leisure is so largely spent on pure entertainment, and passive entertainment at that. In the U.S.S.R. leisure is spent, in principle and partly in fact, in accumulating human capital; in the United States it is simply free time.

The farmer, socialist or collective, lives in far more primitive circumstances. His leisure is still largely forced upon him, or seized from him, by the seasons. Indeed when crafts were not persecuted or frowned upon, winter unemployment was lower. One of the very greatest wastes that Stalin imposed was the drastic reduction of winter crafts.

The Doctrine on the Future

We now turn to the farther future, about which Marx did indeed have much to say. In the U.S.S.R. the memory of these predictions is very green; quotations from Marx, Engels, and Lenin on Full Communism are constantly bandied about.[3] It would be tedious and unfair to inquire whether the regime has attained Full Communism: it neither has nor claims to have. But on that subject it is important to note that the ultimate goal has not been abandoned. Each tactical twist is performed *sub specie aeternitatis;* the beatific vision remains and the observer who neglects it is much in the position of a sociologist in a monastery who studies the kitchen but not the chapel. "Socialism" as we have discussed it is a genuine, and well thought out, way station on the road to Full Communism. To the extent that "socialist" goals have been achieved Full Communism is nearer. Indeed the very ordering and priority of these goals is due in part to the ultimate aims. This is pointed up by what we have already said on the ultimate fate of the collective farm and what we shall have to say on leisure.

Under Full Communism, then, collective classless altruism, not individual material gain, would be the driving economic motive. Reeducated out of all capitalist selfishness into "socialist consciousness," men would do work because it was a pleasure, a duty, and an honor. Payment would be not for work but according to (socially defined) need. It would also be very high because productivity would rise faster than ever after the revolution. The "alienating" division of labor would cease, and in its place the new integrated man would be master of all trades; in particular there would be no difference between intellectual and manual, urban and rural, labor.

Under such social circumstances there is no need for compulsion any more, and the persuasion of one's comrades can take its place. The "state," defined here as the compulsive organs of society such as police, law courts, army, would "wither away," and a voluntary "social organization" remain. Its principal function would be economic planning. This planning would however be very detailed, since there would be no money. Everyone would have his post— or rather his bewildering succession of posts!—assigned to him, and be told exactly what to produce. Thus the planning would be only persuasive, and the comrades would go joyfully to perform duties with which they were in entire agreement. This, of course, entails

[3] Listed in my *Political Economy of Communism* (Oxford: Clarendon Press, 1962), Chapter 17.

a colossal administrative task to which Marx was absolutely blind.

Crime is a consequence of "alienation." Bourgeois society is not constructed around man but around the goods he produces—the so-called fetishization of commodities—and it leaves no room for a fully developed and integrated person but values a human being only as a specialized producer. Moreover, bourgeois individualism is immoral. No wonder, then, that many live antisocial lives. Under Full Communism crime will cease, since everyone will appreciate his social duty, and accept it gladly.

The family is another bourgeois institution: women are sold as part of a property bargain. This too must slowly cease, giving way to a responsible, puritan, equal, outward-looking but nonetheless revocable union, or series of unions, between male and female. As in so many antifamily theories, the position of the child is left vague. Social care is evidently foreseen, but it is unclear just to what extent individual parenthood shall wither away. Above all the family shall lose its economic role. Domestic work is women's slavery, and should be performed by factories or other communal organizations, releasing women for "productive" tasks.

Leisure, or more precisely time away from work, has a quite special role in Marxism, as we have seen. Its emotional importance is derived from the labor theory of value: the longer his hours of work under capitalism the more grossly a man is exploited. Therefore socialism and communism will demonstrate their value largely in shorter hours, constructively spent. This indeed is the meaning of human freedom in Marxism: spending one's time for the edification of self and society instead of working for one's subsistence. Hence the surprisingly short hours the Soviet worker is expected to put in.

Since all are paid "according to need," all are not equally paid, but nearly so. "Paid," however, is really the wrong word. Consumption is a social dividend to which citizenship entitles everyone. As an ideal, all literally help themselves in the stores; in practice each will probably receive a free ration (as did happen under War Communism).

Such, then, were the major doctrines projected to the far future. Believing in them passionately, Lenin and his comrades took power. It was for this noble and absurd vision that they fought, killed (even each other) and died. It is amazing how little these ultimate aims have subsequently been modified. We can point to only a few cases:

(i) Much the most important of these modifications is the one for which Stalin personally is notorious—the survival of the state as a coercive machine. For until encirclement by capitalist states ceases, one needs an army and a counterespionage police. The domestic withering away of the state, say in the economic field, is thus also set back. This extension from security to economic matters may not be very logical (indeed, Tito found it very illogical, and in 1950–1952 undertook a drastic decentralization in the economy in face of extreme foreign danger), but it is natural enough. It follows from the "encirclement" doctrine that Full Communism is almost of necessity worldwide. Stalin is the "socialism" expert, the man who kept things going during the unexpectedly long and unpleasant transition. This particular amendment was his main contribution to Marxist ideology as a whole. It was also, in moderate form, the merest common sense. Where Stalin went wrong was in his paranoiac strengthening of the terror as time went on, based on the absurdity that the class war actually became sharper after the Revolution.

(ii) Many, but not all, Soviet ideologists recognize that Marx was talking nonsense about the division of labor. This may indeed be an "alienating," that is, dehumanizing, force under capitalist exploitation—the Marxist picture of labor under capitalism is sufficiently portrayed by Charlie Chaplin in *Modern Times*. But advancing technology makes it not more but less easy to transfer from job to job; the enactment of Marx's vision would catastrophically reduce productivity. Moreover, under "socialism" labor is not exploited, therefore the specialization of highly qualified socialist labor is quite different and fully justified.

(iii) Some ideologists, trying to present Full Communism as something actually attractive to ordinary mortals, have kept the family in being. They have thus come full circle from War Communism, when the family was under deliberate attack. In that period free divorce was legal and free love widely practiced. But the attack broke down, because of the "backwardness" of the average Russian, the basic puritanism of many leaders, and the unprecedented wave of homeless children. It was decided quite early that the family should survive under "socialism." People are imperfect, and the state cannot provide a substitute for parents.

It would be much too expensive, and the citizens would not tolerate it. The new development is the possible survival of the family forever.

A Managerial Revolution?

The state as a protection against foreign enemies has not, of course, withered away at all. But since the death of Stalin much less paranoia has been shown about internal security. What, then, about the economy? Has command yielded to persuasion? Has the state's economic bureaucracy been transformed into a "social organization," whatever that means? Has the Party tended to interfere more or less?

By a fundamental paradox of Marxism, these questions are emotionally and ideologically unconnected with the onset of a market economy, described above. For Full Communism is by rights both highly centralized and entirely persuasive; there is no bureaucracy only in the sense that everyone by turn is a bureaucrat, and everyone else always agrees with the central plan. It is Titoism, and highly unorthodox, to decentralize and call that Full Communism. In economics, the state withers away not by decentralizing but by substituting consent for command.

Now in a very general way we consent to whatever is customary or inevitable; and in the U.S.S.R. communist planning is both. But in a more specific sense there is not and cannot be detailed planning by consent. Things are unpredictable and spot decisions must be made. These come down as direct orders: local participation can only be minimal, since local people have not the required information. If they do have it, and act upon it independently, there is *pro tanto* a market and no planning, whether by consent or by command. Detailed central planning must entail a bureaucracy issuing orders.

Nevertheless Khrushchev took orthodox doctrines very seriously. He did indeed reduce the role of the state bureaucracy, and he further showed his contempt for it by reorganizing it drastically about once a year. But he retained an ace up his sleeve: the Party. The Party was to be the organ of persuasion; it was to get stronger as the state got weaker. (Under Titoism, characteristically, the Party also must wither away.) At the same time he resisted every expansion of the rights of managers, that is, all decentralization. Yet since he wanted the small Party apparatus to take over from the large state apparatus he threatened ultimately to make detailed central planning impossible—or to turn the Party into a full-fledged state.

The notion of nonbureaucratic detailed central planning is a fundamental absurdity. Marx was wrong, Tito is right, and Khrushchev was trying to square the circle. The state may wither away in the economic field, but only if a market is substituted. We may, then, indeed speak of some small success in the goal of withering away, but not at all in the sense Marx meant, nor in a way that would satisfy an orthodox Communist. The ideology here is self-contradictory, and must itself be changed.

Is, then, a "managerial revolution" inevitable in the U.S.S.R.? By this I mean, will good, gray neutral experts displace Party fanatics at the center of power? The question is fraught with great historical importance, since such people, being more cynical and more moderate, will only pay lip service to Marxism, just as American politicians go to church. They will, then, Russian nationalism apart, be easier to get on with. They will be easier, too, for Russians —but not necessarily for minorities within the U.S.S.R.—to live under.

It seems to me that in foreign policy this has already happened, at least since the Sino-Soviet split, and possibly since Stalin first took power. Russian interests, unpleasant and awkward as these may be, always outweigh communist interests. Communist orthodoxy has migrated to China. In affairs of art, literature, and security, on the other hand, a brutal, philistine, Stalinist reaction is still possible. This is the least "managerialized" field. Economics lies in between.

The top economic specialists nearly all belong to the Party: but what does this mean? They are certainly very poor Communists. In ideology they are conformists, but conformists to whom? So long as a hard core of full-time, dedicated *apparatchiki* remains—to them; but how long will this core be big enough? In a general way we cannot tell, but in economics we can—the core is rapidly melting away. The Party's last desperate bid to stop the managerial revolution was precisely Khrushchev's reforms described above. But his successors have repealed the lot, and reverted to Stalin's administrative hierarchy, in which top ministerial bureaucrats in Moscow outranked local Party bosses in the provinces. In terms of power, this is fateful indeed. Again, in terms of ideology, not a single classical proposition of Marxism is undisputed, and many are already overthrown. It is only a question of what they will be replaced with.

For if all managers and experts reject the Marxian theory of value, they do not agree on much else. Land and capital must have prices and costs be rationally counted, yes; consumers' wishes must be respected, yes. But is the new system to be one of central command or of decentralized market? Technocratically minded engineers prefer the former; so do financial experts who fear a Yugoslav-type inflation and the waste of investment resources that will surely follow the withdrawal of central discipline. Pure managers, unless perhaps they are personally incompetent or manage enterprises already subsidized, prefer to be independent in the market. This attitude is most pronounced in retail trade, where the absurdity of the present system is most apparent, and least in heavy industry.

So there is certainly a managerial revolution in full swing; and of the many possible ones it leans heavily toward decentralization. This is economically good for the Soviets (though it has drawbacks such as inducing greater inflation), and ideologically good for the West, since it confirms many Western criticisms. But in ideology and power politics the real victors are the east European revisionists, and the real losers the Chinese dogmatists. It is still basically a family quarrel. Genuine capitalism, we have seen, will surely only take root in the U.S.S.R. in the peripheral areas like consumer durables and craft production. The question in other sectors is whether capitalism *in the West* can survive the Managerial Revolution there.

Appendix

STATISTICAL NOTE

The Formulae Chosen

Sovietological statisticians have always been in advance of their purely Western colleagues in one respect: due acknowledgment of the paramount importance of the *weights* chosen. The meaning of this all-important concept can be illustrated thus: Suppose that in 1928 we produced 2 tons of steel and 10 tons of grain, and in 1937, 5 of steel and 9 of grain, how shall we determine the behavior of overall production? One simple answer is to treat all tons as equal, so that in 1928 we produced $2 + 10 = 12$ tons and in 1937 $5 + 9 = 14$ tons. But a ton of steel costs far more to produce, and we are willing to pay far more for it, than a ton of grain. So the simple addition of tons of such disparate value is worthless. Suppose the price (or cost) was 6 times as much for steel as for grain in 1928. Then we can say that we produced $(6 \times 2) + 10 = 22$ tons of grain-equivalent in 1928. Moreover, in 1928 the cost for the 1937 outputs of steel and grain (or what we would have been willing to pay for them in that year) would be $(6 \times 5) + 9 = 39$ tons of grain-equivalent for the steel and grain outputs of 1937.

But by 1937 mass production lowered the cost and the price of steel in terms of grain, say to 3 of steel to 1 of grain. So in 1937, by the values of 1937, we produced $(3 \times 5) + 9 = 24$ tons of grain-equivalent. And the output of 1928 would have fetched, or would have cost, $(3 \times 2) + 10 = 16$ such tons.

So we have at least two equally plausible ways to determine overall production:

	TONS OF GRAIN-EQUIVALENT		INDEX (1937 AS PERCENT
	1928	1937	OF 1928)
with 1928 weight of 6 grain = 1 steel	22	39	117.3
with 1937 weight of 3 grain = 1 steel	16	24	150

The index numbers of production are the percentages, given here in the third column. The two weighting systems chosen are generally considered more logical and plausible than many others possible, for example, to weight each ton equally. While they are obviously of equal logical value they yield different answers. When the relative prices (or costs) and relative quantities of the things produced change rapidly, different systems of weighting give staggeringly different results. In 1928–1937 Soviet industry (but not agriculture, construction, or exports) went through just such changes; hence the distressing variability of the results for industrial production and for other magnitudes of which it is an important constituent: national income and the cost of living. For instance, the answer to so vital a question as whether Stalin depressed real wages in those years depends on our choice of 1928 or 1937 weights. There is no one right answer, but two answers equally defensible. Happily, calculation has shown that other periods in Soviet and indeed Russian history present fewer problems. The same variation afflicts the measurement of other economies, probably to a smaller extent, but this is not commonly recognized.

In another respect our calculations for the U.S.S.R. are very poor, and at least as poor as those for other countries: they make inadequate allowance for new goods, and new qualities of old goods. This is particularly true for arms production. Until someone can tell us the value of an H-bomb in terms of field guns we shall never have a meaningful index of arms *production,* only of arms *effort,* that is, we shall only know the resources devoted to this production, not their output. But in fact all series are affected by quality change. The very grain probably has more water and earth in it than it used to in 1897–1928. There are innumerable new consumer goods that would have delighted the subjects of Lenin or Nicholas II, but they would also have been shocked at the quality of modern buildings and boots.[4]

It is generally accepted that the quality and variety of nearly everything has risen almost continuously in the advanced capitalist countries. The amenity of the landscape, the efficacy of teaching at universities, the craftsmanship of repair work, the taste of bread— indisputable falls in quality are rare. This did not happen in the U.S.S.R. During the N.E.P. period, quality was worse than under Czar Nicholas II, and during the first Five Year Plan it was worse than during the N.E.P. We can therefore be quite certain that mere quantitative progress, from 1913 to 1932, understates true progress in other countries; but it might even overstate it for the U.S.S.R. (Table 1). From 1932 onwards, however, quality has improved. By exactly how much, we cannot say for any country.

Intertemporal comparison is probably less certain than interspatial. Thus if in 1955 the average Soviet citizen disposed of R X per head per year and his American contemporary similarly disposed of $ Y, the comparison presents serious problems. The American did not buy the same goods as the Russian, and the ruble

[4] Cf. my *Political Economy of Communism,* Chapter 12.

prices of the cheap goods that poor Russians bought were lower than average, while the commonest American goods had higher-than-average ruble prices. In brief, we are faced here again with a weighting problem, which can be well understood by substituting "U.S.S.R." for "1928" in our previous example, and "United States" for "1937." Using ruble weights we get an answer favoring the U.S.S.R., while dollar weights favor the United States. The same applies for 1913: using contemporary ruble weights, the comparison would no doubt give us a different advantage for the average American than by the use of dollar weights. But at such a great remove in time I am not able to guess at the difference, and present perforce an average.

Incidentally, in terms of pure consumption the American's advantage is somewhat greater, since his defense and investment burdens are proportionately smaller.

But even these complications do not end the matter. Just as in the passage of time from 1928 to 1937 new goods entered consumption, so they do in the spatial transit from Moscow to New York. In any year there are vastly more types of goods on sale to consumers in New York, and—in whichever country quality is now improving faster—the absolute quality is still much better in New York. Here again, then, economic statistics let us down badly. We can only say that the comparisons presented in Table 4 greatly overestimate the Soviet income, but by no certain proportion: not even by a constant proportion.

TABLE 1   Growth of Industrial Production, National Income, and Population in Russia and the U.S.S.R.

	(1)	(2)	(3)
	ANNUAL PERCENTAGE GROWTH OF		
YEARS	INDUSTRIAL PRODUCTION	NATIONAL INCOME	POPULATION
1897–1913	5	2.75	1.66
1913–21	fell to about 25% of 1913 level	fell to about 30% of 1913 level	0.35
1921–25	14	22.0	
1926–27	13	—	—
1925–28	—	11.0	—
1927–28	19	—	—
1926–29	—	7.5	1.30
	1928 weights / 1937 weights	1928 weights / 1937 weights	
1928–32	18 / 7	9.0 / 3.0	1.00
1932–37	18 / 12	12.0 / 4.5	
1937–40	9	2.0	1.17
1948–50	24	—	1.00
1950–55	13	7.0	1.90
1955–58	10		
1958–61	7	7.0	1.70
1961–63	8	3.4	

TABLE **2**   Indices of Agricultural Production, Commodity Exports, Real Wages of Urban Workers, and Consumption

	(1)	(2)	(3)		(4)	
		INDICES OF				
YEAR	AGRICULTURAL PRODUCTION	COMMODITY EXPORTS	REAL WAGES OF URBAN WORKERS[a]		CONSUMPTION, PER HEAD, ALL INHABITANTS[a]	
1897	74	—	—		—	
1913	95	248	75		—	
1917	71	3	78		—	
1921	48	67	28		—	
1926	95	85	79		—	
1927	98	—	—		—	
					1928 weights	*1937 weights*
1928	100	100	100		133	94
			1928 weights	*1937 weights*		
1932	86	138	—	—	—	—
1937	108	68	57	81	100	
1940	114	—	52	74	—	
1946	—	72			—	
1948	124	—			—	
1950	—	208			122	
1952	132	—			—	
1955	157	368			176	
1958	199	—			—	
1960	—	620			—	
1961	213	—			234	
1963	184	—			—	

[a] Since it excludes peasants, who are a large but diminishing part of the total, the real wage is a far less accurate indicator than consumption per head. The latter concept also includes the large "social wage."

The — means data not available.

TABLE 3   Ownership of Cultivated Land
(*In millions of hectares, within contemporary boundaries*)

YEAR	TOTAL	PRIVATE PEASANT FARMS	PRIVATE PLOTS Collective Farmers	Others	COLLECTIVE FARMS (public fields only)	STATE FARMS	OTHER STATE BODIES
1897	about 95	—	—	—	—	—	—
1913	118.2 (105.0)ᵇ	—	—	—	—	—	—
1918		—	—	—	0.2	0.7	—
1920	97.2	—	—	—	—	—	—
1921	90.3	—	—	—	—	—	—
1926	110.3	—	—	—	—	—	—
1928	113.0	108.7	1.2	ᵃ	1.4	1.7	‥
1932	134.4	27.1	—	—	91.5	13.4	—
1933	129.7	19.6	—	—	93.6	14.1	—
1935	132.8	6.8	—	—	104.5	16.2	—
1937	135.3	—	—	—	116.0	12.2	—
1938	136.9	0.1	5.3	1.1	117.2	12.4	0.8ᶜ
1939	134.0	—	—	—	114.9	—	—
1940	150.4	14.1	4.5	0.8	117.7	11.6	1.7
1950	146.3	1.9	5.9	1.6	121.0	12.9	3.0
1953	157.2	(0.03)	5.5	1.5	132.0	15.2	3.1
1954	166.1	—	—	—	—	—	—
1958	195.6	‥	5.5	1.9	131.4	52.5	4.5
1962	216.0	‥	4.2	2.5	114.2	86.7	8.1

PERCENTAGE OF OUTPUT

YEAR	TOTAL	PRIVATE PEASANT FARMS	Collective Farmers	Others	COLLECTIVE FARMS	STATE FARMS	OTHER STATE BODIES
1937	100	‥	21.5	6.3	62.9	— 9.3 —	
1962	100	‥	— 24.5 —		47.0	— 28.5 —	

ᵃ Included in private peasants. ᵇInterwar boundaries. ᶜ Residual.
The — means data not available; the ‥ means data negligible.

TABLE 4   "Catching Up and Surpassing"
(*Percentages of United States figures*)

	1913		1955	
	Russian Weights	U.S. Weights	U.S.S.R. Weights	U.S. Weights
(a) Industrial production	11	14	56	47
(b) National income	— 16[a]	—	48	24
(c) (a) per hour worked	18	24	43	21
(d) (b) per head of population	— 11[a]	—	41	21

[a] It has proved impossible to assign definite weights to these comparisons.

TABLE 5   Performance of Other Countries
(*Annual percentage growth of G.N.P. per head of population*)

	1870–1913	1950–1960
United States	2.2	1.6
United Kingdom	1.3	2.2
France	1.4	3.5
Germany	1.8	—
West Germany	—	6.5
East Germany	—	6.5[a]
India	—	2.0
Sweden	2.3	2.6
Japan	3.0[b]	8.8[c]
Russia/U.S.S.R.	1.1	5.1

[a] Somewhat approximate: includes estimations of my own.
[b] 1878–1917. [c] 1953–1963.

TABLE 6   The Efficiency of Agriculture

The efficiency of agriculture is fairly adequately measured by comparing the growth of output to the growth of input into agriculture. Inputs are land, labor, capital, and currently used industrial materials like fuel and fertilizers. The following figures are known to me:

ANNUAL PERCENTAGE RATE AT WHICH GROWTH OF
OUTPUT EXCEEDS GROWTH OF INPUT

U.S.S.R.	1961–65	1.3
	1956–59	2.0
Ukraine	1937–55	0.0
	1928–37	−2.0
United States	1939–58	1.0

IV

The Social and Cultural Record

by WRIGHT MILLER

Convinced of the scientific nature of dialectical materialism, Marx and Lenin viewed the visionary, reformist conceptions of the "utopian socialists" with the greatest contempt. Lenin wrote in 1899,

> Marx's theory has made clear what is the real task of a revolutionary socialist party—not to set up projects for the transformation of society . . . but the organization of the class struggle of the proletariat, the final aim of which is the seizure of political power by the proletariat and the organization of a socialist society.

Planning for a socialist society, it was frequently said, would divert energy from the struggle, and the vision of a future socialist, egalitarian society was left remarkably vague until after the Revolution of 1917.

After seizing power the Bolsheviks had war, famine, and disease on their hands, but in March 1919 they published the first communist program for Russia. It contains a great deal of rhetoric about making safe the victory over the bourgeoisie, but it is also a very practical document. It exhibits a typical bolshevik combination of concern with urgent measures for immediate problems with long-term, more visionary planning. The program for housing speaks almost entirely of confiscating and converting bourgeois dwellings and improving the hygiene of existing workers' housing; "new dwellings appropriate to the new conditions of the workers' existence" are mentioned last. The plan for education—free, universal, coeducational, and compulsory up to the age of seventeen—has eleven headings, including the attracting of literate but untrained workers to teach others. The health program gives priority to the control of the major infectious and "social" diseases, the nationalization of pharmacy, the building of hospitals and convalescent homes, the duty of all medical personnel to work for the new regime, and the establishment of sanitary regulations. Culture appears only as the tenth item in the education program: "the treasures of art, formerly the property of the exploiters, are all to be made accessible to the workers."

And there is much more. A good deal of this program has been realized and some of it has been greatly extended through later programs. Even defectors from the Soviet Union are, in great majority, still appreciative of what the Soviet government provides in welfare, in educational services in the widest sense, and even in intellectual and cultural life. The organization of all these aspects of Soviet life is, of course, centralized and largely bureaucratized; these services are, very broadly, directed toward goals decided at the top, and they are subject to a control of priorities according to the needs of the state. But this is only the frame, and to imagine that the frame makes the whole picture is to ignore not only the realities of life in a nation of 230 million, but the very facts of human nature.

There are roughly three periods in the history of Soviet social and cultural life: (1) the improvisation, enthusiasm, and experiment, even wild experiment, of the twenties; (2) the oppression and often savage discipline of the thirties and forties, though at the same time there was progress in science and in social welfare; (3) the comparative relaxation since Stalin's death in 1953, a period that shows some significant expressions of individuality and freedom, some limited opening up to foreign influences, but in no substantial way a return to the experimental early period, for this would now be impracticable as well as politically unthinkable. Progress now proceeds on a more mature basis. However, the latest period is still characterized, though on a milder scale than formerly, by that "concertina" pattern of repression-relaxation-repression in various spheres which seems inevitable under a system that has no proper channels for opposition.

The three periods correspond to the periods of Soviet economic and political development; when policy changed in one field it usually changed for all fields. The present essay will deal with these changes only with respect to health and welfare services, education, some branches of science, and literature and the arts.

Public Health

Plague, cholera, and typhus have disappeared from the U.S.S.R., smallpox almost completely so, and malaria and venereal diseases are reduced to small proportions. Children are immunized against smallpox, tuberculosis, and poliomyelitis. The death rate is less than 7 per thousand, which is below that of the United States, though the figure is hardly comparable since the proportion of older people in the Soviet Union is at present low. Life expectancy is 70 years, against 73 in Sweden and Norway, and the Soviet authorities do not hesitate to publish the comparison in their reference works; during the period 1926–1929 the Soviet life expectancy was only 44 years. There are more qualified doctors in the U.S.S.R. per thousand of the population than in the United States or most other Western countries; in 1965 the figure was 23. There are also more hospital beds: the 1965 figure was 9.2 per thousand without counting convalescent homes.

Every Soviet citizen has a health card from birth and is assigned to a pediatric polyclinic until he is sixteen, after which he is assigned to a convenient doctor and attends an adult polyclinic. He can change his doctor if he gives notice in writing. He pays nothing for any medical services or hospital care, nor does he pay medical insurance; for most medicines, however, a charge is made. At the polyclinic he may find, in towns, a radiologist, a pathologist, eye, skin and gynecological specialists, surgeons and nurses; the polyclinic is a cross between a health center and the outpatients' department of a hospital.

The country patient, however, may not be so fortunate. Newly

trained doctors are often directed to country work, with the understanding that they cannot graduate until they have had experience
in their first position, but after this the doctor seems to be directed
no further, though appeals and pressures are tried. In spite of higher
salaries in the country, many doctors try to return to the towns,
where life is better in almost every way. So the medical press
reports whole rural districts without a physician, and the countryside
still has to rely greatly upon the traditional part-trained medical
assistant, or *feldsher,* and his companion, the midwife. This is the
greatest discrepancy in Soviet medical services, and it will take a
long time to remedy, though there are some good medical units in
the countryside.

There is ordinarily less discrepancy in towns, where all enterprises above a certain size must have their own doctor, and the
largest enterprises have their own hospital. The person who works
for a small or out-of-the-way enterprise may not come off so well
in comparison—not only in medical care but in access to convalescent homes, etc.—and yet he may still have an excellent doctor
where he lives. Finally, there is the differentiation between the ordinary clinics and the "closed" clinics which, in several grades, serve
such notables as top officials, well-known writers, ballerinas, and
their families.

The original program for free medical services has thus been
almost realized; as to the universal aspect, the rural third of the
nation is still underprivileged; and the privileges of the small top
class continue a preference that Lenin began in the days when
medical service of any kind was scarce. The average Soviet citizen
is less annoyed at the closed clinics than the foreigner is; he is more
impressed by the progress made in his own lifetime. The foreigner
may point out the frequent sloppiness and lack of elementary pre-
cautions, and the red tape, and may call attention to the dozens
of press reports about local shortages of materials, equipment,
medicines, and personnel, which seem to him scandalous. But in
these local though widespread deficiencies Soviet medicine does not
differ from other aspects of Soviet life, and the native will continue
to expect improvement (though it may be sporadic) and to admire
the system in general. He might quote the World Health Organization Team that concluded in 1958 that "the U.S.S.R. is probably
the first country in the world to accomplish the unification of

medical care, in the sense that treatment and prevention form one single entity"; or the American Mark Field, who, while critical of a thousand practical points, says that "the extent goes beyond anything attempted."

The preventive side of public health, actually, is not yet up to the standard intended. Soviet doctors have to choose, in their third year of training, whether they will be children's doctors, adult doctors, or specialists in public health and sanitation. They remain in these categories all through their working lives, and the third choice is said to be the least popular. All public-health work in the U.S.S.R. is done by qualified doctors, who act as sanitary inspectors, for example. Clean water supplies and canalized sewage disposal do not exist yet in a number of large Soviet towns, not to mention smaller places; consequently the commonest diseases are bacterial dysentery and other intestinal infections. Cure here has run ahead of prevention, probably because it absorbed fewer resources, but the problem is recognized, and in 1964 workers in water supply and sewage were given a startling raise of 24 percent in wages, no doubt to encourage recruitment.

In the early days as much as 80 percent of doctors were women, but the proportion is now only half. All doctors are salaried, and it is not even a high salary—less than the earnings of the most highly paid skilled workers. The difference between the salaries of doctors and nurses is thus much less than in the West, but both professions are highly respected and do not seem to be short of recruits. There is a very small amount of private practice, but the proceeds are heavily taxed, and the W.H.O. team judged that private medicine could not possibly affect the general picture. Medical administration is the responsibility of doctors, and every doctor has many records to keep and forms to fill. He is less often conflicted over the signing of health certificates than he was in Stalin's time, but he may be subject to pressure from his local Party and governmental organizations. In this, as in other areas of Soviet life, the Party is a channel for complaints from the public, and it has a general commission to see that planned services and supplies are provided—which is not to say that they inevitably are.

The six-year medical training has usually been thought satisfactory by foreign visitors, and Soviet surgery has made some daring advances. Foreign medical literature is now much more available, and at the same time Soviet chauvinism has relaxed its claims for Soviet priority in discovering penicillin, streptomycin, and other antibiotics. The psychologists, who discussed every known theory in the twenties, including Freudian psychology, were limited to a strict following of Pavlov's neurological model under Stalin, though during that period they produced some useful research. Today psychotherapy is employed more, and though Freudian views are still unaccepted, it is pointed out that Pavlov recognized that in man verbal stimuli can be a substitute for physical stimuli such as he employed with dogs. Psychotherapy uses words, and hence to practice psychotherapy is still to be a Pavlovian! The incidence of mental illness in the U.S.S.R. is reported to be low, and we need not be surprised at this. Russians have a long traditional experience of "making do" in community, and they have been able to cope with the overcrowding in Soviet cities better than people reared in more individualistic societies would have been. Alcoholism is a serious problem, but the U.S.S.R. includes under this term not only the pathological alcoholics but also the heavy drinkers. Heart diseases, as might be expected, are on the increase, and city strain surely contributes to these.

The Soviet health service, in short, presents a typical Soviet picture of first things first—mass organization in order to cover the whole country (at the expense of comparative neglect of some features), and concentration of some of the best services for the benefit of the small minority most prized by the state.

Housing and Welfare

The most chauvinistic Russian communist would not pretend that housing conditions have not been, through most of Soviet history, appalling. As a result of the scale and speed of industrialization, farm laborers were taken off the land in huge numbers, and the city population increased from 28.1 million in 1926 to 121.6 million in 1965. Between 1926 and 1940 the living space per head decreased from 6.45 square meters to 4.09 square meters, and most families lived in a single room, sharing a kitchen and other facilities with others. It was not until ten years ago that a really massive housing program was begun, and the construction of dwellings now goes on at the rate of between 2 and 3 million a year. Industrial methods of building are used, and since all land belongs to the state there are few difficulties about sites. The striking fact about the new dwellings is that they are not the "communal houses" dreamed of by the first bolshevik planners, but individual apartments of reasonable comfort. Though small and monotonously alike, they usually consist of two rooms with separate kitchen and bathroom and separate lavatory. Rent is very low, obviously subsidized— 4 to 5 percent of income on average; central heating is usual, and district heating frequent.

Sick pay and pensions have been on a fairly generous scale since the 1930s, though both depend on years of service, with a minimum qualifying period. It is possible to receive sick pay as high as 90 percent of earnings, and as long as one is a member of one's trade union the minimum is 50 percent. Retirement pensions have been on an equitable basis since 1956, with a minimum of about thirty rubles a month. (A low wage is forty to fifty rubles.) Higher wages earn higher pensions, but on a scale of decreasing fractions. In 1965 pensions were for the first time paid to the 6.5 million collective farmers, though on a less generous scale. There are no insurance deductions from wages for pensions or sick pay.

Paid holidays compare favorably with those in Western countries. Miners, steelworkers, bus drivers, and others in occupations considered arduous are allowed up to four weeks a year; others get two to three weeks. The work week is now forty-one hours (in five days for most people, from 1967), while ten years ago it was forty-six hours. For heavy work the hours are shorter.

In Czarist Russia there was very little emphasis on sports, and the Soviet state was at first more interested in physical fitness than games. The great growth of sports came after World War II, and though one may believe that Soviet leadership in the Olympics has been achieved by a concentrated effort to boost national prestige, this is hardly enough to account for the 40 million who take part in Soviet national competitions. The Soviet people have taken naturally to sports, and unlike the sportsmen of some new nations, they usually show dignity in defeat and generosity in acknowledging a better opponent.

Why does the Soviet government increase its expenditure on all these services year by year, at a rate much greater than the rate of population increase? We shall certainly go wrong if we are, to use the words of Professor Daniel Bell of Columbia University, "so mesmerized by the idea of 'power' alone as to forget its impact on people." Even from the ideological standpoint it is important for the leaders to show improvement in Soviet living conditions. Also, the outside world does get to know about these conditions, and does learn, for instance, how the home population becomes restive when things temporarily get bad again, as they did in some areas after the disastrous harvest of 1963. Incentives, in general, are more and more used throughout the Soviet system today, the size and powers of the police have been cut down, and if workers are not satisfied they can change their jobs freely. Soviet citizens also know much more about foreign conditions than they once did. And is it not plausible to suggest that there are leaders in the Kremlin who actually take pleasure, as long as the requirements of defense, space research, Soviet prestige, and general planning are not being threatened, in realizing that life for the ordinary citizen is getting better? One may believe this and yet be anti-Communist.

Education and Science

Soviet education is a unified national system, like that of, for example, France, but its aims are very different and permeate the entire system to an extent that is not encountered in any Western democratic educational system. To quote a recent pronouncement:

> The colleges must turn out people who have mastered their speciality well, who are active and passionate champions of Lenin's ideas and the policy of the Communist Party, who are bold and enthusiastic, and are profoundly convinced of the triumph of our cause, . . . irreconcilably opposed to bourgeois ideology.

Exhortations and directives of this kind are repeated *ad nauseam,* but they do not indicate either the content or the achievements of Soviet education; and the foreigner who meets Russians informally may well be surprised to find how few of them—perhaps one in twenty?—will treat him as a subject for indoctrination.

In Czarist Russia a huge proportion of the population, variously estimated at from 60 percent to 79 percent, was illiterate, though in its last few years the Czarist state was providing more and more schools. Today illiteracy has disappeared, even, it is said, for tribes that had no written language until Soviet times. In 1964 there were 68 million students in educational institutions of all kinds, 46.7 million of them in the general schools. Some 30 percent of all books produced in the U.S.S.R. are textbooks; the textbook figure for 1963 was 381 million.

In the early bolshevik period there was enormous enthusiasm for education (partly inherited from Czarist days), but there were few teachers, insufficient buildings and materials, and several million homeless, marauding children. It was not practicable even to make education compulsory until 1930. Yet there was much experiment in education; psychological tests were developed to pick out gifted children; children of the old bourgeoisie were excluded from higher education; and the schools attempted "polytechnical" education proposed by Marx, to train young people in the skills of a number of trades.

All four of these features were abolished in the late 1930s, and it has been anathema ever since, at least in principle, to talk of tests or differentiation on grounds of ability, apart from the special schools for art, music, and ballet, and also for defectives. Experiment in educational methods is often called for, but experiment can be such a delicate ideological matter that (according to Professor Frederic Lilge of the University of California) the Academy of Pedagogical Sciences has done very little in this area since its foundation in 1944. Great resources were early put into universities and other higher institutions, mainly, it would have been said, "to help in the task of outstripping capitalist countries." Under Stalin, fees were imposed for the three top grades in school as well as for universities, but Khrushchev dispensed with them.

Khrushchev inherited an already well-developed upper educated class, with the best-trained children usually despising manual work, and the children of the majority not getting a proportionate share of higher education. He therefore instituted a break of two years between high school and college, and "involvement in productive work" for children from their early teens, but this proved too difficult to organize. The two-year break has also lapsed, partly through complaints about the deterioration in quality of university entrants. What remains is the eight-year school as a basic school for the compulsory ages, that is, seven to fifteen. The polytechnical principle has been brought back, and schools are supposed to provide workshops for crafts in both wood and metal, though a recent Soviet journal complains that "in most school workshops there is not enough workspace for either." Children may be required to clean their school, and in the country they work in agriculture. Normally all young children must attend the eight-year school nearest their home; but some children may be permitted to attend certain special schools where most instruction is given in a foreign language, and this contains the potential for special distinction; the boarding schools, still largely experimental, seem less open to this danger.

After the eight-year school there are four alternatives: vocational technical courses of one to three years, which seem to absorb about a quarter of the children; specialized four-year schools for higher grades of training; evening or shift schools to provide supplementary general education for those already at work; and general secondary schools that give three more years of general education, usually in the same building as the eight-year school, with four hours a week, in principle, devoted to "apprenticeship in factories, offices, or farms." Universities and the specialized higher (mostly technical) institutions, which outnumber universities by about four to one, are now open to the secondary-school graduates and "working youth" who earn the highest marks in entrance examinations. At the very top of the secondary schools there are some special arrangements for discovering the most promising talents in mathematics and science. Thus, without psychological testing, some kind of separation of abilities has been established, though choice between the four types of secondary education is said to be open. Schoolchildren (except those from the specialized secondary schools) are not supposed to be directed into jobs, as higher-education students usually are, and there is no such thing as a career adviser. The Soviet view, in theory, is that almost any kind of child can be trained for any kind of work, and whatever the work may be they should all "glory in labor." In spite of this propaganda, and the many films and plays that show the attractions and usefulness of manual work, there is a social hierarchy of jobs (apart even from the pay) much like that in other countries.

It is too early to say how the education system will work out. Some school subjects, especially languages and history, have suffered a curtailment as a result of the polytechnical principle. There is a shortage of science teachers, many schools still have to work double shifts, and the press constantly reveals shortages of textbooks and materials. So although it is undeniable that Soviet education turns out a higher proportion of engineers, scientists, and technicians than do most Western countries, it appears that the quality is not necessarily high. Foreign visitors say the best are second to none, but the great output is of technicians and technologists trained as a rule in rather narrow specialities, and there are still not enough of them for Soviet needs. "We can't find enough workers to improve accuracy or speed," is the typical complaint.

What is heartening about Soviet education is the general enthusiasm and respect that it commands. It is true that education offers the only way to rise in Soviet society (unless one wants to climb the Party ladder), but the old Russian regard for enlightenment also plays a part, as well as the traditional Russian benevolence and encouragement for all children; and the Soviet system itself has generated a widespread passion for knowledge. Teachers are on the whole respected, though, like doctors, they are not highly paid, and parents are usually much involved in the school. Children from west European countries who join Soviet schools—and I do not speak of the children of communist parents—find the work and discipline easy, the atmosphere warm and friendly and not as solemn as might at first appear. There is far too much rote learning and very little of the "eliciting" that American teachers love. School examinations are easy and mostly oral, and the graduation standard at age seventeen seems equivalent to the west European standard for children a year younger. There is much pressure on teachers to give all their pupils good marks. The theory is that every child should be able to reach the standards set; even drawing and the appreciation of music are not to be regarded as special gifts.

Lenin presides over every classroom, and political teachings about the Soviet state and the capitalist world are formally and exclusively Marxist, but these probably have a less profound effect than the general communal atmosphere, which many children have experienced in kindergartens or nurseries from an early age. "We educate," says Deputy Minister of Higher Education Gerashenko, "so that our young people can combine their individual interests with social interests." This is a conventional communist dictum, but it would take a long essay to disentangle how much is due to the group pattern and how much is an individual response to the state's plans. There is one special incentive to individual effort—the selection of gifted or well-behaved or hard-working children for spare-time visits to the Pioneer Palaces, where they may practice arts and crafts and hobbies as well as take part in group activities.

If any of those Bolsheviks survive who drew up the 1919 program they must feel proud that universal, free, and coeducational schooling has been attained; but they must be disappointed that it has not yet become universal to the age of seventeen; in the country-side even the eight-year school is not universal and in many places only seven-year schools are in operation.

There can be no doubt, however, about their enthusiasm for one result of specialized education, namely the Soviet achievement in science. In 1918 Lenin laid down a draft plan for scientific and technical work, and during the next two years 117 scientific institutions were founded in spite of civil chaos. It was typically Marxist to give priority to science, the key to man's control of his environment, and to initiate an effort supported by huge government funds ever since, in contrast to the suspicious and niggling attitude of the Czarist authorities. All the same, Czarist scientists laid firm foundations in all branches of science and engineering, and Soviet scientists were able to build on the work of men of world reputation such as the chemist Mendeleyev, the mathematician Lobachevsky, the aeronautical pioneer Tsiolkovsky, Dokuchaev, the founder of soil science, and Yablochkov, who invented the electric lamp before Edison. The new government bought foreign equipment and materials and sent young specialists abroad to study, and it continued to do this even during the worst Stalinist years.

The Academy of Sciences has been the organizer and initiator of much research, but as industry grew, the volume of technical research in hundreds of institutes increased until it exceeded by far the work of the Academy and its dependent bodies, though nowadays the Academy retains some general control. By 1964 the country had 4,597 scientific institutions, employing 326,800 scientists in research or teaching.

Soviet science now has to its credit the whole spectacular space program, dating from the launching of the first Sputnik in 1957, and other discoveries such as Cherenkov radiation and the control of thermonuclear reactions within magnetic fields, as well as inventions such as surgical staplers, the kerosene-lamp power source for radio receivers and refrigerators in distant places, and hundreds more. During the last few years Nobel Prizes have been awarded to five Soviet physicists and one Soviet chemist.

The present position has been reached in spite of the suppression, imprisonment, and even execution, during the Stalin period, of scientists who followed the "heresies" that were then held to be incompatible with dialectical materialism—Einstein's relativity, the "indeterminate" physics of Heisenberg, Norbert Wiener's cybernetics, and, best known and longest suppressed, the genetics of Mendel, besides Freud's psychology, which is still rejected. Under Stalin some scientists were able to survive by paying lip service to official views, and cloaking their research in deceptive terms.

But the very great biologist N. I. Vavilov died in a Siberian prison camp. This was the man who built up the Academy of Agricultural Sciences, established the origins of the world's principal food plants, and collected specimens from all over the world in order to experiment with new strains from wild stocks. Only in 1965 were his name and work generally rehabilitated, and the charlatan Lysenko finally discredited. Lysenko was a plant breeder who had green fingers and a very few practical successes, on the strength of which he built up a whole edifice of anti-genetics, claiming swift results for environmental influences when in fact he had been lucky in selecting the right hybrids. Today good work is again being done in genetics and molecular biology.

In many other branches, besides agriculture, Soviet science is not to be judged by the standards of the space program. Priority was quite rightly given from the beginning to physics, mathematics, engineering, and (since mineral resources were largely unsurveyed) to geology. The most able men trained large numbers of less able ones in these specialities, but the prestige attached to the Five Year Plans in itself attracted large numbers of the most gifted and most vigorous men and women to these branches of science, so that other branches suffered by contrast. It is only in recent years that more emphasis has been given to chemistry and the chemical industries, and in some degree to biology: a recent president of the Academy of Sciences, Professor Nesmeyanov, wrote that "the study, from the point of view of the physical aspect, of intimate primary processes of life and the simplest forms of life, such as viruses, holds out no less promise for science and technology than the study of the atomic nucleus and elementary particles."

British scientist A. W. Haslett points out that "in those sciences which deal with organisms as a whole it is difficult to move at a pace suited to planners; and when quick results are produced they are found only too often to have been based on over-simplification or wrong interpretation." There has been a more patient objectivity and less demand for quick results in the last few years, particularly since Khrushchev was removed. There has even been some development of sociology in limited ways—demography, and a good deal of what we would call consumer research. And though it is still unthinkable that the independent writings of some Soviet David Riesman or Lewis Mumford should be published, there has been some discussion, in specialized contexts, of attempts to adapt Marxism to the realities of scientific investigation instead of the other way around.

Soviet scientists are far more in touch with their foreign colleagues than they were formerly permitted to be, and there is actual collaboration with, for example, American scientists in certain fields: in meteorology, where there have always been interchanges; in studies of the earth's magnetic field; and in communication by satellites. In the Antarctic there is constant personal contact.

As we learn more of Soviet science we appreciate its weaknesses as well as its achievements. Recently it earned a somewhat exaggerated respect from many Americans, through the simultaneous impact of the space triumphs and a realization of the wide scale of Soviet scientific education. But many foreign observers feel that if the potentialities of Soviet science are to be realized fully there will have to be more initiative allowed at lower levels, and education will need to be less formal. Even the percentage of gross national product devoted to research is not overpoweringly greater in the U.S.S.R. than in the United States. An Organization for Economic Cooperation and Development calculation in 1965 gave a tentative estimate of "between 2 percent and 3 percent" for the U.S.S.R., against a declared 3.1 percent for the United States, pointing out at the same time that the cost of research is lower in the U.S.S.R.

The cultivation of science in Soviet Russia has some other advantages, however, which must cause Western countries to take a fresh look at themselves. The term "pure science" is not used; the distinction between "fundamental," "basic," "theoretical" science and applied science does not amount to a distinction of social class, as it often does in the West, though the organizational distinction between them is becoming sharper in the U.S.S.R. There is a respect for science, as well as for technology, and some understanding of it among most of the general public. The intelligentsia are far from despising science—more than half of them are scientists anyway— and there is no serious problem of the "Two Cultures." Scientists and technologists often transfer to administrative or diplomatic posts. Kosygin is the first head of the Soviet government to have had a university education (at an industrial institution), while Brezhnev was trained long ago as a metallurgist. Scientists in general lead fairly privileged lives and are probably the most fortunately placed of Soviet citizens.

Arts and Letters

Writers and artists, on the other hand, are viewed by foreigners as oppressed by political control. There are many other aspects to the cultural scene than this—some of them rather ignored by foreigners —but first it would be useful to look at one of the likely basic reasons for control, though there is only room here for the most elementary outline.

The refusal to admit the unconscious psychology, the timidity of the steps in sociology, and the suppression or persecution of many advanced writers and artists appear to have this in common—the fear of being forced to recognize features in human nature, even in one's own nature, that are incompatible with the Marxist view.

But what is that view? Marx and Lenin saw all around them the debasement of human nature in industrial barracks and in peasant misery; they insisted that human relations were conditioned for the most part by economic relations, by the ownership of the means of production. Change these economic relations, and the natural good-ness and comradeship of men and women, which Marx and Lenin could also see, at least potentially, around them, would be released. But the full nature and motivations of human beings when released from economic pressures were spoken of in no more detail than the plans for a socialist future in welfare, education, and so forth. Today the desires of human beings to love, to marry, to raise good children and not injure their neighbor are taken for granted. But the reasons that may drive men to injure their neighbor, to be grasping, self-seeking, sadistic—these are considered as "bourgeois survivals." Parental influence over children is of course recognized, and much exhortation is expended on parents who are neglectful, overindulgent, or oversevere, but these traits in parents are also "bourgeois survivals."

Meeting intelligent Soviet citizens, one finds them at least as sensitive and aware of individual problems of human adjustment as intelligent people elsewhere; and the ordinary Soviet citizen, it seems to me, is rather more capable of warm personal relationships than the ordinary person in many Western countries. What is lacking, except in a few who have come under strong foreign influences, is a view of human nature that can allow for natural aggression, or mother-attachment or father-attachment, or the desire to be alone or to follow the crowd, except in terms of social conditioning. Perhaps in time it will be thought desirable to develop Marxism so that it can accommodate a more fundamental and less class-oriented view of human nature. Some attempts, with a basis in the earliest writings of Marx, are already reported from Poland. But conservative Soviet thinkers must feel menaced by the suggestion that personal motivations, even in Soviet society, can be more fundamental than social forces. The dilemma is crucial for traditional Marxist thinking, but this is a political question that must be left to other authors. This dilemma may help to explain the rationalization by which books such as *Dr. Zhivago,* which have not directly attacked the Soviet Union, may be regarded as treasonable. In this connection it may be worthwhile to note, however, that many Russians, quite apart from their communist training, are obsessed by the fear of being isolated from the crowd. The reasons for this lie deep in the history of Russian society, but the more sensitive and original natures are now trying painfully, just as in many other countries, to express their individuality more fully and more richly; and in this conflict lies the essence of one of the great Soviet problems.

In the first years after the Revolution there were individuality, experiment, and eccentricity in plenty. Most of the intelligentsia were enthusiastically in favor of overthrowing the old order, and in the bolshevik regime many of them saw, with typically Russian all-or-nothing comprehensiveness, the promise of being able to make all things new. Creative artists, such as those who had gathered around Diaghilev, were inspired by the liberation of a new public and the crusade for an industrial society. (For a short time the theaters were open exclusively to the working class, and Stanislavski himself has told how educable the new audiences were.) There were concerts of factory sirens and steam whistles, conducted from a rooftop by a man with flags; there were vivid political posters; there were the theatrical productions of Meyerhold and others, where the whole audience might be involved in the action, or the cast entered through the auditorium on motorcycles, or bizarre constructions took the place of scenery in order to force the spectator out of the attitudes that familiar objects might induce. Chagall and Kandinski, the first abstract painter of all, were organizing art teaching; the "suprematist" Malevitch and Tatlin and others were producing works of art as startling as any of our own day; Eisenstein was using untrained crowds in films such as *Battleship Potemkin*; the volcanic young futurist Mayakovsky was declaiming his revolutionary verses like a street-corner orator; the "marvelous peasant boy" Yessenin was giving a new voice to old Russia in his poems; and the established poet Blok fused Christ and communism together in his outstanding poem "The Twelve."

Lenin disliked modernism but he did not interfere. From 1928 onwards, however, with the first Five Year Plan begun, and Stalin in full control, all this experimentation was by degrees suppressed. Mayakovsky committed suicide, Yessenin had already done the same, Kandinski and Chagall had gone abroad, many writers and artists were arrested or executed, and the rest had to learn to toe the line of the new "socialist realism." The workers, it was said (probably with much truth), did not appreciate experimental art forms, and if artists and writers were to have the privilege of leading their comparatively free and leisured lives their duty was to inspire the workers to "build communism" and to sing the glories of the "new Soviet man." Writers were "engineers of human souls." All forms of art must be intelligible at first contact and must have a mass appeal; experiments in style were anathematized as "formalism." A favorite phrase, used not only with respect to music, was that things should be "in a major key." During World War II there was some relaxation, particularly as patriotism of a Russian national kind became a desirable theme, and for a very short time after the war more foreign influence was admitted. Then in 1946 the grim campaign under Zhdanov enforced controls more rigidly than ever. Great composers like Prokofiev and Shostakovich had to make public confession of their "errors," writers such as Akhmatova and Zoshchenko were suppressed, and painters were condemned for having been seduced by the degenerate Cézanne who "put men on a level with beer mugs."

For more than twenty years there was a great output of artificial novels and plays about characters fulfilling quotas or being disciplined by "self-criticism," or paintings of similar subjects, or attempts to achieve a similar effect in music. Some work that stands the test of time did appear: films by Pudovkin, for instance, Sholokhov's novels about collectivization and the Don Cossacks, which later earned him the Nobel Prize for literature, and some beautiful writing about nature by Prishvin and Paustovski.

The public were sometimes inspired by works of strict socialist realism, and were amused by the occasional productions that were allowed to satirize the worst of these, but they turned much more to the great classics, and political leaders repeatedly criticized Soviet writers and composers for not creating characters like Tolstoi's or symphonies like Tchaikovsky's. Classics—nearly always printed without cuts—were and still are published in larger editions, on the whole, than Soviet writings, and even editions of a million soon vanished from the shops, while the works of classical composers formed the greater part of most concert programs. Dostoevski's works were indeed almost unavailable (though nowadays published in an edition of three hundred thousand), but there were the other great Russians, and translations of Shakespeare, Dickens, Galsworthy, Balzac, Whitman, Mark Twain, Jack London, and dozens more, so that Soviet citizens were never short of books which implicitly suggest a non-Marxist view of the world, or attitudes not "in a major key." There were many attempts to reinterpret the great works of the past on "class" lines, but the basic motive for publication must have been the original desire "to make the world's culture available to the masses."

Much of the country's best cultural energy went into raising technical standards and providing the physical means for public enjoyment of the arts. The five-year or seven-year training in music, ballet, or theater laid the foundations not only of the supreme talents of a Ulanova or a Plisetskaya, an Oistrakh or a Richter, but of tens of thousands of lesser talents that evoke the admiration of those who come to see them in the U.S.S.R. Amateur talent, especially in the theater, has also been raised to very high standards. By 1964 there were 513 permanent professional theater companies performing to 58 million spectators in 308 theaters, and 798 lesser theaters for local or visiting performers. In the same year 78,204 books and pamphlets were published in a total of 1,252,934,000 copies, 32 percent of these copies being works of pure literature.

The prices for the arts have always been kept low—quite disproportionately low in comparison with the price of clothes, for instance. Someone on an average salary—say a young teacher—can by spending only 2 percent of his weekly salary visit the Bolshoi Ballet or Opera once every two weeks, or any theater or some other ballet or opera company once a week. If he buys the very best seats he spends between 6 percent and 10 percent of his salary, though he may find it difficult to get hold of these, since many are reserved for privileged persons or foreigners. In Moscow he might have a choice of two hundred stage performances, including opera, ballet, and puppets, in a period of ten days, but only fifty films. In smaller centers the choice is very much smaller; films, operettas, folk dancers, comedy acts, form a larger proportion of the fare, and people often feel rather short of entertainment. There is often some political content even in these lighter forms, but it can hardly show itself in social dancing, which is the most popular entertainment with the young and is to be found everywhere. A good deal of foreign jazz is played, though the bands are usually poor. There is no pulp literature, nor is there its equivalent on the radio or on television (which now covers half the country). For the most part, these media merely present films or stage performances, with little broadcasting embellishment.

The well-known thaw after Stalin's death has not meant a green light in all directions for all the arts, and it has been interrupted by trials of writers accused of "anti-Soviet" work, which have served only to intensify anti-Soviet attitudes in the West. The thaw as a whole, however, is typical of the more tentative, more realistic attitudes of today.

The present cultural situation has at least five main features.

(1) The need for "various trends" is recognized. "True crea-

tivity," said *Pravda* in 1965, "is only possible in an atmosphere of quest, experimentation, free expression and the clash of opinions." Not all trends, of course, are licensed: twelve-tone music and abstract painting and sculpture are heavily frowned on, to say the least, though some may practice them in private and even (quite legally) sell their works to fellow citizens. The recognition of "various trends" naturally implies freedom also for the more reactionary and hidebound practitioners of socialist realism. Their works do not usually sell very well, and their indignation and self-righteousness are an important element in the repressions that from time to time so scandalize the West. The old machinery of censorship—largely operated by members of the artistic professions—still exists in all forms of art, although today there is more scope allowed to the artists. But by no means are all of these men in key positions liberal.

(2) The darker passages of Soviet history may not only be illuminated but condemned, at least by implication, as in Solzhenitsyn's *One Day in the Life of Ivan Denisovitch*. In such contexts, however, it must often be difficult to know what criticisms might be regarded as comprehensively "anti-Soviet" and so taboo. There has been a rehabilitation of most of the men and women of the early period whose work was suppressed under Stalin—the late poetess Akhmatova, for instance, who at the age of seventy-seven was honored with a selected edition. The paintings of Malevitch and Tatlin are not shown to the public, however, though Cézanne and Gauguin are hung in places of honor, and there is a whole roomful of cubist Picassos in the Hermitage. But abstract art, it seems, must still be derided as foreign.

(3) The arts concern themselves much more with individuals and their personal problems. These are novels, plays, and films without a "hero," in which the chief character is an imperfect being who drags down others through his imperfections. (There are no "antiheroes," however, nor any of those characters so dear to the West at the moment, who try to define themselves and to live without any social relations.) The theater has always been the place to look for a suggestion of new social and political trends and one finds these not only in contemporary plays of social criticism but also in such plays as Radzinsky's *Once More About Love,* which deals with nothing but the heartaches, romance, and tragedy of young people just like those in the enthusiastic audience. There are

short stories as inconclusive and as real as daily life, and occasionally an impressionistic film such as *I Walk Around Moscow*. There are also moralistic, neatly trimmed films and fictions of the older type, but characters are no longer plain black or white, as a rule.

The great heroes of the new generation are the young poets such as Yevtushenko (whose first editions run to a hundred thousand copies), Voznesensky, the poetess Akhmadulina, and the ballad singer Okudzhava. Their personal poetry recitals can fill halls with an ecstatic eleven thousand listeners. Their works show a hatred of phoniness and a many-sided sensitivity. In technique, though original, they are less startling than Mayakovsky. Mass audiences of young people have had some influence on officialdom at times, for example, in keeping open the exhibition of the artist Glazunov who had been judged too avant-garde.

(4) Much more foreign influence is allowed to infiltrate. The B.B.C. is no longer jammed, though some other foreign broadcasts are. Russians returning from abroad have brought in a fair stock of foreign books and records, and the Central Library of Foreign Literature has a weekly accession of hundreds of volumes. Even a well-read foreigner might find it hard to keep up with some of the sophisticated minority who read, say, the latest Harold Pinter, John Updike, or Arnold Wesker in the original. A larger public avidly reads a selected number of translations—some of Hemingway and such works as *Look Back in Anger, The Catcher in the Rye, The Quiet American,* and *Our Man in Havana.* A few foreign films are shown, usually with slight cuts, including *The Magnificent Seven, It's a Mad, Mad, Mad, Mad World, All About Eve, Room at the Top,* and *Oklahoma!,* as well as French and other films. The authorities are clearly more sensitive to foreign opinion, as was evident at the Sinyavsky-Daniel trial (though it did not affect the verdict), but they still keep a pretty strong control over the entry of foreign works, and if outsiders try to force the pace of the thaw in this respect they will help no one.

(5) In one field the state has taken a progressive lead against majority opinion—that is, in trying to raise the general standards of design, away from the prevailing taste for "cabbage and chrysanthemum wallpapers" or china ducks on the wall. Good design flourishes in the three Baltic republics (owing to Scandinavian influence between the wars) and is encouraged to spread from them. The

British, by invitation, put on an exhibition of industrial design in 1964. A few new buildings of elegant appearance are going up, besides the monotonous apartment houses, and one can see a perfect contrast between the best face of contemporary Russia and the worst of the Stalin period if one compares the soaring glass of the Soviet pavilion for the Montreal Exposition of 1967 with the bombastic, overloaded concrete of the Soviet pavilion at the Paris Exhibition thirty years earlier.

Writers and creative artists, unlike performing artists, are not salaried, though they can be tided over between works from a central fund. Poetry and specialized publications are remunerated at three times the rate of royalty for fiction, and a few writers are ruble millionaires through their royalties. (Work for television and radio is poorly paid in comparison.) In living conditions, vacation homes, and so forth, artists and writers are also privileged, and I doubt whether these privileges arouse much resentment, for though there is some philistinism among the Soviet public, the general atmosphere is not favorable to it.

The creative intelligentsia are mostly respected and admired, not only for what they produce but because so many of them show a social conscience and use their position to present, even though in a veiled way, some of the grievances and aspirations of the people. Furthermore, as the most individual types of individuals, the writers and artists and scientists can offer models, in their own persons, to inspire millions of the more perceptive and sensitive who are struggling to express more of their own personalities.

Not only has the Soviet system provided minimum standards of material living and social security, but—paradoxical though this may seem to many foreigners—it has also provided opportunities for the differentiation and development of individuals that could hardly have been imagined by the average citizen of Czarist Russia. Soviet citizens have received these opportunities first through their jobs, and nowadays through the greater privacy they enjoy in the new apartments, where families are so much more separated from each other than they used to be. Consequently more attention can be concentrated on the rearing of children, ordinarily one or two.

Yet the pride of the new Soviet individual is not much like that of the Western self-made man; the people in the new apartments do not seem to be much more acquisitive than they were, and Marxists may take satisfaction in the realization that they neither show much of the puritanical, hoarding characteristics of early Western "bourgeois" societies, nor much of the ostentation of the affluent "bourgeois" society. Keeping up with the Joneses is not a great factor, because in all these new circumstances the Soviet people still retain much of the traditional Russian egalitarianism, and the largely unconscious sense that they are all members of one community. They do not see "society," in the manner of so many Westerners, as something deliberately created by free individuals, but more as a natural mode of being from which they themselves spring—and this no doubt has much to do with keeping them less tense than many Western peoples are.

The other aspect of these group attitudes, however, is that they generate a lot of the laziness and apathy on which petty bureaucracy feeds, while it is only the more politically conscious or the more perceptive who feel that their own efforts can contribute to an improvement of the general situation—economic, political, or cultural. And herein lies a great dilemma for the Soviet leaders: they need all these new individualities and yet—because of their political philosophy and because they also are Russians—they must fear almost any loosening of communal ties. There is a growing danger that a minority with hereditary privilege may be established, based less on money than on the inevitable facts that high officials and intelligentsia—largely constituting a social group apart—can help their sons to get a better education and better jobs.

Soviet society is more complex than it was in early days, and it is likely to become more complex still. That is the sociocultural picture, and it affects the political picture much more than it used to.

V

Reflections on the Soviet System: The Durable Core of Totalitarianism

by BERTRAM D. WOLFE

In Mexico City there is a *pulquería* or *cantina* with the intriguing name, *Memorias del Porvenir*—Memories of the Future. Not having access to *pulque* at the moment, I have no such memories on which to draw. Moreover, if there is one thing that has impressed itself upon me most forcefully in a quarter-century of striving to write, with the aid of archaeological methods, the history of a living society, it is precisely this:

> More than the historian likes to admit, at every turn he finds the unexpected and the unpredictable: contingency, historical accident, biological accident intruding into history, as when the death of a history-making personage brings a change in direction; sudden changes of mood and flare-ups of mass madness followed by mass passivity; emergence of totally new and unanticipated situations; leaps that seem to turn disparate series of ambiguous little events into a definitive large one; the unintended consequences of intended actions. . . .[1]

[1] From the Introduction to the Fourth Edition of *Three Who Made a Revolution*, Bertram D. Wolfe (New York: The Dial Press, 1948).

125

A similar *caveat* appeared in a paper I prepared for St. Antony's College, Oxford, ten years ago, when I ventured out on the precarious limb of prophecy to suggest that the "collective leadership" succeeding Stalin's death was transitory, and that the man with his hand on the power lever of the party machine was already "more equal than the others."

The conference at Oxford had been optimistically entitled "Changes in Russia Since Stalin's Death." My *caveat* was the more necessary since I had provocatively entitled my opening-day paper "The Durability of Soviet Despotism." The paper attracted more attention than I had expected, first as the blank of target practice for a week, then because one of its predictions seemed to get "experimental verification" three days after the Conference's adjournment, when Khrushchev expelled Malenkov, Molotov, and Kaganovich, and a short time later, Zhukov and Bulganin, from their posts.

For a variety of reasons, the present moment is a more uncertain time and the extrapolator, to use an academic term, must of necessity speak with a more uncertain voice. Hence I have settled on a more limited task, namely the reexamination and "updating" of my 1957 paper to determine how much of its picture has withstood the wreckful siege of ten dynamic and battering years.

In my Oxford paper I wrote:

> Brought up in a world of flux and openness, we find it hard to believe in the durability of despotic systems. Our hopes and longings are apt to betray us again and again into a readiness to be deceived by others and to deceive ourselves. The "journalistic" nature of our culture has made us too ready to inflate the new because it alone is "news," while we neglect to put it into its "tiresomely repetitious" historical and institutional setting.

> From the N.E.P. to Socialism in One Country; from the Popular Front and Collective Security to the Grand Alliance and One World; from Peaceful Coexistence to the Geneva Spirit and the Spirit of Camp David—the occupational hazard of the Western Intellectual has been not to read too little but to read too much into planned changes, involuntary changes, and into mere tactical maneuvers and verbal asseverations.

> Each has been hailed in turn as the softening of the war of the total state on its own people and the world; as the long awaited "inevitable change" and "erosion"; as the "fundamental transformation" that would make them like us; "the sobering that comes from the responsibility of power"; the "response to the pressures of reality"; the growing modification of totalist power by a "rationalist tech-

nocracy"; the "sobering effect of privilege upon a new privileged class"; the "rise of a limited and traditionalist despotism"; "a feeling of responsibility to Russia as against World Revolution"; "the quiet digestion period of a sated beast of prey" no longer on the prowl; "the diffusion of power which could lead to a constitutional despotism"; the "mellowing that sooner or later overtakes all militant movements"; the second thoughts on the struggle for the world that have come at last "from a recognition of the mutual destructiveness of nuclear war"; the "inevitable work of erosion upon the totalitarian edifice." [2]

Now, ten years later, at the risk of being "tiresomely repetitious," I must begin by repeating these thoughts once more.

Is this distinction between "closed" and "open" societies still a useful one? To me it seems that it is, and that the making of that distinction is helpful in conjectures on the future of the Soviet system. Here then are the relevant passages from the Oxford paper of 1957:

> Though all lands go through a history, and all orders and institutions are subject to continuous modification and ultimate transformation, there are some social orders or systems that are more markedly dynamic, more open, more mutable, even self-transforming, while others exhibit marked staying powers, their main outlines continuing to be discernibly the same through the most varied vicissitudes.
>
> It may be difficult to determine except in retrospect just when a system may be said to change in ways so fundamental as to signify its transformation; still it is possible and necessary to distinguish between self-conserving and self-transforming systems, between relatively open and relatively closed societies, and between changes so clearly of a secondary order that they may be designated "within-system changes," and those so clearly fundamental that they involve "changes in the system" or basic societal structure. That this distinction may in practice be hard to make, that there may be gradations and borderline cases and sudden surprises, does not relieve us of this obligation. Merely to reiterate endlessly that all things change, without attempting to make such distinctions, is to stand helpless before history-in-the-making, helpless to evaluate and helpless to react.

[2] From "The Durability of Soviet Despotism." Reprinted from *Commentary,* by permission; copyright © 1957 by the American Jewish Committee. Reprinted in *The Soviet Crucible, the Soviet System in Theory and Practice,* edited by Samuel Hendel, third ed. (Princeton, N.J.: Van Nostrand, 1967).

I then gave examples of long-lasting historical configurations such as the Roman Empire, which over three or four centuries, despite historical vicissitudes and changes, continued "in a meaningful sense to be the Roman Empire"; the Byzantine Empire, with a half-millennium of continuity; Western monarchical absolutism, with a continuity of several centuries; the Russian autocracy; and the Chinese system, which reckoned its continuity not in centuries but in millennia.

Between these long-lasting systems, the paper drew some important distinctions. Thus of west European monarchical absolutism I wrote:

> If we take one of the most dynamic regions, that of Western Europe, in one of its most dynamic periods, we note that monarchical absolutism had a continuity of several centuries. This is the more interesting because, though it was one of the more stable and more politically exclusive power systems of the modern Western world, it distinguished itself from the others by being a *multi-centered* system in which the monarch was checked and limited by his need to seek support from groups, corporations, and interests that were organized independently of the central power: the castled, armed, and propertied nobility with their retinues of retainers; the Church with its spiritual and temporal authority; the burghers of the wealthy, fortified towns.
>
> It is the presence of these independent centers of corporate organization that makes Western monarchical absolutism an exception among the centralized, long-lasting power systems. It was these limiting forces that managed to exact the charters and constitutions, the right to determine size and length of service of armed levies, size and purpose of monetary contributions, thus ultimately transforming the absolute monarchy into the limited, constitutional monarchy of modern times. And it is from our own Western history, with its exceptional evolution, that we derive many of our unconscious preconceptions as to the inevitability, sweep, and comparative ease of change. To correct our one-sided view it is necessary to compare the characteristics of multi-centered Western absolutism with other, more "complete" forms of single-centered power and despotism.

Followed a comparison and contrast with the Russian autocracy, and a comparison and differentiation between Russian autocracy and Soviet totalitarianism, which must be quoted at greater length since it takes us to the heart of our subject:

> Unlike Western absolutism the *samoderzhavie* of Muscovy developed into a single-centered power structure. The Czar early managed

to subvert the independent boyars and substitute for them a state-service nobility. The Czar possessed enormous crown lands and state serfs. Bondage was instituted by the central government and adjusted to the purposes of the recruiting sergeant and the tax-gatherer. When Emancipation came, it was decreed from above, developed under state supervision retaining collective responsibility of the peasant to the village *mir* and of the village to the central government.

Industrialization, too, was undertaken at the initiative of the state. From Peter I to Nicholas II, there were two centuries of state-ordained and state-fostered industrialization. The state owned and managed a number of basic industries—mining, metallurgy, munitions, railroad construction and operating—and some commercial monopolies, all crowned with a huge state banking and credit system.

The rudiments of a multi-centered life were just beginning to develop in this powerful, single-center society when World War I added to the managerial state's concerns the total mobilization of men, money, materials, transport, and industry.

The "model" country in this new form of state enterprise was wartime Germany. The system of total management by the state for total war has been variously, but not very intelligibly, termed "state capitalism" and "state socialism." In any case, Lenin was quick to welcome his development as the "final transition form." In it, as in the heritage from the Czarist managerial autocratic state itself, he found much to build on in making his own transition to the new totalitarianism.

From Ivan the Terrible on, for a period of four centuries, "the state had been stronger than society" [3] and had been ruled from a single center as a military, bureaucratic, managerial state. Amidst the most varied vicissitudes, including a time of troubles, wars, conquests, invasions, peasant insurrections, palace revolutions and revolutions from above, the powerful framework endured. Weakenings of the power structure, even breaches in it, were followed by a swift "restoration" of basic outlines. When the strains of a world war finally caused its collapse, there came a brief interlude of "loosening of the bonds." Then Lenin, even as he revolutionized, likewise "restored" much of the four-century-old heritage. It was this "socialist restoration of autocracy" which Plekhanov had warned against, as early as the 1880's, as a danger inherent in the longed-for Russian revolution. He admonished the impatient Populists and then Lenin that unless all the bonds were first loosened and a free "Western" or "bourgeois-democratic" order were allowed to develop and mature, the seizure of power by would-be socialists could not but lead to a restoration of Oriental, autocratic despotism on the basis of a pseudo-socialist "ruling caste." Things would be even worse, he warned Lenin in 1907, if this new "Inca ruling caste of Sons of the Sun"

[3] The formula is that of Miliukov.

should make the fatal mistake of nationalizing the land, thus tightening even more the chains that bound the peasant to the autocratic state.

Followed a brief examination of the Chinese system (called in Soviet political literature "Oriental despotism") which, despite its turbulent history of invasions, conquests, changes of dynasty, rebellions, interregnums, and times of trouble, represented a continuity of several millennia, so that a Chinese villager or official of the nineteenth century, could he have been transported into the China of two thousand years ago, would have felt completely at home. The key to this continuity lay not in lack of a history but in the fact that the need for centralized direction of the whole population for the purposes of vast irrigation and flood-control projects made for an eventual "restoration" after each interregnum or upheaval.

This section of my Oxford paper concluded with the following generalization:

> With the exception of Western monarchical absolutism, what all these enduring social structures had in common was a single power center, a managerial state, a lack of independent social orders and forms of property, an absence of checks on the flow of power to the center and the top, and an overwhelmingly powerful, self-perpetuating institutional framework.

Is the term "totalitarian" still useful in describing the Soviet system? At the International P.E.N. Club Congress held in New York City in June 1966, the Chilean communist poet Pablo Neruda called the Italian novelist Ignazio Silone an unreconstructed "cold warrior" for referring to the struggles of intellectuals against domination by the totalitarian state. To this Silone replied, I think quite properly, that "totalitarian is a necessary descriptive term for a state that controls every aspect of life."

In this respect, too, although no little of the demonic element in totalitarianism has diminished as the paranoid system of chain-reaction purges of Stalin was tacitly and even publicly replaced by gentler forms of institutional monopoly and institutional controls, the basic formulations of the Oxford paper are still applicable:

> Modern totalitarianism, I believe, is one of these comparatively closed and conservative societies, with a powerful and self-perpetuating institutional framework calculated to assimilate the changes which it intends and those which are forced upon it, in such fashion

that—barring explosion from within or battering down from without —they tend to remain *within-system* changes in an enduring system.

At first glance the word conservative may seem out of place in speaking of a society that is organized revolution. And indeed there is a striking difference between Communist totalitarianism and all previous systems of absolute, despotic, undivided (and, in that sense, total) power. For whereas despotism, autocracy, and absolutism were bent on preserving the status quo (such regimes as those of Peter the Great, Alexander II and of industrialization under Witte constituting partial exceptions), Communist totalitarianism is dedicated largely to "the future." This powerful institutional structure which tolerates no rival centers of organization has a vested interest in keeping things in flux. The omnipotence of state and ideology is maintained by carrying on a permanent revolution. Like Alexander's it is a revolution from above. But unlike Alexander's, its aim is nothing less than to keep a society atomized and to create, as rapidly and as completely as the recalcitrant human material and refractory surrounding world will permit, a new man, a new society, and a new world.

Like the earlier systems referred to, it possesses a state that is stronger than society. Like them it represents a system of total, in the sense of undivided, power. Like them it lacks any organized and institutionalized checks on the flow of paper to the top. Like them it possesses a state-centered, state-dominated, state-managed, and, for the first time, a completely state-owned economy.

But if the other societies are distinguished by the high specific gravity of state ownership, state control, and state managerial function within the total activity of society, under Communist totalitarianism state ownership and state managerialism aspire to be total in a new sense. In the other cases, we have been contemplating total power in the sense of undivided power: power without significant rival centers of organization. But now, to the concept of *undivided power,* we must add that of *all-embracing power.*

No longer does the state limit itself to being "stronger than society." It now strives to be *coexistensive* with society. Whereas the earlier power systems recognized certain limitations on their capacity to run everything, leaving room, for example, for pocket-handkerchief farms and the self-feeding of the *corvée* population, for private arts and crafts unconnected with the managerial concerns of the state, for certain types of private trade, and even finding room for village communal democracy under the watchful eye of the state overseer —what Wittfogel has aptly called "beggars' democracy"—the new totalitarianism strives to atomize society completely, to coordinate the dispersed villages into its centralized power system, to eliminate, insofar as it seems possible to do so, even the small private parcel of the *kolkhoznik* and the urban worker, already reduced from a "pocket handkerchief" to a mere swatch. (On this matter there has been much vacillation since the statized and pseudo-collectivized farms, despite tractors and chemical fertilizer and the unremitting attention of "planners" has always been of a low order of productivity per capita, while the small parcels have been far more productive though men worked only with bent back, watering can, such fowl and cattle feed as could be grown or scratched together, plus the zeal that comes from feeling that you are working for yourself and your family or for sale on a free market.)

For the first time a total-power system in the earlier sense of undivided and unchallenged power aspires to be totalist or totalitarian in the further sense of converting the state-stronger-than-society into the state-coextensive-with-society.

The paper then turned to the view, widely held ten years ago and again being urged today, that "the attempt to embrace the totality of social life and social activity is somehow incompatible with the complexity of modern industry, advanced technology, and a literate working population. I reminded my listeners that Germany adopted totalitarianism when it was the foremost country of Europe in industry, technology, literacy, and higher education.

Indeed [I wrote] it is precisely modern technology with its all-embracing means of communication, its high-speed transmission of reports from the localities and of commands from the center and of armed forces to any part of a great country, its mass-communication and mass-conditioning techniques, that for the first time makes it possible for despotic (undivided) power to aspire to be totalist (all-embracing) power. That is what Herzen foreboded when he wrote: "Some day Jinghiz Khan will return with the telegraph."

And so far as universal literacy is involved:

Once more it is Germany that serves to remind us that modern totalitarianism requires that everybody be able to read so that all can be made to read the same thing at the same moment. Not the ability to read, but the ability to choose between alternative kinds of reading is a potential—and only a potential—liberating influence.

The "Law of Diminishing Dictators"

There is a principle of selection in personal despotism [I wrote] which surrounds the despot with courtiers, sycophants, executants, and rules out challenging and original minds. . . . I would not write these "smallish men" too small, however, for when you have a sixth of the earth, a population of over 200,000,000, a total state economy, and a great empire to practice on, you may learn other trades besides that of courtier or faction lieutenant. Even so, not one of [Stalin's lieutenants] exhibits the originality and the high charge of energy and intellect that characterizes Lenin, or the grosser, but no less original, demonic force of Stalin.

With a longer time span and a third exemplar to contemplate, I should like to amplify this "law of diminishing dictators." Like other generalizations that prolong the past by extrapolation toward the future, this "law" should be formulated with the anticipation of possible surprises, such as the appearance of a new dictator, who, after attaining power, may display a demonic dynamism or a complacent benevolence hitherto unknown. It is essential to note that although Stalin has been written smaller now and the leaders have made public if faltering pledge not to restore "Stalinism," no institutional safeguards have been set up to make a new capricious or cruel or even paranoid dictator impossible. Beyond a doubt, however, Stalin was smaller than Lenin, Khrushchev than Stalin, while Brezhnev, Kosygin, and the men in the present, I think transitory, "collective leadership," seem smaller still.

With the diminution in the size of the dictators there goes a diminution in content and dynamic charge of the ideology in the name of which they claim the right to rule over a great nation. A Marx or Lenin in any case is not born every day. Though circumstances may permit a wielder of power to grow with his exercise of power, the appearance of a great man is a genetic accident, not, as Engels and Plekhanov would make it, a law of history. Circumstances do not set their impress upon men so much as great men set their impress upon their age and circumstances. Undoubtedly, Marx was greater than Engels in his passions and the sweep of his more lawless, less systematic, and more demon-possessed intellect.

Though Lenin liked to think of himself as the successor to both Marx and Engels, he actually represents an amalgam of the voluntarist and inevitabilist aspects of Marxism with the extremist revolutionary and organizational traditions of Russian populism, on which explosive mixture he set the stamp of his own unique personality. His Marxism was so different from Marx's that an amused but not unfriendly observer, Charles Rappaport, called it *Marxisme à la tartare*—Marxism with tartar sauce. Stalin's Leninism, in turn, differed enough from that of Lenin that we might term it *Leninisme*

à la mode caucasienne—Leninism marinated in a sauce of moun-
taineer blood-vengeance.

As for Nikita Khrushchev with his proverbs and clichés, his
random remedies, his bumptious outbursts of temper and bossy
humor, his shoe off at the United Nations, his "state of all the
people," "butter on the bread of communism," "we will bury you,"
and "I have seen the slaves of capitalism and they live well"—
though he belongs in the succession of diminishing dictators, we cannot really find a place for him in the series of ideological titans.
Brezhnev, who at this writing would seem to have his uncertain
hand on the power lever of the Party machine, appears to be no
more than an insignificant transition figure in a new interregnum
and a succession crisis that has not yet come to a head.

The Erosion of Ideology: Its Extent and Limits

In view of the tendency inherent in "the law of diminishing dictators," and the accumulation over five decades, not of countervailing
institutionalized powers as is sometimes suggested, but of countervailing pressures for relaxation inside the U.S.S.R.; and in view
also of the, in the main successful, if vacillating and hence not
always complete "containment" by outside resistance and outside
countervailing power, it is not surprising to find seeds of doubt and
signs of erosion in the fanatical, crusading ideology. Facts, too, are
stubborn things and contribute to the work of erosion.

Yet it is well to remember that this process of erosion began
not with Stalin or Khrushchev but with Lenin himself, at least as
early as two years after he had seized power in 1917.

His first "eroding" discovery was made even earlier, namely
that the "peasants had voted with their feet" against the continuing
of the war and its conversion into civil war and world revolution.
The result was his surrender of much of the Russian empire at
Brest-Litovsk merely to hold on to power until the world revolution
should spread to the West. (Actually he got most of the lost land
back not because of world revolution but because of the victory of
the Allies over the Central Powers.)

For two years Lenin saw world revolution everywhere. His
ideology was a compulsive monologue in which he persuaded himself

and his followers that capitalism was finished, that World War I was the "final crisis," that the seizure of power in Russia was only the first act in a worldwide or at least Europe-wide revolution, that the Second International and the mass unions were dead and discredited beyond revival. The masses needed but to be summoned to battle, "International Menshevism" isolated and destroyed by the purge net of the Twenty-one Conditions, set up to admit minnows and exclude whales, and insurrections and soviets would spring up in every land in a worldwide international dictatorship.

Since the old order was breaking down in the central empires, what could take their place but soviets? Lenin could not understand why the Soviet system should fail to elect Spartacans to its leadership (Rosa Luxemburg and Liebknecht did not even win mandates to the Congress of Workers' and Soldiers' Councils), nor why it should vote by 400 to 50 in favor of the convening of a constituent assembly in place of taking all power for itself, or for the Spartacan party, which was not even represented in it. "The Soviet form has conquered not only in backward Russia," Lenin told the First Congress of the Comintern, "but also in the most developed country in Europe, Germany, and in the oldest capitalist land, England."

Genuinely imprisoned in the envelope of his ideological misunderstandings, he misread the British Shop Steward movement, too, fancying its strikes to be revolutionary, and seeming to anticipate a march on Westminster with rifles and cold arms to disperse the ancient Parliament and set up rule by the shop-steward councils. On March 12, 1919, he told a credulous Petrograd soviet that "at present soviets are being established in America." The only correlate I could find was the setting up of the General Strike Committee during the Seattle General Strike to run the municipal services of food delivery and garbage collection "by Order of the General Strike Committee."

Thus the first "erosion of ideology," or as it is sometimes called, "relativization of absolute ideas," began a half-century ago, in the mind of Lenin himself, when he recognized "the delay of the revolution in the West," the revival of the mass unions and parties, the need of "united front" tactics and "infiltration of mass organizations," and of a New Economic Policy in Russia.

With the first erosion arose the first erosion illusions. It is sobering to think how the world might have been saved the cold

war and eastern Europe decades of subjection, if we had not nourished so many illusions about Lenin's and Stalin's ideology, and
had so planned the acts of World War II that our soldiers would
have been at the war's end in positions that could have guaranteed
a decent peace in Prague, Berlin, Bucharest, and Belgrade. And it
is no less sobering to remember that this work of erosion has been
going on now for half a century, yet totalitarianism as a structure
still endures. We must ask once more, as ten years ago, what is it
that still endures, and for the foreseeable future, seems likely to continue to endure, in this institutional system?

The Durable Core of Totalitarian Ideology

Lenin's brief period of "absolute expectations" was over within two
years of his seizure of power. They were illusions promoted by the
ease with which he had conquered power ("as easy as lifting up a
feather") and the certitude that that seizure was but the first act of
a drama whose second act would begin almost immediately in
another part of the forest: namely, Germany. Once these "infantile
leftist" illusions were over, he returned to the durable core of his
earlier Leninism, his doctrine of total and totally centralized organization.

Marx had been vague on how the working class takes power,
though he stressed that it was to be through a party embracing the
entire class. The few other remarks he made when pressed by
Duehring or Lasalle were taken literally by Lenin and Stalin; even
now their successors, though aware of the mischief some of these
precepts are occasioning, seem unable to shake off their spell.

Lenin soon recovered from the dogma of labor-time receipts
instead of money, and from centralized distribution of every hunk
of bread and pen nib. On the abolition of the market, he beat a
partial retreat with the N.E.P. ("Seriously and for a long time.")
In this respect it is well to remember that there has been *not erosion
but reinforcement* in the form of central-command planning of
everything and abolition of the N.E.P. At most, in these fifty years,
there has been ebb and flow with more flow than ebb. On the doctrine of the withering away of the state there has also been the
reverse of erosion. "The state of all the people" is only an enlarge-

ment of the state's claims to speak for everybody, claims first staked out for the Party's dictatorship by Lenin himself in 1902, when he wrote:

> "The Social Democrats must *go into all classes of the population* . . . to dictate a positive program of action alike to rebellious students, to dissatisfied Zemstvo-figures, discontented religious secretaries, and indignant school teachers, and so on."

In Lenin, Marx had an innovating disciple who was a theoretician, a technician, a militant defender, propounder, and virtuoso of organization and total power. Conspirative secrecy, centralized organization, command performance, military discipline, detailed instructions, the ability to mobilize, manipulate, and organize discontent and hatred—a technique, indeed an elaborate technology and pedantic systemization of the art and science of seizing power, extending power by frontal attack or by zigzag and by feeling out the weak spots in the adversary, a technique and technology for holding power, utilizing power, regularizing and bureaucratizing power, extending power in width and depth even unto the affairs of the spirit—what are these if not the levers of modern totalitarian revolution and totalitarian rule?

Centralism

The first peculiarity that strikes one in Lenin's organizational doctrine is his centralism, and his extreme distrust not only of whole classes (the intelligentsia, the petty bourgeoisie, the peasantry, and the working class itself), but even of the rank and file of his own Party, and his own local organizations. In 1904 he wrote:

> Bureaucratism *versus* autonomy, such is the principle of revolutionary social democracy as against the opportunists. The organization of revolutionary social democracy strives to go from the top downward, and defends the enlargement of the rights and plenary powers of the Central Body.

In the third year of his rule, with his power secure and the civil war at an end, far from permitting the principle of centralism to "erode," he reinforced it by plugging the last vents of public discussion with cement. It was then that he abolished the very basis of such Party democracy as had existed in the early years before he could complete the act of *Gleichschaltung,* by prohibiting Party groupings, platforms for proposal of changes, gatherings of like-minded Communists to discuss their views, with expulsion provided for any violation. Having already drained the constituent assembly and the soviets of political power, he now did the same with the trade unions and his own Party.

In power, Lenin was fulfilling the dream of his early "Letter to a Comrade on Our Organizational Tasks," which had so impressed Stalin:

> We have arrived at an extremely important principle of all party organization and activity. In regard to ideological and practical *direction,* the movement and the revolutionary struggle of the proletariat need the *greatest possible centralization,* but in regard to *keeping the center informed* . . . in regard to *responsibility* before the party, we need the *greatest possible decentralization.*[4] . . . The movement must be led by the smallest possible number. . . . But the largest possible number of the most varied and heterogeneous groups drawn from diverse layers of the proletariat (and other classes) should take part in the movement. . . . *Now* we have become an organized party and that means the creation of power, the transformation of the authority of ideas into the authority of power, the subordination of the lower party organs to the higher ones.

Here, as early as 1902, is Lenin's whole schema: the dictatorship of the Party over all classes of society, the transmission-belt system of implementing that dictatorship, the rule of the many and most diverse groups by the fewest and most homogeneous, the transformation of the authority of ideas into the authority of power in all the manifold activities that were to concern the Party—and which activities were not?

Lenin's cry for an organization of revolutionaries to turn Russia upside down did not cease when he had indeed turned Russia upside down. As before, he continued to call for "organization, organization, organization." To his old dream of centralized organization of the Party, he added the new dream made possible by power: the dream of total organization of all life by the Party in accordance with its—that is, his—blueprint for society and man.

Now he would remake the spirit of Russia, its industries, its

[4] Some of our sovietologists now call this participatory democracy.

agriculture, its interchange of goods, its foreign trade. He would remake the Oblomovs, the Lopakhins, the Ranevskayas, the Stroganovs, the Morozovs, and the Ivan Ivanoviches, all according to his blueprint of the New Soviet Man. He would remake Russia's emotions, her thoughts, her feelings, her habits, even her dreams, eliminating by total organization all slackness, all waywardness of will, all indifference to or tolerance of other ways. "We must organize everything," he said in the summer of 1918, "take everything into our hands." To the authoritarianism inherent in an infallible doctrine, possessed and interpreted by an infallible interpreter who rules an infallible party infallibly from above, Lenin added this further dream.

Thus the most obvious trait setting Lenin apart from his associates in the Russian intelligentsia and the revolutionary movement was his absorption with the mechanics and dynamics of organization and power. In a world where most intellectuals were in love with ideas, and accustomed—whether by temperament or the pressure of circumstances—to a distinction, even a yawning gap, between the dream and the deed, Lenin was an organization man— indeed, *the* organization man of whatever movement he took part in. When he broke with his colleagues on *Iskra* it was on the question of organization. Amidst men dedicated to dreams, organization was his dream. But such an ideology, the ideology of complete control of society by the Party, and complete centralization of power within the Party, does not erode as easily as do other ideas such as egalitarianism or international socialism or communism.

In other words, totalitarianism has an ideology that is essentially an ideology of structure. What is growing thin, shallow, passionless, and lacking in conviction is the ideology of the structure's *purpose.* Every effort is made to diminish or check this process of "erosion" by the enforcement of *partiinost,* by the exclusion of the foreign press, radio, and television, by the deliberate suppression of articles of criticism or challenge, by a continuing war on freedom in the arts, and where they impinge on matters of power, in the sciences, by the outlandish denunciation of "archive rats" (Stalin), "historians" (they are "dangerous people"—Khrushchev), "bourgeois objectivity," "bourgeois falsification," and "vulgar factology."

There seems to be no good reason why those who enjoy the prerogatives of absolute power should give it up merely because they have become somewhat vaguer as to why they are exercising it. As I wrote in my 1957 paper:

> If in general it is dangerous to relax the screws ever so slightly or to measure out homeopathic doses of freedom, there is an additional specific danger that big announcements and big promises may seem to mean more than they intend. Illusion, to paraphrase Marx, once it takes possession of great masses of men, becomes itself a material force.

One has only to look at the troubles caused by "destalinization" both in Russia and in its satellites, and the consequent awkward efforts at partial restalinization, to convince one's self that to play with freedom is to play with fire. In my Oxford paper this was formulated as follows:

> It is these concepts of organizational structure, party monopoly of power, and the dictatorship of an infallible élite that set their limits on the possibilities of *organized* public opinion. Resentments, pressures, discontent, longing for a less oppressive régime and an easier lot, exist under despotisms, autocracies, total-power states and totalist states, even as in other social orders. . . . The problem of "statecraft" in a despotism is that of preventing the discontent and longing from assuming *independent* [independent from the party] and *organized* [nonstate and non-Party organizational] form. Since the totalist state penetrates all social organizations . . . it is particularly adapted to keeping discontent thus fragmented and unorganized. Earlier despotisms spied on people not merely to weed out trouble-makers, but often to find out what changes were desired that did not affect its fundamental powers and aims. Here, too, the totalist state is better adapted by virtue of its universal police and espionage system than was the primitive "espionage" of an incognito Haroun-al-Raschid or a Peter the Great.
>
> By 1936, Lenin's idea of an elite, single-centered dictatorship had gotten into "the most democratic Constitution in the world" as Article 126, which proclaims the party to be "the vanguard of the working people [now the entire people] and the leading core of all organizations, both social and state." And in the summer of 1956, when Khrushchev and Company were summing up [as they have had to do repeatedly since] their continued wrestling with Stalin's ghost, they declared in *Pravda*: "As for our country, the Communist Party has been and will be the only master of the minds, the thoughts, the only spokesman, leader and organizer of the people."
>
> It is foolhardy to believe that they did not mean it, self-deluding to convince ourselves that the forces pressing for concessions within the country are likely to find the road open to separate and effective

corporate organization, which organization is the condition precedent to the development of a limited, multi-centered state and society.

The Monopoly of the Means of Communication

One of the key powers of a totalitarian regime is the absolute monopoly of all means of communication. The rulers own and control the newspapers that should criticize their mistakes. They control the critics; they decide who is to be criticized for what, who made the scapegoat, who lauded to the skies. They control the printing plants, the publishing houses, the libraries, the bookstores, the reviews, the reviewers, the size of editions, what shall be published and what remain unpublished; they control the telephone, the radio, television, the loudspeaker on the public square. They control procurators and lawyers, police and mass meetings, the staging of mob scenes, the packing of the courtroom with unconditional adherents, the exclusion of friends and relatives of the accused.

I remember how shocked I was in my youth to read the title of a wartime indictment: *The People of the United States versus Eugene V. Debs.* It is better, I thought then, to be accused by a monarch or a despot. But Debs could speak out, he could address mass meetings while out on bail, his friends could hear him in the courtroom, he could publish his defense, even get it reported, in a not-too-friendly press and in a friendly press as well. He, too, could invoke the name of "the people" and urge that he served their interests and that the indictment found in their name did not express their true feelings or hopes or needs.

But in a totalitarian land, the rulers can dictate the editorials which misrepresent the accused and their deeds, can intimidate the judges, dictate the verdict before the trial, deny meeting halls to the accused, pack the courtroom with secret police dressed as workingmen, peasants and intellectuals, to drown the words of defense and to clamor for punishment. The victorious clique or single leader can put words of guilt and confession into the mouth of the accused, allegations of opposition to the nation, or to "progress," or to whatever else, and for all the public can know, these words of self-accusation were words actually spoken by the accused, for he cannot repudiate them or answer them in the totally controlled press.

Will the Soviet people ever know what Bukharin really urged as a program for them? Or what Malenkov, Molotov, and Kaganovich actually proposed, or what it was that made them "anti-Party"? If we know what Sinyavsky wrote, it was because of his heinous crime of getting published abroad—an honor for the writers of other nations—and because some courageous friend, at the risk of his own freedom, smuggled his courtroom defense out of the country. Inside the U.S.S.R. the ordinary mortal has not heard or read his speech of defense, or the work that he succeeded in getting published in other lands when it was self-evident that he could not publish it in his native tongue for his own people in his own country. Is there any plight more terrible than to be charged with infamous imaginary crimes in the name of a voiceless people who are not even permitted to hear one's answer to the charges that they did not really make?

There is no sign of erosion of this monopoly of the means of communication. Authors, emboldened by the lapsing of the death penalty for unpublished and unpublishable writings, pass tiny hand-written or mimeographed editions around, but this they did even under Stalin and under Lenin, though under Stalin the punishment was more awful when the dictator's sickly suspicion or resentment was aroused. Even the bit of freedom thus assumed by authors in their corporate solidarity arouses the fury of the Party potentates, though many of our commentators like to speak about the scant freedoms taken, without noting the crackdowns that follow.

At present no lover of freedom can take comfort in the brutal treatment of Russia's great poet Pasternak; in the critical pearls concerning him that issued from the mouth of the youth overseer and secret police chief, Semichastny; in the unfeeling rantings of Sholokhov against defenseless colleagues at a Party Congress; in the trials of Sinyavsky and Daniel and their condemnation to long terms of hard penal labor for the crime of practicing their profession; in the incarceration of Tarshis and the mathematician-poet Yesenin-Volpin, and the promising young poet-translator Brodsky, in a mad-house; in Tarshis' subsequent deprivation of citizenship by tyrants who rule the land in which he was born; in the sentencing of the gentle poet Brodsky to shoveling manure in a forced-labor camp in the Arctic Circle, a barbarous sentence that only one who hates culture and poetry could have thought appropriate for the crime of wanting to be a poet. (One looks in vain for an analogue in the treatment of men of letters under the czars; the only analogy I can think of is that of Baldur von Shirach proclaiming, "When I hear the word *Culture,* I cock my revolver.")

I am deeply shocked when callous colleagues write that once the U.S.S.R. too has modern industry, poetry and literary freedom will take care of themselves (the "convergence theory"). Indeed, heavy industry can get along very well without freedom for poets, who do more for industry when they shovel manure.

It is dispiriting to find the publication of *One Day in the Life of Ivan Denisovitch* printed and critically praised one day at the whim of a boss whose only knowledge of literature is the knowledge that comes from power over everything, which is *ipso facto* expert knowledge of everything; and then to find the same work condemned at the Twenty-third Congress at the whim of another boss whose power over everything enables him to know that the work is a bad work.

It is a cheerless task to read the speeches delivered in that great "deliberative body," the "supreme authority of the Party," the Twenty-third Party Congress. It is even worse than preceding Congresses, for it was not even used as a sounding board to propagate a new line. For all the "deliberations" that took place in this august body, its almost five thousand "delegates" and its two thousand honored guests might have been replaced by so many phonograph records, since each speaker took the floor only if assigned to do so, and developed the point assigned to him to develop, in the language prescribed for him by previous decision of the higher body, which decided everything in advance before it convoked the Congress. It would be deadly dull were it not so frightening.

We must take note of the fact that the tolerant and courageous editor of *Novy Mir,* Alexander Tvardovsky, was not even on the roster of delegates or invited guests. He was a delegate to the Twenty-first and Twenty-second Congresses, where his knowing voice contributed something valuable to the omnipotent Party's discussion of literature, but this time his voice was silenced, his wisdom suppressed, and the incoming Central Committee no longer lists his name as a candidate-member so that his voice will not be heard in their meetings either.

This time, in place of Khrushchev, the man who knows all about art and literature is Brezhnev, for as before, power over everything gives knowledge of everything. He told the Twenty-third Congress in 1966:

> Unfortunately such practitioners of the arts are to be found who, instead of helping the people, choose to specialize in denigrating our regime and slandering our heroic people. Of course, these are only isolated cases, by no means expressing the feelings and thoughts of our creative intelligentsia [does not he decide what these feelings and thoughts are permitted to be?]. . . . These renegades scoff at what is most holy to every Soviet man—the interests of the socialist homeland. It goes without saying that the Soviet people [that is, the police] cannot ignore the shameful activities of such people. It treats them as they deserve.

This is not merely a reaffirmation of the sentences meted out to Sinyavsky, Daniel, Brodsky, Tarshis, and Yesenin-Volpin, but a warning to those Soviet writers who would like to support them or follow their example. If this be "erosion" or "convergence," then some of my colleagues have found new meanings for old words, or developed a new indifference to freedom and to the differences between regimes.

Of course, other appropriate delegates were assigned to echo Brezhnev. Yepishev, head of the Central Political Department of the Armed Forces, called for stricter control of writers, and of "the ideological content of works of literature," the elimination of works that are "apolitical" or "lacking in ideological principle" or "simply anti-Soviet." He said:

> Those who lack ideological integrity and are guilty of petty-bourgeois dissoluteness reveal themselves in the fact that under the banner of freedom of creation, or under the pretext of fighting consequences of the personality cult, or under the cloak of championing historical truth and authenticity, they are preening themselves like coquettes before the mirror of history and trying to detract from the heroic history and struggle of our party, our country and its army, the glorious fighting traditions of the older generations, denigrating Soviet reality, minimizing the greatness of our victory over fascism in the last war.

Such is the voice of licensed literary "criticism," while the voices of Tvardovsky and Sinyavsky are silent. The communist youth has produced a literary critic to take the place of the egregious Semichastny, First Secretary Pavlov, who pontificated on the "artist unable or *unwilling* to get a clear idea of the dialectics of life, who takes refuge in a small and musty world of self-analysis, defamation, modernist philistinism."

The First Secretary of the Moscow Oblast Committee of the Party, Konotop, told off *Novy Mir* and *Yunost* for "publishing certain works of literature . . . which give a distorted idea of our Soviet life, present isolated shortcomings and difficulties with relish, cultivate skepticism and apoliticalness . . . publish ideologically harmful works critical of responsible officials . . . and depart from the Leninist principle that literature should show *partiinost* and be rooted in *narodnost*."

The First Secretary of the Moscow Party Committee was sharper still, speaking of "a conciliatory attitude toward alien views and feelings," "elements of nihilism and skepticism," "ideological saboteurs," and those who are more concerned "with what is said of them abroad than with their duty to the people [that is, the Party]."

More disturbing was the fact that a literary policeman, Markov, now functioning as overseer of the Writers' Union, was delegated to speak in its name and attack all the recent achievements of Soviet literature, while the ill-mannered Sholokhov, made arrogant by his being the "first Soviet writer to receive a Nobel Prize," defended the repression of other writers in these words:

> I am not ashamed of those who have slandered their homeland and dragged in the mud everything that is most sacred to us. They are amoral. What I am ashamed of is those who are trying to defend them. . . . And I am doubly ashamed of those who offer their services and make application for condemned renegades to be entrusted to them on bail.

He openly longed for the street justice (lynch law) of the twenties which would not have been so squeamish in dealing with these "werewolves."

A "non-Party" speaker, one N. Sobelev, was permitted to tell the Writers' Union what the Twenty-third Congress had decided for them, and to warn them that departure from the "Leninist principles" reasserted by the Congress would lead to "dangerous results"; while another reporter, M. Alexeev, told them that the Congress "obliged writers to put their entire literary household into a state of complete military preparedness and to mobilize all types of weapons, all genres of literature." [5]

Needless to say, a voice was found, or appointed, one Galanshin, to bid the Writers' Union become the censors of their own members and "stop such works from reaching an audience." The use of a prosecutor from the Writers' Union in the case of Sinyavsky and Daniel was but one example of this new procedure intended to make the writers their own policemen. The final resolution was written in the same prescriptive and threatening spirit. Thus does freedom, in place of broadening down from precedent to precedent, get jerked back by zigs and zags, while indifferent spirits and wishful thinkers among our Sovietologists cheerfully extrapolate each zig into outer space, where they are caught, unprepared, by the subsequent zag. The partial removal of a gag is "news" but its subsequent tightening over the mouth and pushing into the throat is "old stuff" not worthy of report.

The Convergence Theory

There are styles in theories as in clothes. Just now it is the fashion to talk of the "convergence" of the Soviet Union and the United States. As near as I can follow it, this theory seems to assert that as soon as two countries develop heavy industry and can land rockets on the moon (some would insist that there must also be an abundance of managers and of consumer goods), the two systems will converge, developing similar institutions, similar traditions, similar ways of life; in short, become like each other.

One examines the history of mankind in vain for confirmation of such simplification. The abstracting mind talks, for example, of "feudalism," but the historian turns to medieval England, France, Germany, Russia, and Poland and finds the most diverse traditions, institutions, freedoms, forms of mutual obligation or lack of it, in the various latifundial lands; finds too the most diverse forms of bondage, of localism, of sovereign power and rebelliousness, of the reign of law and of arbitrariness, and so on through all facets of life. One need only study the disparate history of those countries

[5] *Literaturnaya Rossiya,* April 29, 1966, and *Literaturnaya Gazeta,* April 26, 1966.

during the Middle Ages, or merely read the symposium edited by Rushton Coulborn, *Feudalism in History,* to convince one's self of man's diversity despite the resemblance, real or apparent—Coulborn's symposiasts cannot make up their mind which—of one or another property relationship and relationship between estates or "classes of men."

So too, the historian watches the rapid industrialization of Germany and England and the United States during the later nineteenth century, and, in the last few decades from 1880 to 1914, of Russia as well, but he cannot find that their institutions or their traditions become nugatory. Germany remained an empire with an autocratic Emperor, *Junkertum,* militarism and Prussian plural voting, while the Britons calculated that their navy would prevent them from ever being "slaves," that a small volunteer army was all they needed; they gloried in their charter of liberties, their reign of law, their supremacy of Parliament, and the steady reduction of the powers of their sovereign until he became little more than a cherished symbol. In matters of the history, traditions, attitudes, and institutions of a country, its philosophy, its intellectual priorities, its freedoms, we must hold with Aristotle that, "Differentiation is the beginning of wisdom." To note resemblances in some economic or institutional feature is barely the beginning of the study of a great nation. To stop there is to abstract from all the things that give color, flavor, distinction, to each of them. One has only begun the real task of studying a people and its history when one begins to note the differentiae, the qualities that distinguish members of a generalized abstract class from each other.

Joseph Stalin once charged me with being "an American exceptionalist." The more I considered this curious charge, the more convinced I became that I was guiltier than the indictment suggested, for suddenly I realized that I was an "exceptionalist" not only for America but for all the lands on earth. I thought of India and China and wondered how one could be content to lump them together under the single rubric of "Asiatic lands," without losing all sense of difference in their spiritual and intellectual life, their social structures, literatures, arts and faiths, in short, the things that made them more different from each other than England is from Germany. To abstract from these differences, as Marx and Lenin did, and at that moment Stalin was trying to persuade me to do, is to miss the essence of each country's life and history. In that moment of challenge to the "terrible simplifiers," and their abstractions, I think a historian was born.

Recently a new generation of simplifiers has appeared. It employs, unwittingly I think, a grossly vulgarized Marxist concept to the effect that "economics determines politics," determines, too, the entire spiritual "superstructure." This vulgarized Marxist abstraction would have made Marx wince and repeat his famous line, "I, myself, am no Marxist." It is terribly easy to forget that technology is neutral as regards freedom, that it may be used either to liberate or to enslave, to inform or to brainwash. "Some day," Herzen wrote in fear and trembling, "Jinghis Khan will return with the telegraph." "Hurrah!" cry our convergence theorists, "Then he will cease to be Jinghis Khan."

Can we forget so soon that it was the technologically most advanced country in Europe, with the best social-welfare laws, the highest degree of literacy, and the greatest number of Ph.D.'s, that developed first the most extreme militarism and then one of the most rabid forms of totalitarianism? Are we to believe that when every man can read, it will no longer matter whether he lives under a system that gives him freedom to choose what he will read or under a system that gives him no such choice but prescribes that he shall be reading the same slogan at the same moment in the same controlled press in every corner of his land?

Are we to believe that because there are mass-circulation journals, a television set in every home, and perhaps a loudspeaker in every square and public place, it no longer matters whether there are many parties or one, rival candidates to choose from or no choice at all, a chance to rebuke, tame, and turn out one's rulers, or no such chance? Is the presence of heavy industry, and perhaps of abundant consumer goods, supposed to make us forget that the central problem of politics is not *Who rules over us?* but *How do we choose our rulers?, How do we tame them?, How do we remove them or replace them?,* and *How do we keep some ultimate control over them in our hands?*

Are we to assume that because mass-circulation journals can make a great sensation out of every court case, therefore it makes no difference whether judges can stop a newspaper from discussing a case while it is under adjudication, as judges can in England, or a judge's only duty is to obey slogans bombarding him in the controlled press and come to the verdict shouted at him in advance in the name of a voiceless people, as was the case in the Sinyavsky trial?

Are we to assume that when in all great lands there is modern industry it will no longer matter whether a single-party state owns all organizations and operates them as transmission belts, or a whole complex of nonstate organizations exists under the control of their members and can be used by them to make pressure on officials, parties, and the state? Can it be that once there is modern industry and abundance of consumer goods (the latter still a mere iterated and reiterated promise in the Soviet Union), then it will no longer matter whether there is a more or less open and pluralistic society or a more or less closed, monolithic, command society with centralized control of everything including what to read, what to think, feel, do, hope, hate, love, and dream about?

Marx was less loose with his dogma that "economics determines politics" than are his unconscious or unthinking imitators. He wrote of English industrialization to tell his own compatriots, *"De te fabula narratur. . . .* The country that is more developed industrially only shows to the less developed the image of its own future." But in the next breath he admonished the Germans that, where there is modern industry in Germany

> the condition of things is much worse than in England because the countervailing weight of the factory acts is lacking. . . . Alongside of modern evils, a whole series of inherited evils oppress us . . . with their inevitable train of social and political anachronisms. We suffer not only from the living but from the dead.

Marx knew the force of historical difference, of restraining laws and institutions, and inherited traditions. He could write of his native land that it suffered from a "political incapacity," that "the political impotence of the German bourgeoisie [meant] the political impotence of Germany"; that every part of German life was a *"partie honteuse"* except for her philosophy, and that even in philosophy

> we are the *philosophical* contemporaries of the present without being its *historical* contemporaries; . . . that in France every class of the people is a *political idealist* and feels itself directly not as a special class but as a representative of the needs of society in general.

. . . In Germany, on the contrary, where practical life is as un-intelligent as intellectual life is impractical, no class of civil society has the need and the capacity for general emancipation.

When Vera Zasulich asked Marx whether she could apply his "convergence theory" to Russia, he wrote many drafts of varying length and sent none of them, responding at last that the " 'histori-cal inevitability' of this movement is *expressly* limited to the *countries of Western Europe.*"

There was really only one field in which Karl Marx devoutly hoped for and believed in "inevitable" convergence, and that was in the class consciousness and class position of the workingmen of western Europe. Since they were all separated from the ownership of their means of production, he reasoned, since they all had to sell their "labor power" in order to live, since all "alienated" both their work and its products, since all produced value and surplus value, since all had employers to face, wages to bargain for, a common need of organization and struggle, a common cause, a common enemy, and a common fate of "increasing pauperization" by virtue of their common increase in productivity—surely their psychology or class consciousness and their struggle would converge into a common psychology, a common class consciousness, and an inter-national solidarity in a common international class struggle. More-over, modern industry had necessarily to teach the modern working-men literacy, whereupon they would all tend to study the same things, namely the classics of "our German theory."

When Mazzini and his disciples, Lubez and Major Wolff, failed to produce acceptable documents for the First International and Dr. Marx was called in to write its Statutes and Inaugural Address, he thought the great day had come. He circumspectly avoided "the bold language" of *The Communist Manifesto,* figuring that he must lead the British and French workingmen who had founded the In-ternational by careful stages to that convergence in theory which he hoped was inevitable. He paid tribute to cooperatives, labor leg-islation, union organization, political democracy, and even—that *bête noir* of his scientific socialism—to moral values. He nourished the hope that the converging way of life of all "proletarians," their cooperation in a common organization, aided by the influence of his guiding presence in the General Council and the consequent "exchanges of ideas and discussion . . . will not fail to produce gradually a common theoretical program."

Yet, though Marx's was by no means a mechanical convergence theory—no mere holding that common economic circumstances must "inevitably" produce a common way of life and thought—and though he added all care and patience to the mechanical similarities he thought he saw, the hoped-for convergence never did take place. Underneath the avowed internationalism of the First International lay the deeper forces of disparate national character and national divergence. The seeds of disunity were in the very foundations of the International, and as the various countries industrialized and their working classes grew, it was their diversity that grew, not their uniformity.

From the First Congress on there contended for mastery a French theory (Proudhonist mutualism and phrase-radical anarcho-syndicalism), a Russian theory (Bakuninist communist anarchism and its Swiss and Latin offshoots), and a German theory (that of Marx, not to speak of the completely diverse German theory of Lasalle). Besides, there was yet a fourth ideology, unnoticed by the other three since it did not possess the generalizing habits, or the inclination to conquest, or the noisy combativeness of the other three, though it was the only ideology actually held by a genuine workingman's mass organization: that of the British trade union and liberal-labor-Christian Dissenter movement.

There was, indeed, no way in which German ideologues could be made to think like French "phrase-radicals," or Russian "gourmets of extremist doctrines," or any of them made to think like the "bourgeois proletariat of England." In the end Marx lost patience with his fruitless labors as a pedagogue and the failure of the hoped-for convergence to come from common features in the life of the workingmen of each land. Then he enlarged the powers of the General Council from a federal servant to a centralizing master, expelled or alienated whole "sections," and packed a Congress with unconditionals of his own doctrine. When the smoke of battle cleared, Marx found himself triumphant and alone with nothing better to do with the empty shell than to transport it to far-off America for unnoticed burial.

The Second International, which began under the sage council of the aging Engels, foundered on the same rock of national diversity. It never achieved a common view on anything, neither on tactics for securing the eight-hour day, nor on general strike, nor on war, concealing from itself and the world its fundamental diversity by bleaching out all practical differences of tactics and outlook in empty and ambiguously denatured but "unanimous" resolutions. When the guns of August began to speak in 1914 the bright birdcage grew still. Workingmen who had so often been told of the convergence of their aims, their common enemy within, and their common solidarity across frontiers looked across no-man's-land at the *enemy,* recruited in "proletarian" and "peasant" masses, well armed, well uniformed, with Red Cards still in their pockets.

Now, what is presenting itself as the most striking feature of the Third, or Communist, International is not the convergence of the common totalitarian structures of the constituent ruling parties, but the divergence and diversity of their national interests, national temperaments, national rivalries, their common rebellion against the Russian national pattern and hegemony that Lenin had built into the very foundation of the International he was determined to protect from nationalism.

Thus, what history teaches us, even in such similar structured institutions as those of totalitarianism and such similar ways of life as those of the workingmen of industrial lands, is not the lesson of convergence but divergence, not abstract uniformity attained by the discounting of all but a single or a few features of life, but the endless diversity that characterizes actual history in every land and in every age. There, visible for all but the willful simplifier to see, is the evidence that the communist ideology and the totalitarian structure of communist China and communist Russia differ from each other even as do the nationalism and the exercise of great executive powers in plural and open societies by Presidents Charles de Gaulle and Lyndon Baines Johnson.

That does not mean that we cannot generalize concerning certain features of closed and open societies and of monolithic totalitarianism and democratic pluralism, but we can do so usefully only if we keep a modest awareness of the diversities of life and its divergences even where certain common institutional and ideological features are present and must be taken into account. Otherwise we lose our awareness of what is valuable in our institutions and traditions, and with it we lose our ability to think in the field of history or of the social disciplines in general. Generalization is useful only if we remember that after we have begun our "definition" by indicating the genus or species, our more pressing task is to become aware of the *differentiae* without which the "definition" is lifeless and incomplete. Aristotle knew his own country's civilization too well to forget for a moment that "differentiation is the beginning of wisdom," and that without it there is no wisdom at all.

Legitimacy and the Problem of the Succession

Fifty years have passed since Lenin seized power and established the dictatorship that has proved by a half-century of continuity and contained change to be the most durable institutional regime, or the most durable "Party" regime, in the modern world. Yet it is striking that in the course of a half-century it has not succeeded in establishing a legitimate mode of succession.

Broadly speaking there are three kinds of legitimacy: the hieratic, the monarchical, and the democratic. In the first case, a leader is chosen by a religiously recognized procedure and invested with religious-magisterial authority. In the second, legitimacy depends upon blood relationship. Where it prevails, when a monarch dies it is clear through blood relationship who his successor shall be. *The King Is Dead, Long Live the King* is a formula which makes it possible for even a minor child under a guardian regent to be invested with royal power. In the third case, the normal procedure for choice of a successor is a popular election. But the rules also determine a democratic succession in the case of sudden death. One cannot imagine Harry Truman or Lyndon Johnson appealing for "the avoidance of confusion and panic" as the frightened lieutenants of Joseph Stalin did in a broadcast to their subjects made after six hours and ten minutes of terrified silence concerning his death.

The Russian democratic Provisional Government of 1917 represents an intermediate stage in the establishment of a new legitimacy after tⁱold monarchical legitimacy had broken down or been termⁱy revolution. The chief characteristic of the Provisional nment from a political standpoint was that it had

the grace to call itself *Provisional*. By this act, it proclaimed itself
as *prelegitimate,* a government that openly considered itself provisional and recognized as its primary task in the sphere of politics
the convocation of a constituent or constitution-making assembly
to be elected freely and democratically, which could write a new
constitution for the Russian land, thus establishing a new democratic legitimacy.

Lenin rightly recognized that he must at all costs prevent the
creation of that new legitimacy. That is why he set so precise a
date for the seizing of power: "History will not forgive a delay by
the revolutionaries who can win today . . . but risk losing everything tomorrow."

Even then he did not take too seriously the ideological program
of the Revolution on a "mere" Russian scale:

> The seizure of power is the point of the uprising; its political
> aim will clarify itself after that seizure.
> It would be ruin or a formality to await the wavering vote of
> the 25th of October, the people rightly and obligatorily decides such
> matters not by voting but by force. . . .
> Any delay in the offensive is like unto death.

Lenin opened that article, written on the eve of the seizure of
power, almost with the same words with which he closed it:

> I write these lines on the evening of the 24th, the situation is
> impossibly critical. The clearest thing of all is this, that now, really
> and truly it is clear that now any delay in an uprising is like unto
> death.

Once Lenin had power in his hands and those of his Party,
he laid his plans to prevent the establishment of a new democratic
legitimacy: "We say to the people that their interests are higher
than the interests of a democratic institution. It is not necessary
to go back to the old prejudices which subordinate the interests
of the people to formal democracy."

With the forestalling of the constituent assembly by his seizure
of power, and the rupture of democratic legitimacy by the dispersal
by force of the only authorized representatives of the Russian people,
Lenin bade farewell to legitimacy and established a permanent
dictatorship.

There no longer was hereditary monarchical legitimacy or democratic legitimacy or any thought of prelegitimacy. In a half-century

the dictatorial regime has not once submitted its actions or its personnel to the approval of the Soviet people in a free election, nor can it, nor has it the intention to do so in the future.

What then was the basis of Lenin's claim to rule over a great nation? Simply this: We have made a revolution in one nation with the intent to use it as a springboard for world revolution. We Communists have seized power over this nation because we possess an infallible doctrine that lets us know what history wants our country to do and to be. We are the sole possessors and only true interpreters of a "scientific" and infallible doctrine that enables us to work out a blueprint for the remaking of the Soviet Union and the remaking of man. It is this which justifies the dictatorship that we have set up over our own people, and aim to extend to all the lands on earth.

Lenin said on December 5, 1919, after he had been exercising power for two years, "Dictatorship is a harsh, heavy and even bloody word." And a year later, on October 20, 1920, he explained with precise pedantry to doubting democrats:

> The scientific concept *dictatorship* means nothing more nor less than unrestricted power, not limited by anything, not restrained by any laws, nor by any absolute rules, and resting directly on force, *that, and nothing else but that,* is the meaning of the concept, dictatorship.

In short, all limitations, constitutional, traditional, legal, or moral, were ruptured. Having taken power by force in the name of their blueprint, the dictators were to apply their blueprint without accepting any restraint upon their use of force. For such a regime, though it last a half-century, no legitimacy is sought nor possible.

Instead, there were four pieces of semantic sleight-of-hand employed by Lenin, but these were only meant to paralyze the enemy and lessen opposition.

The first is the confusing of the proletariat with the people. The second is the confusing of the Party with the proletariat. The third is the confusing of the Party Machine with the Party. The fourth is the confusing of the *Vozhd* or Leader or Boss with the Party Machine. All four of these semantic tricks are inventions of Lenin. As hypocrisy is said to be the tribute that vice pays to virtue, so these subterfuges are the tribute that dictatorship pays to democracy. They have grown stale by endless repetition but Lenin's heirs do not dare dispense with any of them lest their world come tumbling down.

As we probe the fictions they dissolve before our eyes. The Party is no party, for a party means a part and where there are no contending parties, life dies out in the single party.

From her prison cell Rosa Luxemburg admonished Lenin:

> Freedom for the supporters of the government alone, freedom only for the members of one party—that is no freedom at all. . . . All that is instructive, wholesome, and purifying in political freedom depends upon this essential characteristic. . . .
>
> With the repression of political life in the land as a whole, life in the Soviets must also become more and more crippled. Without general elections, without unrestricted freedom of press and assembly, without a free struggle of opinion, life will die out in every public institution. . . . Public life gradually falls asleep, a few dozen leaders . . . direct and rule . . . an elite of the working class is invited from time to time to meetings where they are to applaud the speeches of the leaders and approve resolutions unanimously . . . not the dictatorship of the proletariat but of a handful of politicians, a clique. . . . Such conditions must inevitably cause a brutalization of public life: attempted assassinations, shooting of hostages, etc.

How grimly has history confirmed her prophetic vision! What she did not foresee, however, was that Lenin himself would finally drain his Party of all political life by prohibiting groupings, and that his successor would kill more members of his own Party than all the enemies of communism in the world put together.

Where then shall legitimacy lodge? There is no provision in statutes or constitution for an infallible leader, yet an infallible doctrine in the long run requires a single, infallible interpreter. If there are a number of conflicting interpretations the doctrine loses its "scientific" and "infallible" character, and the voiceless people may make one of the rival factions its mouthpiece, so that pluralism will break out in the monolith.

When a leader dies, who shall name his successor? The soviets have been drained of life, the Party has been drained of life, the unions have been drained of life, the Central Committee has been replaced by the Politburo or Presidium, and that by the Secretariat. Only a "little clique of leaders," as Rosa Luxemburg termed it, can proclaim its collective dictatorship, concealing its internal difference until a new dictator emerges to declare his rivals to have been anti-

Party or enemies of the people. Given the law of diminishing dictators, given too the muted discontents and pressures within, and the external pressures without, there is no telling how long this "system" will endure. But one thing is certain, within it there inheres no true legitimacy nor any intention of seeking it from a free discussion and vote of its people or a free function of its "public" bodies. What I wrote ten years ago I am afraid is still true:

> As long as collective leadership does not swiftly and determinedly broaden itself instead of narrowing; as long as it does not openly treat itself as "pre-legitimate" in the sense of aiming to replace itself by broader, non-dictatorial organization of power; as long as power does not flood down into the basic units of the party (where it did not inhere even in Lenin's best days), and as long as it does not then overflow the party dikes and spill out into self-organizing corporate bodies independent of the state and party; as long, in other words, as there develop no organized institutionalized checks upon the reflux of power to the top, not a mere slowing but an actual reversing of the whole trend of totalitarianism—there is no reason to regard any directory or collective leadership as more than a mere interregnum between dictators . . . and there will be no legitimacy to provide a lawful succession.

And at this moment I cannot imagine any faction in the Communist Party that would make as its program the devolution of power to the limbs and parts of the body politic, or a genuine consultation of its people to establish a new democratic legitimacy. Nor can I presently imagine such a set of circumstances as might engender such a faction.

VI

Reflections on the Soviet System: Toward a More Human and Equal Society

by WILLIAM M. MANDEL

Point of Departure

Essays such as this are read almost exclusively by college-educated people or those in process of getting such an education. Even in wealthy California, with its exceptional junior college system, it is only among families earning $12,000 per year or more that a majority of children so much as enter college,[1] not to speak of subsequent drop-out due to financial problems among lower income groups. But only one fourth of the families in the United States earn even $10,000 a year.

Does coming from a prosperous family mean that one's information is *fundamentally* better than that of those whose source of knowledge is confined to the noncultural mass media? The encyclo-

[1] From the Coordinating Council for Higher Education, *An Evaluation of the Tuition Free Principle in California Public Higher Education* (May 1965), p. 33, table T.

pedia most widely found in both schoolrooms and homes in the
United States is the *World Book*. Here are excerpts from its article
in the 1965 edition, "Communism," written by Dr. William Eben-
stein, Professor of Political Science at the University of California:

> Communism . . . has no respect for family life . . . Commu-
> nism ignores what we consider normal standards of morality and
> ethics. . . . Communists believe that force will some day settle all
> relations among nations in favor of communism. . . . People who
> oppose the government in any way may be tortured, murdered, im-
> prisoned, or sent to slave-labor camps without a trial. . . . To a
> communist: . . . Antimilitarism is the arming of a communist na-
> tion, or the preparing of a communist country for war. . . . Dis-
> armament Proposals are efforts to keep noncommunist countries
> from preparing their own defenses. . . . Warmonger is a person or
> group that tries to defend itself against communism.

Textbooks are no better.[2] I am left with no choice but to take
among my starting points the assumptions: (a) that my reader will
evaluate every fact and statement about the U.S.S.R. from the standpoint of his own experience as a member of the comfortable upper
strata of American society, not that of its median citizen, and (b)
that his views on the Soviet Union, as a communist-led country,
have been shaped at least to some degree by writings such as that
just quoted. This will compel me, again and again, to cite data
about the United States, so that evaluations may be made against
the standard of a real society, and not its most favored fragment.

What, for example, is the meaning of my estimate that the Soviet
living standard will have caught up with all aspects of that of the
United States in about thirty years, and will have passed it in many?
What living standard, that of the readers of this book or that of the
median American? If it will take that long, then why all the fuss
about the Soviet Union? The answer to this lies in the first of our
comparisons.

In its annual report to Congress in January 1964, the United
States Council of Economic Advisers said that thirty-four million
Americans were living in poverty. This means, it concluded, that
they inhabit "a world where Americans are literally concerned with
day-to-day survival—a roof over their heads, where the next meal
is coming from. It is a world where a minor illness is a major tragedy,

[2] See William M. Mandel, "The Soviet Union in Junior High Texts,"
California Social Science Review (April 1967).

where pride and privacy must be sacrificed to get help." Two years later, Michael Harrington, whose book *The Other America* first focused national attention on poverty in the United States, said the figure is actually fifty million, if one includes those whose income is so low and precarious that they are "one illness, one accident, one recession" away from the dividing line.

The average *family* income of the bottom thirty million Americans in 1964 was about $1,800, which is not very different from the average for the *entire* Soviet people urban and rural. But Soviet people are *not* concerned with day-to-day survival: a roof over their heads, the next meal, a doctor, hospitals, or medicine. Nor need they sacrifice dignity to get help. What Soviet socialism has done—what it pioneered in doing—was to outline a human quality of life when it had an economy only a fraction as productive as that of our own country. Yet ours has not succeeded in doing this and shows no signs of being able to. The Equal Opportunity Act of 1964, launching the "war on poverty" in 1965, was called by *The New York Times* "too limited in means, too timid in ideas, *even as a jumping-off point.*" (My emphasis.) After a year of that "war," James Reston reported in the *San Francisco Chronicle* (November 28, 1965) that "the gap between the rich and the poor is greater than it was a year ago." Mississippi had plain starvation in 1967.

It is this difference in what is done with the nation's wealth and for its people that constitutes the real challenge of the Soviet Union, and not the fact that it showed how to industrialize a backward country most rapidly. Yet consider this challenge against the following editorial from *El Malcriado,* the newspaper of farm laborers on strike in California, 1966:

> For nearly all people there is a thing that is more important than money. It is a thing called dignity or self-respect or honor. . . . We who are farm workers have all been insulted. We have seen ourselves treated like cattle. . . . We have seen our children treated as inferiors in the schools. . . . Our color or our language or our job have kept us apart. . . .

Edward Hallett Carr, whose six volumes on early Soviet history are in a class by themselves, summed up this difference twenty years ago in a slender book titled *The Soviet Impact on the Western World*: "But equality, in the sense in which it is one of the fundamental purposes of Soviet social policy, means non-discrimination between human beings *on irrelevant grounds* such as sex, race, colour or class." (My emphasis.)

The examination of the Soviet future in this essay will be based, then, on several premises. One is that it is a revolutionary society *in toto,* a new way of life, whose challenge does not lie in its economic growth rate or any other single factor but in the underlying fact that the means of producing goods, wealth, and services have been socialized in their overwhelming preponderance, regardless of whether the forms are cooperative or governmental, federal or dispersed to the effective control of local managements.

Corollary to this is the premise that to speak of convergence between Soviet socialist and Western capitalist society is to judge by superficialities, not fundamentals. Just as the Soviet Union, for reasons clearly set forth by Marx in his *Critique of the Gotha Program* of 1875 and Lenin in *State and Revolution* in 1917, not only can but must employ the mechanisms of money, price, profit, and the like to operate its economy essentially free of *private* profit, so capitalism can and has borrowed social welfare and planning pioneered or fundamentally enlarged in the Soviet Union, but remains capitalist as long as the acquisition of *private* profit remains the basic economic law of society.

Another premise is that we are in no position to view the U.S.S.R. in a condescending manner based upon our continuing higher output and the existence of certain freedoms Soviet citizens do not fully enjoy. All too often, this attitude is what underlies the appearance of academic objectivity and dispassionateness in this field.

A final premise is that, despite the need for self-critical and uncondescending comparisons between the United States and the U.S.S.R., the Soviet Union must be understood within its own frame of reference, its own time and place, its own previous history, its national psychology, and also the degree to which its policies in the past and today are, or are believed by its leaders to be, responses to external situations compelling internal policies other than those they might otherwise desire. Consider first the last of these. In December 1965, Premier Kosygin granted an interview to James Reston of *The New York Times,* in which he said:

> You have the multilateral force, the allied nuclear force, the McNamara council or committee [of allied defense ministers] . . .

any unification of forces in that camp must be directed against us. It compels us to muster our own forces and react to what you do. We are against this concept, but it is very strong in the United States, and we have to take it into account in thinking *ten or fifteen years ahead*. . . . One prospect is for the arms race and the increase in military budgets. [My emphasis.]

The war in Vietnam had precisely that effect upon the U.S.S.R. If this affects Soviet planning today, how much more strongly was that the case when, in 1931, Hitler was on the verge of coming to power in Germany and Stalin made the most prophetic of all his speeches, precisely accurate as to time:

> To slacken the tempo would mean falling behind. And those who fall behind get beaten. But we do not want to be beaten. No, we refuse to be beaten.
> The history of old Russia is one unbroken record of the beatings she suffered for falling behind, for her backwardness. She was beaten by the Mongol khans. She was beaten by the Turkish beys. She was beaten by the Swedish feudal lords. She was beaten by the Polish and Lithuanian gentry. She was beaten by the British and French capitalists. She was beaten by the Japanese barons. All beat her— for her backwardness. . . .
> We are fifty or a hundred years behind the advanced countries. We must make good this distance in ten years. Either we do this, or they crush us.

That, then, has been and remains the reasoning governing the modification or even distortion of Soviet internal policies in response to external situations. Now consider the impact of the past, the nature and pace of movement away from it, and, very important today, the fact that the present leaders of the U.S.S.R., born about 1905, chiefly into families of the poorest peasantry, are old enough to have keen personal memories of that past, and would unhesitatingly subordinate all other values to prevent the reimposition of that past from without, as was attempted in the intervention of 1918–1920 and Hitler's invasion of 1941. This was stated to me in precisely those terms in 1966 by men in their forties—ordinary citizens—who had fought in World War II, and still think of their country as being in its prewar status of, in their words, capitalist encirclement. Even the thinking of those under thirty is colored by memories of war. A twenty-eight-year-old taxi driver in Leningrad had as his earliest recollection the famine conditions during the German and Finnish siege of that city for nine hundred days, and a woman the same age recalled being led out of Stalingrad by her mother with the city burning all around.

Probably no Westerner knew prerevolutionary Russia as did Dr. E. J. Dillon, an Englishman who spent forty years there prior to the outbreak of World War I, and who knew Russian well enough to be a professor at Russian universities and even editor of a newspaper. The distinguished anticommunist historian Paul Milyukov, who was Minister of Foreign Affairs in the Provisional Government before Lenin, regarded Dillon's *Russian Characteristics* as the most accurate description of the Russian people. Here is Dillon's description of the Russian peasant—the "average" Russian was a peasant—before the Communist Revolution, in his book *The Eclipse of Russia* (1918):

> Too often the Russian peasant dwells in a hovel more filthy than a sty, more noxious than a phosphoric match factory. He goes to bed at six and even at five o'clock in the winter, because he cannot afford money to buy petroleum enough for artificial light. He has no meat, no eggs, no butter, no milk, often no cabbage, and lives mainly on black bread and potatoes. Lives? He starves on an insufficient quantity of them. . . . And yet those starving men, women and children, had raised plenty of corn [British usage for grain] to live upon. . . . But they were forced to sell it immediately after the harvest in order to pay the taxes.

Ten years later, in 1928, Dr. Dillon visited communist Russia when it was still a peasant country and wrote from his half-century of perspective, in *Russia Today and Tomorrow*:

> Everywhere people are thinking, working, combining. . . . If one could obtain a bird's-eye view of the numerous activities of the citizens of the Soviet Republics one would hardly trust the evidence of one's senses. Nothing like it; nothing approaching it in variety, intensity, tenacity of purpose has ever yet been witnessed. Revolutionary endeavour is . . . fusing heterogeneous elements into . . . a strong people cemented by quasi-religious enthusiasm. The Bolsheviks . . . have mobilized well over 150,000,000 of listless dead-and-alive human beings, and infused into them a new spirit.

Yet this was written when the country had just pulled itself out of the ashes of three years of World War I followed by three of foreign intervention superimposed on and prolonging civil war. Industry was barely above its prerevolutionary level, and the industrialization policy was in its first year. It was a period when, as I was able to see during my own first, year-long stay, the peasants still wore birch-bark sandals, rag leggings, and homespun.

The industrialization of the next thirty-five years was conducted under the world's first planned economy. The ridicule with which the very idea was greeted in the West changed in later years to lofty condescension as scholarly nit-picking accumulated truly endless examples of inefficiency and waste in what it came to call a "command economy." Was a command economy necessary? Consider a quite recent event.

In 1961 the U.S.S.R. manufactured no Big Inch pipe whatever, and therefore placed orders abroad for much of what it needed to build its first pipelines to the east European communist-led countries. Standard Oil and other major American, British, and Dutch interests feared the pipelines would facilitate Soviet exports outside the communist bloc, and openly pressured Western countries to cancel those orders. In 1963 West Germany did forbid its steel mills to supply the two hundred thousand tons of pipeline for which they had contracted. Thereupon the Soviet "command economy" went into action, undertaking a crash program to build mills to produce immense quantities of oversize pipe. Western steel experts ridiculed the goals and schedule. The outcome? In 1965 the U.S.S.R. emerged as the world's largest producer of steel pipe. The pipelines, thousands of miles long, had been built.

Obviously, this could only have been done by disrupting all sorts of previously laid plans in other fields. But the job was done. Societally, waste was reduced because the U.S.S.R became capable of purchasing abroad, with the money earned through increased petroleum sales, products that it would have taken greater relative effort to produce at home. The living standard was improved, because much of the purchasing in the mid-1960s consisted of entire plants—British, Italian, German, French, Japanese—to make synthetic fibers, automobiles, and other consumer goods. But in the process of doing the job, innumerable local cases of waste were caused because pipeline manufacturing was given emergency priority. And such priorities on a large scale could only be enforced by a system in which plant managements were rigidly controlled. This limited the workers' initiative, and fostered bureaucracy and excessive authority for superiors.

Agriculture, which is Exhibit A in Western "proofs" of the non-viability of Soviet methods, suffered—and ultimately benefited—in the same fashion. Soviet economist M. Breev states flatly in *Problems of Economics* (December 1965), p. 10, that "the transition in the 1930s to methods of direct state planning in agriculture and the pronounced intensification of the mechanism of planning by fiat in this branch were among the chief reasons for the retardation of the development of agriculture for several decades." In this particular application, the command economy was harmful. But in the same overall field, agriculture, it meant that 100 million acres of virgin soil were planted under Khrushchev, and these virgin lands produced 52 percent of the total grain marketed in the U.S.S.R. from 1954 through 1964. Likewise, it was due to the technique making possible the building of fertilizer factories at so extraordinary a rate that production rose 50 percent in the two years from 1963 to 1965, attaining the United States output level of 1958. Western experts expect the U.S.S.R. to be selling fertilizer in the world market by 1970, a very important factor in relations with the underdeveloped countries. (For the future, it is worth noting that neither farmers into whose villages I hiked at random in 1966 nor other rank-and-file citizens I met casually regarded agriculture as operating under a command economy any longer.)

In 1965, the United States Department of Agriculture found that the U.S.S.R. produced 5.2 million tons of milk more than the United States. Only twelve years earlier, it was the United States that had produced 50 percent more milk than the Soviet Union. While the United Nations sets 2,350 calories per day as the minimum food requirement, the Department of Agriculture reports present Soviet intake at over 3,000, almost precisely the same as in the United States, where poor people die of hunger "throughout the rural South," by doctors' Senate evidence (*San Francisco Chronicle,* July 10, 1967).

The Soviet peasant of today produces on his private plot (independent of the collective farm) and retains for his own consumption *all* the diet components that the system existing before the Revolution made it impossible for him to have, and also sells a great deal of this to supply the cities. Nor does he go to bed at 5 or 6 P.M. any longer for want of artificial light in the winter. Over 90 percent of peasant homes have electricity at this writing, while the remainder, in the most remote areas, have ample supplies of kerosene. This, plus the *kind* of cultural emphasis placed by the Soviet regime from the very beginning, as well as a reduction to city levels in actual daily hours worked, has produced a quality of rural life that vastly richer societies of another order have not been able to achieve.

T. Mistriukova, chief bibliographer of the Lenin Library, Moscow, made a study of reading in the collective-farm village of Guliai-Borisovka in southern European Russia (reported in *Komsomolskaya Pravda,* July 31, 1960), after determining that it did not differ from other villages in terms of its public library, book sales, and similar pertinent data. The village is fifteen miles from the nearest paved road and railroad. In its 390 households, there are 369 adults and 240 children who hold the Soviet equivalent of library cards. The records show their average reading to be 11 or 12 books per year. The library has 7,000 books. In addition, most of the families own books, and 60 of them had fair-sized collections, averaging 37 each. It should be added that Soviet libraries do not carry much in the way of light reading, and while there are plenty of girl-meets-boy-meets-tractor novels, publishers' complaints of their failure to sell would suggest that library readers may not like them either. Serious literary classics are very widely read.

U.S.S.R.-wide figures are extremely close to those of this single village. Village libraries alone showed an average of 5,500 books each in 1963, 500 card-holders per library, and 15.5 books and magazines checked out per person per year.[3] It is interesting that urban libraries show figures only one third higher for items checked out per person, indicating that the cultural lag in the villages has been very sharply reduced.

The situation in the United States contrasts very sharply with this. A Gallup poll of a cross section of Americans, urban and rural, from college graduates to illiterates, taken the same year (1963), showed that only 16 percent could think of a book they would like to read, although 46 percent claimed they "read a book all the way through last year" (*San Francisco Chronicle,* February 24, 1963). Sociologist Mirra Komarovsky of Columbia University, in her book *Blue-Collar Marriage,* writes of semiskilled, white workers making $2,500 to $8,000 per year, who have not been to college, and half of

[3] *Narodnoe Khoziaistvo SSSR v 1963 godu* (Moscow: Statistika Press, 1965), p. 603.

whom have not finished high school. Speaking of her survey at a University of California symposium (quoted in the *San Francisco Chronicle,* January 24, 1965), she said:

> They are like people living in some past era. . . . As the interviews progressed, I felt further and further away from the 20th Century. . . . Nothing is visible in the vast darkness beyond this limited circle (family, relatives, a few friends, etc.) but a few movie stars, athletes, and some national office holders. . . . *They do not read books.*

The people she speaks of *are,* in income, education, and the rest, the average American. Her survey was not made in a Louisiana bayou, but in an Eastern suburb.

What of the leisure-time activity of people in Soviet cities, where reading faces the competition of TV and other forms of diversion? (In 1963, TV was a rarity in the countryside, except very close to the largest cities.) The Sociology Laboratory of Leningrad University made a survey of leisure-time activities of the personnel of one of that city's greatest industries, the Kirov Works. The researchers discovered only a 5 percent extreme difference in time allocation to such activities by sex, age, and between manual workers on the one hand, and engineers and technicians on the other. For the whole, TV, radio, movies, and theater received 19.6 percent of leisure time (of which TV and radio accounted for 12.1 percent), while reading represented 13.2 percent. In contrast, the Gallup poll showed that 67 percent of all Americans preferred to spend Saturday night watching "TV westerns," specifically.

From Today to Tomorrow

In terms of living standards and culture in the sense in which we have been discussing it, few will disagree that the changes to be expected in the U.S.S.R. in the foreseeable future will constitute progress as we understand it, not essentially different from that which has already occurred. But there is another area, in which a sharp break occurred a decade ago with the removal of Stalin from the pedestal of deity, and in which a new significant change subsequently got under way, expressed most clearly thus far at the Twenty-third

Congress of the Communist Party in 1966. This is the change from dictatorship to consensus, in which the Party is now the agency through which the organized structures of a stable and complex society, showing unmistakable signs of a pluralist mechanism, arrive at a set of working policies.

For a long period the Party *was* the state (in foreign relations, at least, it still is) and Russian journals of government and law admit that the soviets withered on the vine. Under Khrushchev they began to revive. The public's recognition of this is reflected in the phenomenal increase in circulation of the government's newspaper, *Izvestia,* as compared to that of the Party, *Pravda,* both of which are sold nationwide. As recently as 1959, *Izvestia* sold 1.5 million copies to *Pravda's* 5.5 million. But in 1967, the government daily's circulation, at 8.67 million, substantially outstripped that of the Party's.

The fact that the Party structure has been the state was expressed by a procedure under which all major decisions at all levels were issued over the joint signature of the parallel Party and government authorities. This constituted an order to the subordinate Party agencies to see that the policy was put into effect. However, at the Twenty-third Party Congress this practice was protested by the head of the parliamentary structure of government, Nikolai Podgorny, himself of course a member of the Party's "cabinet," the Political Bureau. While he did not object to joint signature at the federal summit level, he held that at all lower levels this undermined the authority of government and made it easier for the Party to bypass the government in its desire to get things done. The results of this policy were disruptive. His view was not opposed.

Pluralism today is expressed by more than merely the rise of government to a status starting to approximate that of the Party in at least some respects. The press, a mighty force, no longer confines itself entirely to loyal echoing of the policies of its publishers. The third greatest daily in the Soviet Union is *Komsomolskaya Pravda* (6.4 million circulation), published by the Communist Youth League. Because the collective farms are still controlled by their founders, now well into middle age, that paper has pressed for a reform that would decentralize decision-making to the level of field team or livestock crew, usually headed by a person under thirty, who is almost always better educated than his elders and superiors.

In my view, this reform is essential if there is to be the truly fundamental improvement in agriculture that is so much needed.

Two magazines, *Novy Mir* (New World) and *Iunost* (Youth), with a combined circulation of 2.15 million, actually constitute what the West would regard as a "loyal opposition" in the Soviet Union, and voiced and built the demand for a substantial number of the changes that have occurred there in the past decade, not only in literature but in such remote fields as genetics, agriculture, and the development of industry in small towns previously by-passed.

Actual organizations, some old, some new, today serve as means of voicing divergent opinions or interests. Because of the traditional prestige enjoyed by the literary profession, the Writers' Union is important in that respect far out of proportion to its numbers. When two writers, Sinyavsky and Daniel, were sentenced to jail early in 1966, the judge who sentenced them found it necessary to accept an invitation to speak before the Writers' Union, where he "was heckled publicly by a large group of Soviet writers," according to the Moscow correspondent of the United Press (*San Francisco Chronicle,* March 19, 1966). But that summer, in many conversations in the Soviet Union, everyone I spoke to accepted the official reporting of the case, which distorted the two men's writing by quoting out of context, depicting them as hostile to Soviet society. Because the folk memory of the massacres of the poor during the civil war and the fourteen-nation intervention, and Hitler's slaughter of civilians twenty years later, is extremely vivid, most Soviet citizens are not prepared to accept the notion of any freedom of a kind that might in their view weaken the nation's unity in a world in which danger of war exists. The very notion of an opposition, loyal or otherwise, is literally abhorrent to most Russians. They simply do not think of this as affecting their personal freedom. To them, the overriding freedom is the right of the U.S.S.R. and its people and social revolution to exist; the right of fundamental dissent is not accepted.

The peasants, fragmented until 1966 on their tens of thousands of collective farms, are henceforth to have a national organization to represent their interests.

Students from five hundred cities and towns with higher educational institutions held their first U.S.S.R.-wide conference in 1966, at which student self-government was one of the issues on the agenda. (At some places, students themselves make the allocation of subsistence grant funds, on the basis of their more intimate knowledge of their fellow students' needs.) Thus they too took their first step toward organization that would represent their interests in a pluralistic structure, although this initial meeting had very heavy overtones of paternalism, with the Minister of Higher Education making the opening address. But he emphasized the need for independent research projects by students (a recent development there) and stated that curricula henceforth would give greater attention to the social sciences.

Although that last had clearly been foreshadowed by several years of discussion in educational circles, by the very recent introduction of a science-and-mathematics or humanities-and-arts option from the fourth year of grade school, and by increasing freedom of controversy in the social sciences as such, the Minister's announcement itself reflected the pulls and tugs, and the consensus arrived at on the basis of pluralistic interests at the Party Congress just held. For the same Congress that heard nought but conservative expressions with respect to cultural freedom heard much advocacy of liberalism for social science (and no contrary voices) within the framework of axiomatic acceptance of socialism, and the communist goal; the same Congress that accepted considerable independence and increased powers for government vis-à-vis Party changed that organization's rules to make it harder to oust entrenched officials in its own structure, easier to oust dissident members, and harder to join at all. It also restored the Stalin-era designations "General Secretary" and "Political Bureau." However, the universal resentment of Soviet citizens against what they regard as the disruptive economic, governmental, and Party reorganizations of Khrushchev's last years in office suggests that this name change simply represents a return to the "tried and true." Those I spoke to all felt that there is more grass-roots democracy than ever before.

All the conflicting notes I have mentioned were present in the keynote speech at the Congress by General Secretary Brezhnev, which had been delivered to and approved beforehand by his colleagues. Moreover, contrary to all previous practice, he simply dodged basic questions of theory, passing them over in silence. One was the matter of the present nature of the Soviet state. Mr. Khrushchev had explained the new voice permitted to a diversity of structures and interests by proclaiming the end of the dictatorship of the proletariat, which he said had been succeeded by the "state of the entire people." However, careful readers of Marx noted that he had ridiculed that notion in his *Critique of the Gotha Program* nearly a century ago. No one was yet prepared to offer a definition on the basis that "pluralism" is a word just as acceptable to Soviet society as "profit," with the understanding that this pluralism represents group interests and structures rooted in the diversities of a socialist society, just as "profit" in the U.S.S.R. is earned by government and cooperative but not by private entities.

Another theoretical issue evaded by Brezhnev was the Khrushchev-era notion that socialism as a power was already stronger than capitalism in the world, an idea that, in the light of the Sino-Soviet split and the war in Vietnam, posed more questions than it answered. The Soviet man in the street does not think of his country as the stronger. A man who lost his own father in a Stalin concentration camp said to me in 1966 that the U.S.S.R. "is in capitalist encirclement," and volunteered that he would personally fight the United States in Vietnam if such help were sought. The pre-World War II back-to-the-wall psychology is a real factor in Soviet politics, whatever the balance of power in the world. But Mr. Brezhnev's position is not that of Lenin, Mao, Tito, Ho, and Castro, who won nearly unassailable lifetime authority by successfully leading indigenous mass revolutions and defending them against the strongest military interventions the anticommunist world was politically capable of mounting in each of these different situations. Nor is his status that of Stalin, who placed himself in the same category as these others by falsifying his not-inconsiderable role in the prerevolutionary Party and the Revolution, and by slaughtering many of those who remembered that organization under Lenin. Nor is it that of Khrushchev, who represented the first step away from absolute monarchy in Russia and functioned spontaneously and naturally in the tradition of the "little white father in the Kremlin."

Mr. Brezhnev came to power as the consequence of an orderly vote by the Party Central Committee, which has been an actual parliament of the Soviet Union at least since 1957, and which was dissatisfied with his predecessor on a number of counts. As the U.S.S.R. is no longer a dictatorship of either terror or of prestige such as Mao and his associates enjoy, he only can emerge as acknowledged guide of its destinies who seems best to understand

and to have the capacities to adjust the differing points of view effectively present, and he can hold that position only so long as that remains the case. (Whether, on a day-to-day basis, the Party's present General Secretary is actually the *real* guide or simply presiding chairman is an open question at this writing, although I think the latter.)

Therefore, when matters are unclear and there is no pressing need to resolve them at the moment, they may simply be set aside. And this was the case at the Twenty-third Party Congress with respect to the nature of the Soviet state and to the current status of the power balance between socialism and capitalism. *Today it is recognized in the U.S.S.R. that human society is at a new level of complexity* and that it is simply no longer possible for a Marx-Engels team to offer answers to everything, or for a Lenin personally to supervise, criticize, and edit theoreticians, historians, and sociologists, in addition to writing himself on economics, politics, and philosophy. So the Twenty-third Congress called, in speeches and its resolution, for sociologists to work out the problems in their fields and for economists to facilitate and draw conclusions from the new noncommand, consumer-choice system. This will require a vast expansion of training in these fields where there has been almost none. The state is recognized to be the province of legal scholars, and the world scene (below the summit level) to be that of specialists in international relations, whether Party, government, or academic.

War Socialism

But the same Congress and the same speaker did sound medieval on literature; greater freedom in government was accompanied by restrictions in the Party. Why? *The* great change currently in progress in the U.S.S.R. is the economic reform ("Libermanism") that gives each government-owned "firm" considerable freedom to make many decisions for itself on a profit-and-loss basis, with volume of sales as the most important government-set target to meet and beat. What is most important is that this change is being carried out during the active lifetimes and very largely through the agency of men to whom its concepts were once anathema. The U.S.S.R. is emerging from nearly forty years of the "command economy" for which I believe a better term would be War Socialism, because economic policy was deeply affected by the need to industrialize hastily in anticipation of World War II, then to wage that war, then to rebuild from devastation without assistance, and then to achieve military parity with the United States, which had developed and stockpiled nuclear bombs and bombers.

At the very outset, the decision to lift itself by its own bootstraps through industrialization meant acceptance of the reality that Russia, whose backwardness its leaders knew only too well, would not have the assistance of revolution in an advanced industrial country like Germany, which had been hoped for in 1917 and for some time later. Nearly half a century would pass before the U.S.S.R. was able to negotiate from strength, with France in 1966, the kind of technological assistance and long-range joint economic planning it had hoped for from a socialist revolution in Germany. The economic development that followed the Revolution was both a great leap and a long march. Although the right to engage in capitalist enterprise was abolished, differentiated payment continued, in pursuit of a continuing policy of stimulating growth by a combination of planning, enthusiasm, and cash incentive. In 1927, at approximately the same time as Dr. Dillon's report of enthusiasm running high, Soviet labor provided seventeen wage gradations, with the highest paid eight times as much as the lowest.[4] Because economic planning was only just then being initiated, unemployment was still substantial, and benefits were one half of wages, so the spread between an unemployed bottom-grade worker and an employed top-grade one was 16 to 1.

Differences in reward were part of the communist program. This was stated publicly and clearly by Lenin in *State and Revolution,* written in 1917 before his party took power. After quoting Marx's *Critique of the Gotha Program* as his authority,[5] Lenin restated Marx's argument thus:

> Hence, the first phase of communism cannot produce justice and equality; differences, and unjust differences, in wealth will still exist,

[4] George M. Price and Alice Hamilton, *Labor Protection in Soviet Russia* (New York: International Publishers, 1928), p. 64.

[5] Ignorance of Marx in the academic world is second to no other factor as a cause for the prevailing misunderstanding of the Soviet Union. See William Mandel, "Translation, Annotation, Scholarship, and Ignorance," *Slavic Review,* XXIV, 4 (Dec. 1965), 714–721.

but the *exploitation* of man by man will have become impossible, because it will be impossible to seize the *means of production,* the factories, machines, land, etc., as private property.[6]

Like Marx in the earlier work, Lenin understood the psychological factors involved:

> If we are not to fall into utopianism, we cannot imagine that, having overthrown capitalism, people will at once learn to work for society *without any standard of right;* indeed, the abolition of capitalism *does not immediately* create the economic prerequisites for *such* a change.

Lenin then explained the "standard of right" by which people would continue to judge their rewards:

> The state will be able to wither away completely when . . . people have become so accustomed to observing the fundamental rules of social life and when their labor is so productive that they will voluntarily work *according to their ability.* "The narrow horizon of bourgeois right" [Marx's phrase], which compels one to calculate with the shrewdness of a Shylock whether he has not worked half an hour more than another, whether he is not getting less pay than another—this narrow horizon will then be left behind.

He also made quite clear that he had no time schedule whatever, and foresaw the attainment of "complete communism" not in terms of calendar dates but of circumstances to be achieved:

> But how rapidly this development [of the productive forces of human society] will proceed, how soon it will reach the point of breaking away from the division of labor, or removing the antithesis between mental and physical labor, of transforming work into the "primary necessity of life," we do not and *cannot* know.

Private Profit Remains Illegal

Both before and *under the current economic reforms, the same basic principles apply: one earns only the rewards of one's personal work, not* (with few and insignificant exceptions) *the results of the employment of others.* However, differences in earnings exist because of differences in natural physical and mental endowment and in char-

---

[6] This and the following are from V. I. Lenin, *Selected Works,* Vol. VII (New York: International Publishers, n.d.), pp. 85–88, passim; Lenin's emphasis throughout.

acter, which largely determine whether one works on an assembly line or in a creative capacity at a time when society still cannot dispense with the former category of work, doubtless a source of alienation in the absence of complete workers' control.

One result of the decades of War Socialism has been the rooting of attitudes making it necessary for the Soviet press, even after the Twenty-third Congress, to carry many articles demonstrating that the "Liberman" reforms—meaning competition for the market among Soviet firms, interest on the capital loaned by government banks, and profit as one criterion of success (sales-plan fulfillment is the major criterion)—do not represent return to capitalism. The interest, profit, and other earnings do not go into private hands but serve more accurately to measure and stimulate production in publicly owned enterprises in accordance, now, with the customers' desires (except for such activities as defense). While managers receive substantial bonuses, they cannot use them to go into private business; nor are these bonuses large enough to retire on, nor do they place the manager remotely in the income bracket of an individual of comparable responsibility in a Western country. Not being an owner, the manager is still subject to removal at any time.

The middle-level Party bureaucracy was worried about the Liberman reform of the economy. That bureaucracy does not consist for the most part of evil people dreaming of an old man with a moustache and concentration camps, but of unimaginative people who have worked hard, suffered through years of building, war, and discipline, and have seen their country grow in the process. It took three years of the most public, most frank, most participatory discussion by everybody (*millions* of people, in the Party and out, in newspapers, meetings, and every other conceivable forum) to get agreement on the economic reforms. But there are many old-timers (in their forties and fifties actually) who were reluctant to make the change, and a little frightened of it. These are the conservatives in the Soviet spectrum, and they are conservative politically as well as economically. (Fifty percent of Soviet management executives are under forty. They are the power base of reform in Soviet society.)

The politicians of this world are not often intellectuals. And at this stage of development, those who are intellectuals (in the Soviet Union or elsewhere) are required to adjust their style to that of those who are not. So there was an unspoken, and perhaps even an un-negotiated, but implicit horse trade at the Twenty-third Party Congress of 1966: a promise of considerable freedom for the economy and for social science, which had come to be regarded as essential to meet pressing needs by a majority, in exchange for tightening-up of the Party machinery and harsh words for outspoken writers, preceded by the jailing of Sinyavsky and Daniel. The well-informed Alexander Werth reported in *The Nation* (September 15, 1966) that Premier Kosygin and Culture Minister Mme. Furtseva voted against prosecuting them, and Party Secretary Brezhnev abstained, but a conservative majority of a special subcommittee of the Central Committee carried the day. He blamed the atmosphere created by the Vietnam war.

Getting Things Done

This move in two opposite directions produces a contradiction. The years ahead will see a struggle to resolve it. Abolition of War Socialism favors ultimate reversal of the conservative trend of the Twenty-third Congress in the realm of political organization and the creative arts. In March 1967, *Novy Mir* editor Tvardovsky, himself a Party member, declared independence of the Party's tutelage in the sphere of socially-critical literature. More important, he was able to get his statement published, and in a weekly of a million circulation with an editor much less liberal than himself. In June, A. I. Solzhenitsyn, himself barred from publication since 1964, urged the Writers' Union to demand abolition of literary censorship.

The Party has always been basically a body for getting things done. One joined under Lenin to make a revolution. One joined at his death (when there was a huge influx) to carry on his work and build socialism. Workingmen Communists went to the villages in the tens of thousands to organize the peasants into collectives, and many were beaten and shot. They were sent to the wildest, most barren places to build the new industries. In World War II, when men had to be chosen to cover a retreat or spearhead an advance, it was Communist Party members who were ordered to step forward. When the fate of Moscow was actually in the balance in October

1941, divisions of draft-exempt overage, underage, and medically unfit Communists, many of them intellectuals and office workers, were organized and stood at the gates of the city until wiped out. They won the time needed for fresh divisions to be brought from Siberia.

With the great dams and other construction projects of the postwar years, the story was repeated. So it was with the opening of 100 million acres of virgin soil under Khrushchev. In each case, however, where Party members were sent under orders to form the backbones of staffs, the Komsomol provided the mass personnel by calling upon the enthusiasm of youth. Sixty thousand students went to the newly broken prairie of Kazakhstan in the summer of 1966 to bring in the crop under frontier conditions; ten thousand went to the most isolated places in the U.S.S.R. to string wires into the last 10 percent of villages without electricity by the fiftieth anniversary of the Revolution.

But "shock work," as the Russians call it, is inefficient, costly, wasteful, although it gets things done. Now that they have more engineers than we and increasingly skilled workers, and masses of machinery, the increasing complexity of their immense economy has caused it to be damaged by the old fire-brigade methods. The economic growth rate declined for several years, although it remained very high by long-term Western standards. (Capitalist countries not in the arms race and stimulated by large investments from abroad have surpassed the U.S.S.R. in this respect for various periods of years, but not over the long run.) Although Party membership has boomed as never before (10 percent of the adult population today), no parallel is to be found between that phenomenon and measurable factors in the country's progress, as was found in earlier periods. Not long ago, it was believed that the inadequacy of Party membership among the peasants was one reason that agriculture failed to show any sort of uniform rate of progress. However, for several years now there has been a Party "club" in every collective farm, but output went from an all-time high in 1962 to catastrophe in 1963 to another new high in 1964 followed by a considerable decline in 1965; 1966 did show a 10 percent rise, so universal in terms of type of produce and weather zones as to give grounds for the belief that a major turning point may have been reached.

In industry, the Party's annual campaign for production achieve-ments in honor of May Day is outweighed by the economic fact that bonuses are paid on quarterly results. Therefore, March, at the end of a quarter, is always a high-output month, followed by relaxation in April, despite the fact that it determines the record as of May Day.

Emotionally, nearly everyone in the U.S.S.R. admires the Party. The overwhelming majority accept and understand its social goal of a communist society. In practice, however, it is beginning to get in the way, although it is doubtful that there is anyone who thinks it no longer needed. Even its own officers for the Party membership of business entities complain of its interference in economic affairs. In *Partiinaia zhizn'* (Party Life), No. 24, December 1965, the head of the Party committee of the construction organization building a power station protests an order by the borough Party committee. The order was to send part of the highly specialized and shorthanded project personnel to a nearby village to build cow barns and pigsties for a collective farm of which the local Party is sponsor. What kind of economy is this, he asks?

In 1967 the Party had a vast organizational machinery for its 13 million members, an enormous press, and overwhelming public sup-port. But one wonders what it accomplishes that government could not accomplish, except that it causes its majority of conscientious members to weigh their own behavior, public and private, more care-fully than they would otherwise; that it raises their morale by provid-ing a feeling of mutual support; and that it provides a check at each level against the authority of executives who tend to see problems solely in terms of the particular responsibilities they bear. Party Congresses meet only once in four years in an immense auditorium and listen to speeches. Central Committee meetings, approximately quarterly, are today the seat of power and do serve as a parliament in that respect. But it is now accepted policy that all the parlia-mentary bodies of actual government (from the Supreme Soviet, the formal parliament of the U.S.S.R., down to the village soviet) shall be reported to regularly by the executives they elect. At higher levels they have larger numbers of standing committees than hitherto, functioning in a manner familiar in the West. Reports by ministries and departments are to be distributed to each member long enough in advance to permit intelligent discussion by others than those who happen to have professional knowledge in the given field. This became the general practice in the Supreme Soviet itself (to which virtually all Party Central Committee members belong) in mid-1966.

I have discussed the parliamentary pyramid of government asking the Party to keep hands off, in Chief of State Podgorny's speech at the Twenty-third Congress. The armed forces, whose officer corps consists almost entirely of Communist Party members, have long since won the right to run their own affairs, except for the naming of the Defense Minister (always a career officer however). A more important independent structure than either of these two is the executive branch of government headed in 1967 by Premier Kosygin and, through his cabinet ministers, directly managing the country's economy. This is the field in which the new principle of judging publicly owned businesses chiefly by their sales and profits is most fully operative. That principle would be reduced to meaninglessness if workers and equipment were taken off a job on which they were working under a contract involving specified sums of money, penalties for late completion and bonuses for finishing ahead of time, to go out to build barns and pigsties free of charge. It is interesting that in the case in question, the manager concerned refused the borough Party official's orders. The consequence was an official reprimand—which hurt him, a Communist, in exactly the same way, no less but no more, than the words of a priest to a religious individual who confesses a sin.

While the "withering" of the Party, which Lenin anticipated as well as withering of the state, will be very long-drawn-out, complex, and probably painful, its foreseeable future would seem to lie in the function of top-level policy-making in determining consensus among structures and interests equally loyal to Soviet socialism but seeing life from different angles. At the grass roots it can serve the function of propagandizer of new ideas and policies. But to get it to abandon its accustomed function of organizer, and organizer by command, will not be easy, even though it already accepts the need for this in principle. In foreign affairs, it makes all the decisions, even on petty matters. While it often rejects the advice of foreign communist parties, it holds their opinions in higher esteem than any other reports from abroad, even where the Communists are too few in number and too weak in influence to have an accurate picture of the situation in their own country.

Greater Democratization

Although the U.S.S.R. is not remotely civil libertarian, there is a vast amount of participatory democracy on many vital subjects, when the decision is made to open them to public discussion. I have already mentioned the breadth of the "Libermanism" discussion. The psychology of Soviet citizens consequently reflects the assumption that government must listen to the people. I have numerous tapes carrying the tone of the nineteen-year-old lounging by the Moscow River who said to me in 1966: "You've *got* to send a message to the President that the American people doesn't want that war in Vietnam . . . he has *got* to listen to you, to the voices of his electors." A woman commented on a similar remark in another discussion: "But the people don't decide much [in America]. Their democracy, in general, isn't as effective as it is with us. For all practical purposes there is no democracy." When I commented that most Americans thought the shoe on the other foot, and cited the differences in elections, a barrage of responses from the crowd offered what the speakers regarded as proofs of the democracy of their elections. They all knew the names of their "congressmen," unlike the experience of the Stanford student (reporting in the *San Francisco Chronicle,* August 14, 1966), that "none of the people I talked to on the streets [of a ghetto in Brooklyn] had any idea who his congressman was."

In 1965 and 1966, a national discussion occurred to frame new model rules for collective farms to replace the existing set, thirty years old. The discussion was carried on for many months in the 5 million daily-circulation national newspaper read by the peasantry, *Sel'skaia zhizn'* (Rural Life), which published in detail a vast variety of notions coming from the grass roots. In November 1965 the U.S.S.R. Academy of Sciences' Institute of State and Law convened a conference on the subject. Its participants were people from research institutes and higher educational institutions in law, economics, and agriculture, the agriculture ministries of the U.S.S.R. and of its Russian Republic, the Moscow Regional Farm Administration, the U.S.S.R. and Russian Republic "attorney-generals" offices (procuracies), publishing houses, newspaper and magazine editorial boards. Although a majority of persons at such a gathering would certainly be members of the Party, hardly anyone mentioned that organization, and no one deferred to the official rank or the structure represented by any other speaker.

Speakers whom one might expect to seek to protect the rights of bureaucracy took precisely the opposite position. The opening speaker, a legal scholar, had proposed that the model rules have the force of law. But then a representative of the U.S.S.R. Agriculture Ministry's Division of Collective Farms held that that would deprive the farmers of the right to change or amend them. An academician with a distinctly Central Asian name, Shaibekov, from the University of Kazakhstan, informed the body that his republic had not waited for a lead from the federal level but had drafted its own proposed model rules, which he urged be considered for the U.S.S.R. as a whole. He protested the tendency, more marked in Kazakhstan than elsewhere because of the vast virgin-soil planting program, to reorganize collective (cooperative) farms into state (government-owned) farms without their consent, and wanted the model rules to specify that the government of the given republic must give its approval. (The Party Congress subsequently fell in line, with a policy of drastically curtailing such reorganizations.)

A federal government spokesman urged that the size of the collective farmer's private plot and the number of livestock he could possess individually be tied to his contribution of work in the collective itself. But, the Soviet law journal [7] reporting this meeting said, "A majority of the participants in the conference held otherwise."

There was sharp difference of opinion over town meeting versus representative democracy in governing the farms. Some held that no farm should be permitted to be so large that all its members could not gather in the local rural hall to decide fundamental problems. A speaker who had formerly chaired a 72,000-acre farm cited his experience in favor of representative democracy. The discussion showed the actual level of attendance at general farm meetings to be extraordinarily high by the standards of membership organizations in the West. Three hundred out of eighteen hundred was regarded as as example of an unacceptably small gathering, not even comprising

[7] The conference report appeared in *Sovetskoe gosudarstvo i pravo,* No. 3 (1966), unabridged translation in *Soviet Law and Government* (White Plains, New York: International Arts and Sciences Press, Summer, 1966).

a legal quorum empowered to do business. (Four percent of membership is normal at trade union meetings in the United States. The most controversial meeting in the history of the Berkeley, California, Consumers Co-op brought out two percent of its 40,000 members in this highly-educated and turbulent community.)

In view of my discussion of the future of the Party, it is exceptionally significant that some speakers emphasized that only a member of the given collective farm should be eligible to be its manager. Hitherto, it had been the Party's practice to send outsiders in, in much the same way as the head of a state farm is named by the superior agency.

A speaker noted that while the work of collective-farm management, professional people (veterinarians, etc.) working on the farms, and equipment operators was guaranteed remuneration by government legislation, the rank-and-file collective farmer had no such protection, and was entirely dependent upon the crop and other products. The Party Congress a few months later committed itself to the institution of a guaranteed wage for farmers during the current Five Year Plan. In May 1966, the Party and government *recommended* to the collective farms that they pursue this policy as of July 1 of that year. The fact that this carried no force beyond recommendation to economically independent entities is evidenced by the publication of reports nine months later that there were still farms not paying a guaranteed wage.

As this book went to press, the new model rules had not yet been adopted. It may be speculated that the extraordinary advance of agriculture in 1966 strengthened the hand of those who wished to leave well enough alone. But the nature, form, and extent of the discussion makes clear that the situation with respect to the rules does represent the consensus of Soviet opinion, very much including the rank-and-file.

To regard democracy as inseparable from confrontation of opposing candidates on election day is hardly sustained by the experience of the West. The *Los Angeles Daily Journal,* a newspaper for lawyers in our second largest metropolitan area, carried in 1965 an advertisement by Hal Evry stating: "Leading public relations firm with top-flight experience in statewide campaign wants attorney general candidate." A reporter's inquiry in the *San Francisco Chronicle* (December 3, 1965) brought the following comment from Mr.

Evry: "People are generally unsophisticated. The issues just confuse them. The best way to manipulate them is with a simple slogan they can understand. And it's better *if they never see the candidate*." (My emphasis.) Mr. Evry managed the successful race in 1958 for congressional candidate George Kasem, a Democrat who won in a district that had previously been Republican territory.

Misuse of the system of competitive elections by the power of the campaign fund shrewdly employed does not mean the system should be junked, but neither does it justify its use as an absolute criterion of democracy. In 1966, for the first time in thirty years, a responsible Soviet political figure proposed that the U.S.S.R. make use of competitive elections. Mr. N. K. Arutiunian, former rector of the University of Armenia and head of state of that Soviet republic at the time of his speech, said to the congress of the Armenian Communist Party:

> It has always been argued that where there are no antagonistic classes, it makes no sense to put up two or more candidates since this would lead to futile rivalry and opposition. . . . Unity does not mean a complete homogeneity of all the opinions and feelings of the people, of their talents and energies, their methods of work and public activity. . . . The nomination of more than one candidate . . . would . . . increase their [the voters'] political activity and interest, would raise the level of responsibility of the candidates toward their electors (*The N.Y. Times,* March 22, 1966).

Support for the idea at least reached a level at which *Izvestia* found it necessary to devote a lengthy article (May 13, 1966) to defense of the one-candidate system. (My own probings that summer did not indicate this to be a live issue among the people, who indicated vocal satisfaction with the present system under which several candidates are named informally and only one appears on the ballot after discussion at meetings.)

The sense of realism that emerges from Mr. Arutiunian's speech, as from the collective-farm rules discussion, reaches into most realms of Soviet life and suggests future trends. For example, the notion that unemployment is simply impossible in a socialist country (except for people who are merely between jobs) has been discarded in favor of the understanding that socialism eliminates its causes but that there may be unemployed unless planning properly distributes industry geographically to the places where population factors have produced an unused labor supply. This knowledge itself is a result of the freedom for sociological research that has developed in the past decade. Given this information, the control over the economy provided by public ownership can be brought into play. In February 1966, a joint resolution of Party and government made provision for schooling and jobs for the extraordinary 70 percent increase in eighteen-year-olds in the two preceding years reflecting the sudden demobilization of the army after World War II. One of its provisions will suffice to illustrate its association with the socialist nature of the economy. All managements were ordered, depending upon the employment problem and skill levels required, to save 5 percent to 10 percent of *total* places on the payroll, as instructed by *local* authorities, for youth newly entering the labor market, with an even higher percentage permissible for 1966 alone, when a school reform put two graduating classes on the labor market simultaneously.

Another example of the unfreezing of attitudes is presented in an article by Yu. Kariakin, a social critic, originally appearing in the *World Marxist Review,* from which it was picked up by *Novy Mir.* The article is in support of Alexander Solzhenitsyn's novel of life in Stalin's concentration camps, *One Day in the Life of Ivan Denisovich.* Those who attack that novel (and one speaker did so at the Twenty-third Party Congress, four years after publication), says Kariakin with bitterness, uphold "the communism of the barracks." He quotes Mao Tse-tung as having written: "Real love of man is possible, but only after classes have been abolished everywhere in the world." To which Kariakin responds:

> The principles of communist humanism must be brought to reality not only in a remote future, but today; *otherwise they will never be.* If they are not observed day in and day out, they will be postponed to eternity. What is most important is that these principles be cultivated from *earliest* childhood. And if we inoculate all children against a number of diseases, and do so successfully, it is all the more important to protect people *from childhood* against the psychology that rules in the "city of identical little men," which unfortunately exists not only in the fairy tale. [My emphasis.]

And he finds a line in one of Lenin's last articles that is a cry for individual dignity: "Lenin said that the destiny of Russia, the fate of the revolution, depended upon those 'of whom one can swear that they will take no word on faith, say no word against conscience.' " [8]

The stand taken by Solzhenitsyn and Kariakin is that widely accepted by thinking Soviet youth today. A literary critic reviewing Yevtushenko's *Bratsk Hydroelectric Station* for the middle-of-the-road magazine *Znamia* says: "The organizing idea of his poem is contained in the words, 'we are not slaves,' and in irreconcilability to all forms of slavery, physical and intellectual, and whether their social form makes the fact of slavery evident, or whether it conceals them. . . ." The critic adds:

> The unifying principle in *Bratsk Hydroelectric Station* is rather the spirit of the ethics of citizenship. Today we perceive acutely that the further development and destiny of the revolution and, consequently, of human history are indissolubly tied to the problem of the moral level of society and consequently to the moral improvement of each individual.[9]

Note that morality is tied to the ethics of citizenship, which in the West we spell out under the concept of democratic values. We have seen the call for competitive elections by the academic and political figure Arutiunian. But it is Kariakin who details in this same article the values in which he believes by attacking those he opposes:

> If someone holds that somebody else doesn't have the right to his own convictions, and the latter is ashamed of his opinion, is afraid to express it and tries to get rid of it (meaning he has blind faith in someone), you have the basic prerequisite for worship of an individual. . . . The champions of worship of an individual want to see everything regulated, but in practice they merely give free reign to lawlessness. . . . The hatred borne him [reference here is to the main character of Solzhenitsyn's novel] by the present defenders of worship of an individual has a social origin. Their attitude toward him is such precisely because he has begun to put questions dangerous for them. . . .

These, then, are Kariakin's democratic values, and those of the editors of *Novy Mir*: the right to individual opinion, the courage to express it, the rule of law, free thought, the right to put questions

[8] *The Soviet Review,* Vol. VI, No. 3 (1965). See also Y. Kariakin and Y. Plimak, *Hans Kohn Analyzes the Russian Mind* (Moscow: Progress, 1966), in English.

[9] A. Makarov, "Thoughts on Yevtushenko's Long Poem," translated in *Soviet Studies in Literature,* Vol. II, No. 3 (1966).

dangerous to those in positions of authority, a political party expressing the perceptions of the people. They clearly believe this possible
within the framework of continued leadership by a reformed Communist Party. And Kariakin asserts with no less vigor his belief that
these values can truly exist for all only in a society in which the
power of private wealth does not render the freedoms of the majority
impotent in practice. (But these views are held in a society that at
present writing still occasionally jails writers; often delays publication by other writers; controls the staging of controversial plays and
films; limits showings of avant-garde art; tightly controls foreign
travel by its citizens; continues to ban dissent in the mass media over
foreign policy, Trotsky, drugs, and sex deviation; and which limits
cultural expression and education in Yiddish. It is also a society
that in fifteen short years has advanced from holding hundreds of
thousands in forced-labor camps to a situation in which there are
hardly a dozen persons detained for reasons of dissent; this change
having been accomplished under the same political party and without violence. I know of no comparable *rate* of *nonviolent* progress
in the history of human political institutions.)

Toward a More Human and Equal Society

How wide is the influence of the types of writing I have been
quoting, that is, what will be their impact upon the future? Yevtushenko's *Bratsk Hydroelectric Station* appeared in a magazine selling 2 million copies and read by practically every young school-
teacher in the country—a country in which literature is revered and
is regarded by all, of whatever viewpoint, as the most powerful of
teachers. *Bratsk* contains, in its forty pages, a long passage beginning,
"I am the dispatcher of light, Izzy Kramer," which is one of the
most powerful statements against anti-Semitism in world literature.
These teachers have had a whole age group of children read that
poem. And thus, although official education has not yet done very
much about it, the most important thing needed to uproot anti-Semitism in the U.S.S.R., concrete education against it, has begun. An
even broader audience was reached with this message by the filming
in 1966 of a novel about the legendary first Five Year Plan, Ka-
tayev's *Time, Forward!,* in which two of the heroes are named Mar-

golis and Weinstein. The government is directly involved in film-making, and the movie got fine reviews. Also that year, the mass-circulation magazine that published *Bratsk* carried a documentary novel on the German massacre of the Jews at Babi Yar and *Novy Mir* published the first essay in the Soviet Union on the roots of ethnic prejudices in social psychology. It dealt specifically with anti-Semitism. *Anti-Semitic Activities of the Ukrainian Nationalists,* published in Ukrainian in the Ukraine in 1967, documents their participation in the slaughter of Jews there under Hitler.

Two other programs, originating in Party and government, are striking at the roots of ethnocentrism and xenophobia, of which folk anti-Semitism is only one manifestation. Father Edward H. Flannery's *The Anguish of the Jews,* and the Glock and Stark work, *Christian Beliefs and Anti-Semitism,* a sociological study published in 1966 by the University of California Research Center, find religion to be the chief vehicle perpetuating anti-Semitism. (Only 25 percent of Americans are entirely free of that prejudice according to the latter book, and it is found to rise in direct proportion to intensity of religious belief.) Like it or not, the antireligious education of the Soviet people has vastly reduced anti-Semitism by largely eliminating religion. However, the crudeness of that effort, particularly in pamphlets directed against Judaism, diminished that result somewhat among the very small proportion of the people (and even fewer non-Jews) who read writings in that latter category. But today one finds a Soviet Ukrainian atheist magazine opening its pages to defense of the ethical values contributed by Judaism, including Christianity itself, at that stage in history when all moral thought appeared in religious form (*Liudina i Svit,* April 1966). One of the difficulties encountered in earlier postwar years in convincing Soviet people (including nonreligious, younger Jews) that anti-Semitism exists in the U.S.S.R. at all is that they know from their own experience how vastly it has declined. In the Russian historical context, anti-Semitism equals pogroms—organized assaults upon Jews—and they are long since forgotten. So is exclusion from membership in voluntary organizations, which is still very common in America. So is residential discrimination, still exceedingly widespread in the United States.

Ethnic massacres are recorded in prerevolutionary relationships among other Soviet nationalities, and these were complicated and given visible symbolism by religious differences (the Christian Armenians versus the Moslem Azerbaijanis, for example). Here again, the substantial elimination of religion has had positive consequences, along with the general policy toward nationalities for which the U.S.S.R. is famed in Asia and, more recently, Africa. It was not merely because it had demonstrated its noncolonialist foreign policy over a long term of years that the "white" U.S.S.R. was acceptable as mediator between India and Pakistan. The fact that the meeting was held not in the capital, Moscow, but in the central Asian city of Tashkent, to which the declaration by the parties owes its name, is an indication of the fundamental understanding of Asian sensitivities possessed by the Soviet Union. It is well known in Asia that the U.S.S.R. continues today to put more money per capita each year into health, education, housing, and economic development in the former czarist colonies than into Russia proper, for the purpose of closing the tremendous gap that existed between them. In Uzbekistan, the Soviet Union's cotton-growing "Mississippi," the number of Uzbek college students rose from 28,900 in 1958–1959 to 79,300 only five years later. Even in the earlier year, there were more Uzbeks in college than there are students in Sweden, although there are 25 percent more Swedes than Uzbeks in the world.[10]

Industrialization, bringing urbanization, has had a major influence in improving ethnic relationships as well as eliminating cultural backwardness. Where industrialization has occurred under conditions of discriminatory wage, housing, employment, residential, and social policy, whether in the United States or Hong Kong, ethnic hostilities have worsened: witness Watts. But where the opposite is the case, as in the Soviet Union, urbanization has been a positive influence by taking people out of rural isolation among members of their own ethnic group. For example, in the cities of Soviet Central Asia, native girls began to approach 50 percent of the high-school attendance as early as a decade ago, while in the villages, where Moslem traditions are strong, they were one quarter to one third, although even this represented a fundamental culture change.[11] It is simply beyond belief that in the American South today, as reported in the *San Francisco Chronicle* (May 9, 1966), "a nurse in

[10] See the article by Ethel and Stephen Dunn, and comment by William M. Mandel, *Current Anthropology* (June 1967).
[11] *Kul'turnoe stroitel' stvo SSSR* (Moscow: Gos. Stat. Izd., 1956), p. 177.

the white wards of the hospital routinely washes a newborn baby, but the Negro mother must get out of bed and walk three floors down to the basement to wash her own newborn child." And the time is long gone when the rural structure included landless farm laborers, of whom three million were "starving to death" in India as this is written, "not so much [from] the lack of food supplies . . . but [from] the lack of money to buy food" (*Chronicle,* May 3, 1966).

In the great construction projects of Central Asia and the opening of the virgin lands of Kazakhstan, a melting pot has begun to arise. Ethnocentrism has been reduced. Marriages across nationality lines have come to occur in significant numbers. These changes are penetrating back to the rural strongholds of tradition. During at least the first forty years of the Soviet regime, the leading tendency in this sphere was for each of the sixty ethnic groups for which it provides schools in their own languages to emphasize its particular culture. But ethnographic studies show a pronounced countertendency in the past five to ten years. People still living in their native villages have become bilingual or, in the Caucasus, trilingual, using the language of an adjacent ethnic group when convenient, whereas linguistic purism had hitherto been preserved for a thousand years or more. Tremendous effort and substantial funds have gone into obtaining competent translation of creative literature, folk and otherwise, from as well as into the minority languages, so as to eliminate any notion that some other group is inherently culturally inferior. It is pertinent to note that the Yiddish classic Sholom Aleichem became known to the ordinary Soviet schoolchild (his name has been mentioned to me in street conversations by persons of diverse nationalities) through required reading in literature courses long before his recent limited vogue in English in the United States. A plaque in Ukrainian on a house on the main street of Kiev tells the passerby this is where he lived.

But where Soviet officialdom has been content with the changes in attitudes following spontaneously in the wake of these ethnic, cultural, religious (or antireligious), and economic policies, social scientists in recent years and thinking youth of the morality-hipped immediate post-destalinization generation are not. V. I. Perevedentsev notes that employment at a hydroelectric plant and a textile mill in Tajikistan is only one-fourth Tajik and Uzbek due to personnel policies based on existing skills and ignoring ethnic considerations. No discrimination is implied. (Translation in *Soviet Sociology,* 1967, in press.) Historians battle for change by demanding the whole truth on the roots of Stalinism (*Survey,* April 1967).

Although women are less confined to the home than in the most advanced Western lands, studies show women have less time to read, to pursue education, to go out. The government is making strenuous efforts to overcome these problems through easing physical difficulties, but almost none to change the attitude of men. Only in 1966 did the general press indicate a concerted policy to change male attitudes. Mass-circulation women's magazines (*The Woman Worker* prints 10 million copies) publicize and encourage organized efforts by women to fight manifestations of male prejudice, or thoughtlessness, at executive levels. By 1970, accommodation in pre-school facilities, already by far the largest on earth, at 8 million in 1967, will rise to 12 million, essentially meeting the full need in the cities and removing dependence upon grandma and her traditional upbringing. (For a while this will widen the culture gap between town and country, until similar rural facilities catch up.) In 1967 there was the almost universal institution of the two-day week-end, most important to working women for whom Sunday has hitherto been house-cleaning, shopping, and mending day. The current drive to raise the number of stores and clerks, the sixfold rise in dry-cleaning services scheduled by 1970, and the multiplication of refrigerator manufacture eliminating the need for daily shopping will greatly further genuine emancipation of the rank-and-file woman. Add to this the financial and organizational provision being made to give every child ten full years of schooling by 1971 (academically equivalent to junior college in the United States) and the basis for a truly major further culture change will have been established.

We have turned to these sociological tangibles from considerations such as democratic values, civic morality, and the impact of literature, because the latter can only have a broad base when the former are provided. The civil rights militants in the United States have learned and are seeking to impress upon the society that a law guaranteeing a Negro's right to eat in a restaurant or buy a house in a Caucasian neighborhood is valueless as long as his earnings average half those of whites, and restaurants or down payments are beyond his means. The U.S.S.R. has left that discrimination far behind, and its ordinary people regard us as savage for not having done so. However, its own problems of building a new man, of developing true love for one's fellow man instead of merely enforcing his right to an even break, or producing the attitude that one should do one's work without thought of the tangible reward, that one should do things without ulterior motives—these hinge on the material factors we have been listing.

What is new today is the belief that, as phrased by social critic Kariakin and the moralist poets, communist humanism must be worked at right now and not have to wait its turn until "the material and technological basis" has been created. One of the most powerful of the poems of Voznesensky is "B'iut zhenshchinu" (Someone Is Beating a Woman). The youth of today respond to wife-beating through a poem like Voznesensky's, and their demand for morality, for not treating another human being as a thing, reaches into yet another aspect of life. In envisaging the future of the U.S.S.R., it should be noted that in 1966 half the population was under twenty-six.

But those abroad who think the young Soviet people born since the war are drifting from communism are quite mistaken. The anti-Stalinist Yevtushenko puts it most simply in his *Precocious Autobiography*: "Communism has become the very essence of the Russian people." What one does hear on the part of particularly sensitive Soviet individuals is a fear that the communist ideal is being vulgarized to equate with material abundance alone. But having also heard plain farm people correct, in Marxist philosophical terms, one of their number who envisaged communism as the end of human development, I found it hard to accept the notion that all it means to them is a car in every garage.

Soviet exchange students have been coming to Berkeley for nearly a decade and I've gotten to know them well. They are doubtless a selected group, but they grew up as part of Soviet society and had no expectation of coming here until a very short time before being chosen. The very much higher living standard here does not disturb them greatly. Their attitude is that their country will eventually have the same and better. They have outright contempt for the desire held, in their experience, by the great majority of foreign students in the United States to get jobs here and stay. They are utterly shocked by the limitations on everyday freedom imposed by private property: the fact that somebody can actually own a beach so you cannot swim or picnic there, or that open country is posted with no-trespassing signs so you cannot hike or camp.

Underlying all else in their outlook was an attitude best expressed in a speech to the Twenty-third Party Congress by a twenty-five-year-old woman describing her trip to the United States. Her senatorial hosts' jaws dropped when she, a member of the Supreme Soviet, told them she was a dairy-barn worker: "There are no dairy maids in their Congress: their kind of democracy doesn't permit that."

Today's Soviet youth will grow to middle age under the conditions of the economic reform now going into effect. By granting a significant measure of independence to the management of each plant and store, and to its personnel as a unit, it already has proven the ability to oil the joints of a system become stiff with the weight of its own growth. The reform will certainly improve the living standard, and thus may well virtually eliminate what remnants there are of the kind of crime that arises out of coveting things we regard as necessities, but by its nature it will increase "business" crime.

It is difficult to think seriously of crime in the U.S.S.R. when one has just returned from a trip in which sixty foreigners, very wealthy by Soviet standards, report one case of stealing in thousands of miles of travel during which personal belongings were left near open cabin windows and in city-tour buses, and Soviet guides found no need to suggest that people lock doors or take things with them for safety. When an item was mistakenly reported missing, the response, *"We don't take things"* bespoke an impressive certainty about the large crew of the Soviet vessel where the incident occurred. Soviet people on a jam-packed city beach showed no sign of safeguarding their belongings, and police—regular or auxiliary—were just not there. Against this background, it is unwise to ignore the taped comment of a teenager engaged in conversation at random:

> The worst that happens is if a man has been drinking a little, he goes home and that's all. . . . That's a common sight in the Soviet Union. But otherwise there is no disorderly behavior. No murders, thefts, breaking in: it just doesn't happen in our country. We regard this, Russian people regard this as though we would be robbing ourselves.

It is easy to prove him wrong by citing Soviet court records and newspaper items, but the question is whether the fact that both he and the foreign visitor form that impression is really not more significant. Statistically, criminal trials dropped by over one third from 1958 to 1963, while the population rose by 9 percent.

If both the status and income of all concerned in each individual enterprise will be increasingly dependent upon its competitive position (profits and bonuses for all if your line of clothing moves in the stores; losses and short workweeks if it does not), the tendency to engage in sharp practices—not unknown in the U.S.S.R. today—will increase. The numerous followers of Yevtushenko and Voznesensky among today's youth demand morality from elders who see themselves as moral in the sacrifices they made to build their country. Yet youth's demand for a higher living standard is a factor in the introduction of this presently necessary economic reform that will undermine morality in the business sphere that affects all of life.

Thirty years hence the reform will have performed its function. Projecting forward the long-term growth rates of industry in the U.S.S.R. and the United States (taking the most optimistic figure for American industry, 4 percent, the least optimistic for Soviet industry, 7 percent, and the consensus of American specialists that our industry is now double that of the U.S.S.R.), that is the maximum period needed for the Soviet Union to overtake the American living standard as it will have improved to that future date. In 1966, Soviet per capita production of major consumer durables (except cars) reached west European standards for the first time. (In 1917, Russian industry produced one eighth as much as American. In 1950, it produced one fourth as much after having been devastated in a war that actually boomed the American economy. Today it produces at least one half as much [Moscow claims two thirds].) This reckoning of the living standard includes the difference in population and the advantage the United States now enjoys in products of past years: roads, utilities, housing and other buildings already in place, and personal-use property (furniture, etc.) presently possessed.

Thirty years is the longest period that can elapse before the Soviet youth of the time will say, "so what?" to affluence. But whatever may be happening there by way of imitation of such harmless aspects of the "youth culture" of the West as folk-rock, jeans, hairdos, and the replacement of accordions by guitars, the Soviet rebels at the end of this century will hardly express themselves via the manifestations of contemporary alienation. For the roots of alienation will be lacking. They will not see the product of their work become the property of private owners of the machinery, nor will dehumanizing routine jobs be necessary any longer. The rebellion in the West is against parents whose way of life compels them to be at war with everyone else—a war reflected into the family with greater or lesser force.

In the U.S.S.R. even today, the factors bringing people together are greater than those tearing them apart. The present economic reforms will intensify the latter, within a framework however in which public ownership remains sacred, although its group aspect will become more prominent, its nationwide aspect a little less so. While in the cities the negative moral consequences of business competition may become significant (although collectivism will be greater within each individual enterprise), the same reforms may cause the change in the morality of the countryside to favor the group rather than the individual.

Nearly half the Soviet population is still rural, and the collective farmer is the most numerous type in the countryside and sets its tone. Soviet sources make clear that Stalin's policy of industrializing by stripping the collective farm of its joint product *undermined* the feeling of collectivism among the peasantry by making the family dependent for its physical survival upon the most intensive cultivation of the *private* garden area it was allowed to retain. (Stalin may have been forced into this by the refusal of any country to make development loans to the U.S.S.R. or reconstruction loans after World War II, but it is the effect upon peasant mentality that concerns us here.)

Khrushchev stimulated agriculture by raising purchase prices, but came a cropper when he tried to reduce the peasants' private garden-plot and milk-cow business. The Brezhnev-Kosygin administration further increased purchase prices, reduced the collective farms' procurement quotas, offering a 50 percent price bonus for produce sold over quota, and pledged not to raise the quotas for five years. If the peasants find that this promise is good, that fact, plus the tremendous government investment in fertilizers, pesticides, defoliants, growth promoters and land improvement, and the new rules of the collective farms, should make work on the collective proper more remunerative for the peasant than the time-waste of pasturing a single cow and cultivating a vegetable patch by hand. The countryside has been the stronghold of individualism until now, and the source replenishing it in the cities as their population has multiplied by drawing on the villages. But if there is success in transforming the collectives into genuinely cooperatively run enterprises in which the members' interest in working exceeds their concern for their garden plot, cow, pig, and fowl, the collectives' moral impact upon Soviet life in a socialist direction will be immense. It would be quite mistaken to underestimate the influence of the rural revolution of the 1930s that causes a middle-aged woman encountered today in a village street by a lone foreigner to respond with ringing pride, when asked how she lives: *"Ya kolkhoznitsa!* (I am a collective farm woman!)"* or that causes state-farm people, offered a comparison between Catherine the Great and Stalin, to respond with resentment that Catherine had given their very village, with all their serf ancestors, to one of her gentleman friends, while under Stalin it belonged to them.

As off-season and processing industries are developed in the villages under collective-farm or local-government ownership, that form of urbanization will diminish the present gap between town and country life. In addition, the 1966–1970 Five Year Plan provides a trebling of housing construction on collective farms and a doubling on state farms, plus the provision of some urban amenities.

The prospect for the next two decades or so would thus seem to be a change from a state-focused economy in the cities and an individually focused one in the countryside (in the sense that collective farmers show more concern for their private plots and animals) to one focused in both cases on the enterprise, publicly owned in town and cooperatively owned in the village. Effective control will be at the enterprise level in both cases. The federal government will guide development through national plans effectuated in financial and investment policy, incentive prices, and in the cities, the appointment of responsible management, under present plans. (A leading economist, Professor Alexander Birman, suggested in 1966: "Perhaps we need a new system for electing particular executives or discussing their appointment.") The working individual will have a greater concern with the success of the enterprise because his own earnings will depend upon that quite directly. Hitherto, the peasant never knew where he stood, except for what he had from his individual plot, and the worker's income depended almost entirely upon his

individual output or that of the work crew needed for the performance of a particular job. The enterprise as a whole could make or
lose money with negligible effect upon him personally, except for
actual cessation of flow of work to do. This is no longer the case
under the economic reform.

Soviet society will therefore become more homogeneous in the
sources of its value structure. This will be facilitated by the building
of a year-round rural and national road system, eliminating the present long isolation of the villages during the mud seasons, reflected in
authoritative advocacy of increased breeding of draft horses as late
as 1966. The 1966–1970 Five Year Plan specifies that its purpose
in doubling production of television sets is to help reduce the cultural gap between town and country, and the figures indicate that by
1975 everyone will have TV. It must be remembered that Soviet
broadcasting is approximately of the nature of American educational
TV: duller than commercial, but not centered on dehumanizing violence and sexual escapism. It fully deserves classification as a cultural medium.

The same date, 1975, will also witness the attainment within the
four walls of the home of the living standard Americans have found
desirable in terms of major appliances: refrigerator, washing machine, and vacuum cleaner, in addition to TV. It is these things that
free the woman's hands and time, and bring the world to her mind
more fully than media relying solely on the word: radio and printed
matter. Lacking them, and given the cultural tradition of male non-
cooperation in the home, the equality with men guaranteed to Soviet
women by law has proved incapable of eliminating the age-old gap.
The remarkably higher level of female achievement in the U.S.S.R.
than in any nonsocialist country (three fourths of the physicians, two
thirds of the teachers, more than half the economists and statisticians, two fifths of the agricultural experts and veterinarians, one
third of the lawyers and judges, and three tenths of the engineers
are women) is, in the face of the physical difficulties of shopping and
housework, an amazing demonstration both of women's tenacity and
capacity, and of the human consequences of virtually eliminating
discrimination by sex. But women are still rare at the very highest
levels: women heads of medical schools yes, women in the Academy
of Medical Sciences very few; women in the cabinets of republics
yes, in the Politburo of the Communist Party—the effective U.S.S.R.

cabinet—not one, and exceedingly few in the effective parliament, the Party Central Committee.

It is hard to see how full actual equality can fail to eventuate in the U.S.S.R. by the turn of the century, given the existing legal equality, women's record of accomplishment in the face of present physical and traditional cultural handicaps, and the elimination of the physical difficulties of housekeeping in the next decade or two. The cultural handicaps of supremacist attitudes on the part of men, and of real feelings of inferiority or lack of confidence on the part of women, will not disappear of themselves, but we have said a good deal to indicate that those whose moral lead is followed even by large numbers of today's youth have strong feelings on this. Perhaps there is no better single indication than the fact that there are so many women poets of high general popularity, from the late Anna Akhmatova to Bella Akhmadulina of the Yevtushenko-Voznesensky generation.

Given a living standard equal to that of America at the same time (the private car is on its way, and ample modern housing, constituting the most serious lack today, will be universal by the turn of the century: the U.S.S.R. produces more cement, window glass, and lumber than the United States even today),[12] what will then happen to Soviet society?

Children born in 1954 and thereafter will all have a complete secondary education, equal to junior college here. We have already spoken of the peasantry and of women. At the beginning of this chapter we quoted a British professor forty years resident in Czarist Russia, whose attitude toward Lenin in 1918 was expressed thus: "In the Bolshevik movement there is not a vestige of a constructive or social idea." Ten years later, this same Dr. Dillon revisited the country, and was utterly astounded: "The Bolsheviks then have accomplished . . . more than seemed attainable by any human or-

---

[12] A. Allen Bates, Chief, Division of Building-Research, National Bureau of Standards, headed technical exchange delegations to the U.S.S.R. in 1960 and 1965. He reported in the *Journal of the American Concrete Institute* (August 1966): "Having lived very extensively around the world, I must say in all frankness I have never seen any other society change and improve as much in any five years as did the Russian from 1960 to 1965. . . . I have never seen in all my years of traveling as much accomplished in providing shelter as has been done in the Soviet Union in the five years between visits. The same could be said with regard to food distribution."

ganization under the adverse conditions with which they had to cope." On a problem racking the rest of the world to this day, he observed: "Their way of dealing with home rule and the nationalities is a masterpiece of ingenuity and elegance. None of the able statesmen of today in other lands has attempted to vie with them in their method of satisfying the claims of minorities."

While women are not represented in the ruling Politburo, non-Russian nationalities are present in force among its nineteen members. The Uzbek Rashidov, coming from a people with an ancient urban tradition who gained representation on that body years ago, was joined after the Twenty-third Party Congress by a second Asian, the Kazakh Kunayev, whose people were actually nomads only thirty-five years ago. Two other members, a Georgian and a Latvian, also come from peoples whose languages bear no relation to Russian whatever. Five more are Ukrainian and Byelorussian, members of Slavic peoples held inferior to the Russians under Czarism.

Although obstacles that we have discussed remain in the path of women, the record with regard to ethnic minorities speaks for itself. The problem of some discrimination against Jewish culture and that of residual anti-Semitism in the population has been mentioned. It would be unfair not to note that the Jews constitute one percent of the population, while similar problems of discrimination and bias with respect to the other non-Russians comprising nearly half the Soviet population have been eliminated for all practical purposes. The results achieved in the Soviet Union are similar to those sought in the United States by the program encompassed in the term "black power." What remains is for peoples completely preindustrial before the Revolution and for fifteen years after it to close the gap between them and the developed Russians in science, engineering, management, highly skilled labor, and to overcome in rural areas the residue of the exceptional oppression of women in Moslem cultures.

In every sphere of significant mass-scale differences in status among human beings—education, urbanization, sexual and ethnic equality—the Soviet Union will be a vastly more homogeneous country a generation hence than it is today. Except for urbanization, it is already more homogeneous, that is, less conflict-prone than any other. Dozens of conversations with individuals and random groups, urban and rural, young and old, in Moscow, Leningrad, the Ukraine, and along the Don and Volga, in the summer of 1966, turned up two expressions of discontent couched in extreme political terms, but the overall impression was one of a simple absence of social tensions. The feeling was one of calm, resting on the conviction that one could plan one's own life, and that the society would help rather than hinder the realization of such plans.

In all spheres, including urbanization, social mobility is without parallel, social stratification least. The majority of the men who rule the U.S.S.R. today (65 percent) come from the most poverty-stricken, downtrodden, and illiterate section of the peasantry. Thirty percent were born into the families of industrial workers in Czarist Russia. Only 5 percent are the children of white-collar people of any kind.[13]

There is nothing in the Soviet Union like the range from people sleeping in doorways to others who have one mansion in Hyannis Port, another in Florida, a $40,000-a-year Manhattan penthouse, a ranch in the West and a home on the Riviera. (It is not only derelicts who sleep in doorways in the United States. *The New York Times* (May 28, 1965) reported: "typical cases; that of the 40-year-old mother who slept with her four children for several nights in tenement hallways after the local welfare office refused emergency assistance.") *No* Soviet industrial "tycoon," including the man who heads the steel industry, bigger than U.S. Steel, nor the head of the petroleum industry, bigger than Standard Oil, nor the head of the merchant fleet, bigger than Niarchos' or Onassis', earns even $15,000 a year, although that is no money at all by the standards of the wealthy in underdeveloped, poverty-stricken countries like India or even Ghana. Nor does any Soviet Party or government official, including the premier, earn that much. Nor does any movie star. A handful of the most creative people do: a few authors, some scientists, and musicians and dancers who perform abroad.

The *entire* Soviet population will be well above that level a century after the Revolution, fifty years hence, given the present rate of rise in living standard and continuing employment of both husband and wife (five hours a day, then?). Considering the virtually complete social homogeneity that can reasonably be expected, and the fact that even today the publicly accepted assumption there is

[13] See Grey Hodnett in *Slavic Review* (December 1965), p. 643, table 4, and footnote 20.

that communism would constitute the good society (receiving what one needs rather than being paid, and working conscientiously as a matter of course), it is difficult to see why communism should not come to be. A vacationing clothing worker on a Black Sea vessel told me in 1959 with naïve optimism: "We're on the very verge of communism." A peasant-faced ten-year-old in a small town in 1962 asked: "Is the American people planning to build communism?" A youth outside my Kiev hotel in 1966 said: "But you can't get to communism on moral incentives alone" to the nodding approval of assembled passersby; and a state-farm worker on the Volga peered into a more distant future: "But when we get to communism, that won't be the end of human development."

Approximately twenty-five years from now, there will be a generation of youth for which affluence by Soviet standards (and by American standards of today) will be a fact. That generation will be repelled by the aspects of business morality resulting from the present economic reform, however limited that effect may be. The government of that day will consist of people of the generation that produced both Yevtushenko and the present head of the Komsomol. This extreme conservative, Sergei Pavlov, represents the simple inability to comprehend freedom of speech and of the press, and the hostility to it, that one might expect in a country that had no chance to become accustomed to anything but absolute monarchy until 1953, and whose recent historical experience contains much that fits the stereotypes of those who think of it as a besieged fortress. There is a marked distinction between the Yevtushenko-Voznesensky generation, now between thirty and forty, which remembers the Stalin era and the impact of Khrushchev's speech, and today's youth, which has never known the fear of concentration camps, or disillusionment, and displays no active interest in any structural movement to prevent the return of those days, which it simply assumes to be gone forever.

In the Soviet Union, the struggle for political freedom and civil liberties necessarily will essentially have occurred between now and the time the split Yevtushenko-Pavlov generation comes to power.

A new factor has been introduced into the prospects of Soviet internal development by the truly epochal agreement between the U.S.S.R. and France reached in 1966. In the words of Premier Kosygin's Paris television address, Dec. 8, 1966:

For the first time two great powers . . . belonging to different social systems . . . have resolutely decided to place their relations on a firm basis . . . The rapprochement between our countries is not of a temporary nature; it is not determined by certain temporary subjective factors [de Gaulle] . . . Our countries can develop individual lines of production and even whole branches of the economy whose output they can supply to one another over a long period of time. During the talks we have agreed on how to begin this important work.

The aircraft and television industries were the first to be affected, with joint space exploration discussed, and a Soviet gas pipeline to France proposed. Mr. Kosygin made a similar proposal to Britain during his visit there two months later, subject to British abandonment of the U.S. alliance, as France had left NATO. He made clear that Soviet policy aimed ultimately at involving all Europe, under the same conditions.

This coordinated economic planning with a non-socialist country, even if limited only to France for some years, will involve mass-scale personal contacts and travel outside the U.S.S.R. on a level utterly without precedent. It will destroy the basis for the xenophobia of such as Pavlov, who worried at the Twenty-third Congress about corruption of Soviet youth by travel even to East European countries. It will put Russians into intimate contact with a civilization in which cultural experimentation and political dissent are deep-rooted traditions. The influences will run both ways. The fact that French per capita production of electricity is no higher than that of the U.S.S.R., while French urban life is more modern, would suggest that, in certain respects, peasant life would have to be more primitive. A team of 50 British engineers who spent 3 months in Moscow on the design of a polyester plant in 1966–1967 had to adjust to the fact that three-fourths of the Soviet engineers with whom they worked were women.

The sociological consequences of such contacts upon the non-Soviet partners are beyond the scope of this essay. But in the U.S.S.R. they will certainly favor the Yevtushenkos over the Pavlovs, particularly in the critical category of technological and managerial intelligentsia among whom direct contacts will be greatest. But French films are already reaching mass audiences in the U.S.S.R. On the other hand, there was evidence from the very first days of the Brezhnev-Kosygin administration in October 1964 that it would seek stability for its foreign policy by basing it upon countries where Communist parties are strong, such as France, and where internal pressures could therefore be counted upon to uphold long-term agreements with the U.S.S.R. once arrived at. It was from this strengthened international power base that Moscow would negotiate with the U.S. and West Germany.

Just how the young Soviet activists of the 1990s will propose to change an economy based on an interplay of self-interest and group interest[14] to one based on true love of brothers cannot be predicted. Perhaps the reward economy actually will be drowned out by a constant rise in the proportion of goods and services distributed free, as projected by the Party program of 1961. Perhaps—in all seriousness —Soviet science fiction, already probing and philosophical, will begin to give us speculative hints. In any case, one must not underrate the long-term effects of the psychological change that has already occurred, in which Soviet people have become noticeably more socially (outer) oriented than people living under capitalism.[15] Nor should one overestimate the time required for the pluralist, consensual, participatory working of Soviet society to restore the level of freedom existing in Lenin's lifetime.[16] This it does by outweighing leaders raised in Stalin's Czarist style of operation. As this goes to press, the *New York Times'* Harrison Salisbury reports from Moscow that Pasternak's *Doctor Zhivago* is to be published there, that the recently-confined poet Iosif Brosky is working freely in Leningrad, and that the freeing of Sinyavsky and Daniel was expected within 3 or 4 months. Most important, he writes that "most of the figures prominent in the attacks on Pasternak have now been de-

---

[14] Consciously recognized in the U.S.S.R. as one of the "dialectical contradictions" through which Marxists believe all progress to occur. See article by M. B. Mitin in translation journal, *Soviet Studies in Philosophy*, Spring, 1967.

[15] The degree to which this does—and does not—apply to the significant peasant fourth of the population emerges in a contemporary study, *The Peasants of Central Russia* by S. P. and E. Dunn (New York: Holt, Rinehart & Winston, 1967).

[16] See *Russia In 1919*, by Arthur Ransome (New York: Huebsch, 1919). This is a forgotten classic ranking with John Reed's *Ten Days That Shook the World*, and demands republication.

prived of major political power, including almost all the leading figures in the Komsomol-state security group of that period." (*San Francisco Chronicle,* Aug. 6, 1967). Without their backing the Pavlovs are powerless.

VII

The U.S.S.R. in World Affairs: An Historic Survey of Soviet Foreign Policy

by FREDERICK L. SCHUMAN

Homo Sapiens—or, as Aristotle preferred to call him, "the political animal"—has from time immemorial achieved peace with his neighbors by uniting them in fear, suspicion, and hatred of strangers, aliens, and enemies across frontiers. This age-old pattern, despite high hopes to the contrary, was no more changed by the Russian Revolution of half a century ago than by Woodrow Wilson's crusade to "make the world safe for democracy" and win "the war to end war." The old Adam is still with us, even though his persistence in the thermonuclear age threatens disaster and possible suicide for all mankind.

Lenin once observed, in a comment quoted thousands of times in the American press:

> We are living not merely in a State, but in a *system of States;* and it is inconceivable that the Soviet republic should continue to

exist for a long period side by side with imperialist States. Ultimately one or the other must conquer. Until this end occurs a number of terrible clashes between the Soviet republic and bourgeois States is inevitable.

Winston Churchill later said:

> I could not help being charmed by Signor Mussolini's gentle and simple bearing and by his calm, detached poise in spite of so many burdens and dangers. . . . If I had been an Italian I am sure that I should have been whole-heartedly with you from the start to the finish in your triumphant struggle against the bestial appetites and passions of Leninism. . . . Your movement has rendered a service to the whole world. . . . Italy has shown that there is a way of fighting the subversive forces which can rally the masses of the people, properly led, to value and wish to defend the honor and stability of civilized society. She has provided the necessary antidote to the Russian poison. Hereafter no great nation will go unprovided with an ultimate means of protection against the cancerous growth of Bolshevism.

Both Lenin and Churchill subsequently changed their minds, thus displaying a capacity unique to great statesmen. Lenin's words were uttered at Party Congress VIII in March of 1919 when American and Allied armies and navies were invading and blockading Russia and subsidizing the counter-revolutionary White Armies of Kolchak, Denikin, and Yudenitch in hope of destroying the Soviet regime. By 1921, when the Red Army had prevailed in a land reduced to ruin and famine by seven years of warfare, Lenin saw hope in "coexistence."

Churchill's words were spoken in Rome, January 20, 1927, when he, among many others, mistakenly believed that the salvation of "Western Civilization" was to be had by an alliance of the democracies with Fascism for "defense" against Communism. The result was World War II.

These fantasies of long ago are still with us. Whether the result will be World War III, which will indeed be "the war to end war," still remains to be decided. Meanwhile, what can usefully be said in brief compass regarding the foreign policies of the men of Moscow over the past half century?

Four Options

The first thing to be said is that the Muscovite policy-makers, despite their Marxist messianic visions of a world reborn, have been obliged to live in a State System whose sovereign members are competitors for power, one with another, in a context of international anarchy. Under these circumstances each sovereignty is, of necessity, insecure (Russians most of all in view of their long and tragic history of invasions and interventions by alien foes usually possessed of superior technology and military might) and the quest for security, albeit futile in such a State System, becomes the central concern and even obsession of those responsible for national decisions.

How to seek security? Only four choices have emerged in centuries and millennia of human experience. One is "Security by Supremacy"—that is, the imposition by a major Power of its authority on all its neighbors and rivals, eventuating in a Universal Empire or World State in which the game is ended. No Power has ever succeeded in arriving at this goal since the Romans of ancient days. A second option is "Security by Balance"—a quest for non-involvement when other Powers are so poised against one another that no power can threaten all the rest; for example, United States foreign policy during 1815–1914, and again in the 1920s and the 1930s. A third option is "Security by Coalition"—a quest for allies among less dangerous rival Powers against more dangerous rival Powers to the end that the more dangerous rivals may be checkmated by the united action of the less dangerous. The fourth and final option is an attempt to play the role of *Tertius Gaudens* or "Happy Third," whereby policy-makers foster war among rivals in the hope of non-involvement and neutrality.[1]

[1] On June 24, 1941, Senator Harry S Truman declared: "If we see that Germany is winning we ought to help Russia and if Russia is winning we ought to help Germany and in that way let them kill as many as possible. . . ." This same conception was expressed in a now forgotten anecdote of World War II. Churchill, Hitler, and Stalin all die on the same day and go to Heaven. Saint Peter tells them that because of their great services below each will be granted one worldly wish. Hitler: "My wish is that all the Russians should be exterminated." Stalin: "My wish is that all the Germans should be exterminated." Churchill: "Are you going to grant their wishes?" Saint Peter: "Yes." Churchill: "In that case, I will settle for a Scotch and Soda."

Chapters of Change

The decisions of Soviet policy-makers over half a century have oscil-
lated among these options—since there are no others, pending the
obviously improbable agreement of mankind to replace the State
System of international anarchy by some form of world government.
At the outset, 1917–21, Lenin sought Security by Supremacy through
world revolution. The Allied and Associated Powers sought the same
goal through the destruction of the Soviet regime. Both failed. The
Allied coalition fell apart and gave up the struggle. The Communist
International, founded in Moscow in 1919 as the "General Staff of
the World Revolution," proved wholly incapable of achieving its
purpose. The short-lived Communist regimes in Bavaria and Hungary in the spring of 1919 were soon suppressed. Following the
Polish invasion of the Ukraine in April 1920, the Red Army swept
into Poland amid high hopes of carrying the revolution into Central
Europe, but was halted and driven back before the gates of Warsaw
in August. The armistice of November was followed in March 1921
by the Treaty of Riga, which coincided in point of time with British
recognition of the Soviet regime, the first Anglo-Soviet trade agreement, and the adoption of the New Economic Policy. With the
postwar "stabilization of capitalism," the prospects for further
"proletarian revolution" rapidly waned. Government by Communists remained limited to Russia.

In this context the Comintern had no meaningful function save
as a source of revolutionary rhetoric. Its Seventh Congress met in
Moscow in 1935 and turned out to be the last. The organization itself was formally dissolved in 1943 as a gesture of inter-Allied unity.
The later organization of European Communist Parties in the Communist Information Bureau, or Cominform, was abandoned in 1956
as a means of placating Tito. No subsequent effort was made to
unite the Communist Parties of the world in any effective global or
even regional organization. By the middle of the 1960s all Communists, to their astonishment, had become nationalists and were
quarreling among themselves, with all thought of world unity through
universal revolution postponed to the Greek *Kalends*.[2]

[2] Pages 209–220 following are reprinted, with slight changes, from pp.
154–166 of *Government in the Soviet Union* by Frederick L. Schuman (New

The fluctuating foreign policy of the U.S.S.R. during the past five decades can be rendered intelligible, as can those of other Powers, by reference to the options suggested above—always bearing in mind that policy-makers, like other humans, are fallible and capable of mistakes of calculation, with results, in a State System based on the assumption of violence, which are often tragic. The history of Soviet diplomacy is readily available in many other books and is no part of our present task. The record may, nevertheless, be usefully reviewed in outline within the context already indicated.

In 1922, at Genoa, Soviet and Western delegates strove without success to negotiate a settlement of financial claims and counterclaims. Georgi Chicherin and Walter Rathenau made use of the occasion to sign the Treaty of Rapallo (April 16, 1922), whereby Moscow and Berlin canceled all claims against one another, entered into full diplomatic and commercial relations, and embarked upon a decade of German-Russian political and even military collaboration between outcasts against the dominant French bloc on the Continent.

In the 1920s and early 1930s both the U.S.S.R. and the United States, in their several ways, were committed to Security by Balance, thanks to the stability of relationships among other Powers in Europe and Asia. But there was no collaboration between them in the absence of American recognition—not accorded until November 16, 1933. Soviet policy, unlike its American counterpart, was by no means strictly "isolationist." The *Narkomindel* (People's Commissariat for Foreign Affairs), directed by Chicherin and subsequently by the wily Maxim Litvinov, sought safety by concluding bilateral non-aggression and neutrality pacts designed to localize any conflicts which might occur and by championing disarmament and the outlawry of war.

The U.S.S.R. was the first Great Power to ratify the Kellogg-Briand Pact of Paris of 1928 for renunciation of war as an instrument of national policy—and the first Great Power to espouse, at Geneva in 1927 and thereafter, complete and universal disarmament

York: Crowell, 1961). Copyright © 1961 by Thomas Y. Crowell Company, reprinted by permission. The author is grateful to the publisher and to Professor Arnold A. Rogow of Stanford University, editor of the Crowell Comparative Government Series, for permission to include this passage in the present work.

(with tongue in cheek in the certain knowledge that the "bourgeois States" would never assent). These hopes of the 1920s came to nothing, thanks to gross mismanagement of human affairs in Russia and the West alike. This period of Soviet foreign policy reached its culmination in the signature of non-aggression and neutrality pacts with Poland (July 25, 1932) and with France (November 29, 1932) and with Litvinov's signature in early July, 1933, at the otherwise abortive London Economic Conference, of bilateral accords with most of Russia's neighboring states, plus some others, defining and renouncing "aggression."

Toward the Abyss

All these bright words were soon to be reduced to waste paper. They took no cognizance of the realities of power politics in a State System of rival sovereignties nor of the need of somehow bringing into being some semblance of World Federal Government as a substitute for the traditional imperatives of *Realpolitik*. The wasted opportunities of the 1920s were doubly or trebly wasted anew during the dark decade of the 1930s.

The earlier Soviet formula for safety served Soviet interests well so long as other Powers were balanced in a more or less stable equilibrium. The pre-condition vanished with the advent of the Great Depression. The New York stock market crash in the fall of 1929 was soon followed by economic stagnation, mass unemployment for workers, mass bankruptcy for businessmen and farmers, and mass misery and desperation for scores of millions of people in all the "capitalist" economies of the world. This *débâcle* was mistaken in Moscow for a vindication of the Marxist prognosis. New images of proletarian revolution loomed up. But such dreams remained dreams. The major political result of the Great Depression was the coming to power in Japan (1930 f.) and in Germany (1933 f.) of local imitators of the Italian Fascists of the 1920s. The new Caesars "solved" all social problems, in corrupt cooperation with industrialists, aristocrats, and the demented masses of the lower middle classes, by preaching a crusade to "save civilization from Communism," to the tune of massive rearmament, military adventures, and open preparations to take over the world from the faltering hands of the Western democracies.

Hitler in *Mein Kampf* had made it crystal clear that his projected path to world power must lead not only to the subjugation of the West but to the destruction and partition of the U.S.S.R. His prospective allies, Mussolini's Blackshirts and the militarists of Nippon, were similarly oriented. In the 1930s, as in the 1960s, in the minds of millions of muddle-headed people in the democracies, anti-Communism was a badge of impeccable respectability—in the name of which sundry lunacies, outrages, and crimes (up to a point) could be condoned and even applauded. The madmen of Berlin, Tokyo, and Rome therefore cloaked their conspiracy from the outset in the garb of the "Anti-Comintern" Pact of November 25, 1936, and shouted daily that their only ultimate objective was "the destruction of Bolshevism." In the face of an ever-mounting menace, Moscow's response was an abrupt abandonment of its previous pattern of policy, a rapid build-up of armed forces, and a search for Security by Coalition.

In the course of the quest, Soviet diplomacy and Communist Parties achieved successes which, had they not later been undone, might well have averted World War II. Anti-Fascist "Popular Front" coalitions won elections in Spain in February and in France in April and May of 1936. Meanwhile the U.S.S.R. joined the League of Nations (September 18, 1934)—from which Japan (March 27, 1933), Germany (October 14, 1933), and Italy (December 11, 1937) withdrew—and concluded military alliances, in the guise of pacts to uphold Arts. 10 and 16 of the League Covenant, with France (May 2, 1935) and Czechoslovakia (May 16, 1935). France was allied with Britain, Belgium, Poland, and the "Little Entente" of Czechoslovakia, Rumania, and Jugoslavia. The United States was paralyzed by "isolationism," reflected in the "neutrality" laws of 1935–39 which, in the name of keeping America out of "other people's wars," helped to make the world safe for aggression. But the new Grand Alliance had overwhelming power at its disposal to "deter" and "contain" Fascist ambitions of world hegemony.

How and why all of this was thrown away, with resultant tragedy for all mankind, is a problem of human irrationality and political miscalculation which men may debate, inconclusively, from now until doomsday. In any case it is clear from the record that the men of Moscow, despite their many mistakes before and after the advent of disaster, bore no responsibility for impending catastrophe during the middle 1930s. Year after year Litvinov's eloquent voice at Geneva pleaded for "collective security" and the solidarity of the U.S.S.R. and the Western democracies in resisting Fascist aggression. Year after year policy-makers in London and Paris rejected all proposals for collective action, acquiesced in Fascist aggression, and finally brought their nations to the brink of ruin. Their motives were mixed, as all human motives are mixed. Some, dreading war, sought peace by "appeasement" of the Caesars. Others hoped that the Western Powers could play the role of *Tertius Gaudens* in the war to come, while Hitler's Germany and Tojo's Japan assaulted the U.S.S.R. All were mistaken in their evaluation of the Fascist threat. All feared and distrusted the U.S.S.R. more than they distrusted and feared the Fascist dictators—which attitude in the end was fully reciprocated by Stalin's policy-makers in Moscow, with ghastly results for all concerned.

Only a few highlights need be noted in the mad diplomacy of the wasted years. Japan's warlords seized Manchuria in September of 1931 and subsequently made military probes into Mongolia and Soviet Siberia. Moscow and Peiping pleaded for international action, through the League of Nations, against aggression. London and Paris refused. Washington was impotent. In 1937 Tokyo's militarists launched an all-out assault on Chiang Kai-shek's China. Pleas for help evoked no response in Western capitals. Moscow extended limited aid to China and beat back Japanese incursions in a series of border battles. Meanwhile, Hitler (March 16, 1935) repudiated Part V of the Treaty of Versailles, providing for German disarmament, and reintroduced military conscription in the Nazi Reich. Moscow urged action. London and Paris did nothing beyond diplomatic protests. In October, 1935, Mussolini ordered his armies to conquer Ethiopia. Moscow urged action. London and Paris, behind a hypocritical façade of League "sanctions," did nothing, wrecked the League, and finally accepted the Fascist conquest. Hitler (March 7, 1936) abrogated the Locarno treaties and began the remilitarization of the Rhineland, thereby making impossible any defense by France of its Eastern allies. Moscow urged action. Paris and London did nothing.

The rest of the tragedy was destined to unroll with the inexorability of a Greek drama. Franco, massively aided by Hitler and Mussolini, undertook the overthrow by armed violence of the Spanish Republic in mid-summer of 1936. Moscow extended help to the Loyalists and pleaded once more for concerted action against aggression. London and Paris, in the name of "non-intervention," connived in the Fascist conquest of Spain, as did Washington in the name of "neutrality." When Hitler ordered his *Wehrmacht* to invade, occupy, and annex Austria (March 12, 1938), the pattern was repeated. By the following summer Neville Chamberlain was thrice flying to Germany—on the principle: "If you don't concede the first time, fly, fly again"—for the purpose of helping Hitler, in the name of "peace," to destroy Czechoslovakia. Moscow proposed common action and offered to defend Czechoslovakia, by war if need be, if the Western Powers would cooperate. Chamberlain and Halifax, Daladier and Bonnet, went instead to Munich and signed the "Peace" settlement of October 1, 1938, whereby Hitler was authorized to annex the Sudetenland, containing all the Czech border fortifications, and to reduce what was left of Czechoslovakia to helplessness. Chamberlain and Halifax signed a neutrality and non-aggression pact with Hitler, October 1. Daladier and Bonnet did likewise in Paris, December 6, 1938.

With the League Covenant and the Grand Alliance treaties all thus cast to the winds while the Fascist Caesars triumphantly rode "the wave of the future," the men of Moscow were obliged to reconsider their course—as Stalin indicated to Congress XVIII in his address of March 10, 1939, denouncing the Western "appeasers" and "Munichmen." Four days later Hitler occupied Prague and extinguished the remnant of Czechoslovakia. Subsequent British efforts to negotiate a new alliance with the U.S.S.R. came to nothing. Western policy-makers so deeply feared and distrusted Communists, who fully reciprocated their sentiments, that the common menace of Fascist aggression, threatening all with destruction, was insufficient to reconstruct the Great Coalition which had so rashly been thrown away. London refused to pay Moscow's price for an alliance: a joint guarantee of Finland, Estonia, Latvia, Lithuania, Poland, and Rumania—none of which desired any such guarantee and all of which dreaded the prospect of being defended by the Red Army. Moscow refused to conclude an alliance on any other terms.

Since Hitler and Ribbentrop were quite prepared to pay a price for Soviet neutrality which Anglo-French leaders were unwilling to pay for an alliance, Stalin and Molotov, in an abrupt reversal of course, abandoned Security by Coalition in favor of the role of *Tertius Gaudens,* thus out-Chamberlaining Chamberlain—with equally dismal results. The Nazi-Soviet Non-Aggression and Neutrality Pact of August 23, 1939, contained a secret protocol contemplating a new partition of Poland and the division of Eastern Europe into German and Soviet spheres of influence. But contrary to contemporary judgments, oft repeated since, the Nazi *Blitzkrieg* against Poland, launched on September 1, was not the consequence of the Nazi-Soviet pact since, as is now known, the decision had secretly been reached and even the date had been set by Hitler and his aides in April of 1939. The pact was the consequence of the decision, and of almost certain Soviet knowledge of the decision, not *vice versa.*

Inferno

The miseries and horrors which engulfed most of the human race, including above all the U.S.S.R., in the wake of the follies which have been reviewed are well known and have been recounted in detail in other places: how the Kremlin sent troops into eastern Poland in mid-September; imposed protectorates on Estonia, Latvia, and Lithuania and, in violation of its own solemn treaty obligations, waged the "winter war" on Finland (with Britain and France absurdly threatening to fight the Soviet Union instead of the Nazi Reich) and, in March, 1940, imposed peace terms and frontier changes designed, like other Soviet moves of 1939–41, to bolster defenses against Hitler; how the "phony war" gave way in the frightful spring of 1940 to further *Blitzkrieg,* with the invincible *Wehrmacht* conquering Denmark, Norway, the Low Countries, and France—as Mussolini entered the conflict for the "kill"; how the United States awakened in alarm from its isolationist dream, extended aid to Britain, and soon embarked on "lend-lease" assistance to all of Hitler's foes; how the U.S.S.R. in alarm annexed Estonia, Latvia, and Lithuania along with Bessarabia and Northern Bukovina while seeking continued peace with the triumphant Reich; how Hitler in 1940, like Bonaparte in 1811, having lost his "Battle of Britain," decided to conquer Russia; how the assault was delayed in the spring of 1941 as the *Wehrmacht* troops entered Hungary and Rumania and struck down Jugoslavia and Greece; and how all the combined armies of Fascist Europe hurled themselves against the Soviet Union on June 22, 1941, in the most savage, deadly, and destructive invasion in the history of modern warfare.

Security by Coalition now became, almost too late, the price of survival. The U.S.S.R., like the United States after Pearl Harbor, was forced by enemy attack to become the full ally of Britain in a new Grand Alliance. Prospects remained dark in 1941–42. Moscow had contracted out of war in the Far East, as Japan contracted out of Hitler's crusade against Russia, in the Soviet-Japanese neutrality and non-aggression pact of April 13, 1941. In all other respects almost all the world was at war in a far-flung combat for mastery of the planet between the Fascist Triplice and the "United Nations" —most of whose lesser members in 1942 were "governments-in-exile." The *Wehrmacht,* having destroyed or dispersed all the Soviet armies in its path, reached the outskirts of Moscow by December, 1941. But here, for the first time, Hitler's hosts were halted and driven back by new Russian armies defending the Motherland. By mid-summer of 1942, however, Japanese forces had overrun much of China, all of Southeastern Asia and Indonesia, and all of the islands of the Western Pacific, while the armies of the European Axis were threatening Egypt and had reached the Caucasus and the Volga in another victory march—soon to be accompanied by the most hideous atrocities in all the record of human brutality as the Nazi psychopaths undertook the systematic extermination of all Jews and most Slavs who had fallen into their power.

In the sequel we must confine our attention—amid a global phantasmagoria of Fascist insanity, heroic underground resistance in the occupied lands, and massive battles between the largest armies of all time—to the pattern of Grand Strategy which was to determine the shape of the post-war world. Despite pledges and promises and urgent appeals from Moscow, Britain and the United States were unable or unwilling to open any effective "second front" against the Reich in the West until the Normandy landings of June, 1944. The North African and Italian campaign of 1942–43, albeit clearing the Maghreb of the foe and bringing Sicily and southern Italy under Allied occupation, offered no meaningful relief to the hard-pressed defenders of the U.S.S.R. Even American lend-lease supplies to the Soviet Union, ultimately totaling $11,000,000,000, still remained a trickle in 1942 and most of 1943. Russia's fighters

—who, in Churchill's phrase, "did the main work of tearing the guts out of the German army"—were long obliged to rely for victory on their own valor and on the output of the Soviet war industries. Both were to prove equal to the needs of a time of desperation.

The turning point of the war in Europe was the savage and protracted Battle of Stalingrad, beginning in August of 1942 and ending with the final surrender (February 1, 1943) of the wretched survivors of Von Paulus's encircled Sixth Army. Henceforth the hitherto unconquerable *Wehrmacht* was to suffer defeat after defeat all across the Russian steppes, with Soviet forces finally overrunning Rumania, Bulgaria, and Hungary in late 1944, and, early in 1945, taking Warsaw, Vienna, Prague, and, at the end, Berlin—where Hitler and Eva Braun, setting the example for Goebbels and his family, committed suicide on April 30, 1945, a week before the unconditional surrender of the shattered defenders of a now defunct Reich.

Churchill had hoped that Anglo-American forces might liberate the Balkans and much of Central Europe before the arrival of the Russians. Washington vetoed the project as militarily impossible. Making a virtue of necessity, Churchill and Eden journeyed to Moscow in October, 1944, and struck a bargain with Stalin and Molotov for a division of Southeastern Europe into "spheres," with Greece to be in the British zone, Bulgaria and Rumania in the Soviet zone, and influence to be shared in Hungary and Jugoslavia—all of which indeed came to pass, except for Hungary, in ways then unforeseen. Washington was shocked at such "immorality." The tangled tale of the Yalta (February, 1945) and Potsdam (July, 1945) "summit conferences," where vague formulas were bandied about, written ambiguously into solemn agreements, and given wholly different interpretations in Moscow, London, and Washington, cannot here be told. Let us only note that the Grand Strategy of the Great Coalition in World War II brought Russian troops and Russian power to the Adriatic, the Danube, and the Elbe.

Aftermath

The first question posed by the fall of the Third Reich and by the subsequent surrender of Japan (August 14, 1945) was the question of whether the U.S.S.R., the United States, and the United Kingdom could continue to cooperate in making a peace as they had cooperated in winning a war. By prior agreement at Yalta, the U.S.S.R. played a brief role in the defeat of Japan through a one-week *Blitzkrieg* into Manchuria, while the United States, not to be outdone by its enemies in the science of atrocity, initiated a new and ghastly era in the arts of war by the atomic bombing of Hiroshima (August 6) and Nagasaki (August 9). The first question was soon answered. Immediately after Japanese capitulation, London and Washington, perceiving that Stalin was resolved to impose Communist regimes on all the lands of Eastern Europe, Danubia, and Balkania north of Greece and to establish a *cordon sanitaire* in reverse against the West, began to challenge Soviet policy and to demand "democracy" and "self-determination" for the new Soviet "satellites," as allegedly pledged at Yalta and Potsdam.

The "Cold War" was thus begun. Its history is not our present concern, since here again the details of victories and defeats, advances and retreats, maneuvers and counter-maneuvers, calculations and miscalculations, are readily available in many other books. Its origin, however, is worthy of further comment. Soviet power was imposed on much of Eastern Europe, 1944–48, by virtue of Anglo-American incapacity to get there first. This disability, in turn, was due to the fruits of the "Peace" of Munich in 1938, for at Munich the Western statesmen not only betrayed Czechoslovakia but surrendered Eastern Europe to Hitler without quite knowing what they were doing. The results, as a few of us predicted at the time, would be either a Nazi-Soviet partition of Eastern Europe, Nazi control of Eastern Europe, or, in the event of the final collapse of the Third Reich, Communist control of Eastern Europe. All of these results materialized *seriatim* in the aftermath of Munich.

In world politics, as in other human affairs, decisions have consequences which are often irreversible. The Cold War began with Western efforts to reverse the consequences of Munich and with Soviet efforts to perpetuate, and capitalize upon, the consequences of Munich. Thus far, by the 1960s, Western attempts to "liberate" Eastern Europe and to "roll back" Soviet power to prewar frontiers have failed altogether of their purposes, while Soviet attempts to maintain the *status quo* of 1945 f. have been largely successful.

The global pattern of Cold War soon became, once more, the

age-old pattern of Security by Coalition in a temporarily bipolar world—in which, thanks to the advent of the thermonuclear age, old patterns and ancient assumptions of violence in international relations are wholly obsolete if the human race is to have any hope of survival. But all humans, Communists and anti-Communists alike, are creatures of habit who, in the face of new dangers, resort to old formulas because they lack sufficient imagination to devise new departures.

In the world following World War II, as in the world preceding World War II, mutual distrust, fear, and suspicion between the Marxist rulers of Russia and the policy-makers of the Western democracies were the dominant themes of their relationships. The Marxists of Moscow feared, with much reason, that the "bourgeois imperialists" of the West were resolved to rob them of the fruits of victory and, if possible, to suppress Communism all over the world and to destroy the Soviet regime in the U.S.S.R. itself. The leaders of the West feared, with much reason, that the "Communist imperialists" of the East were resolved to "take over the world" and to crush democracy, civil liberties, and private business enterprise all over the globe. Both fears, however justified by a selective compilation of supporting evidence, were unrealistic and, indeed, irrational in terms of the immense dangers to all concerned in action thus motivated by fear. But Twentieth-Century Man, as Spengler, Toynbee, and the psychoanalysts have long since pointed out, is less rational than non-rational or irrational and therefore seeks to solve new problems with old solutions.

The result was a new arms race of unprecedented magnitude, intensity, and peril and the emergence of two rival military coalitions, each determined to "deter" the other from "aggression" by accumulating thermonuclear weapons, and each quite capable of destroying the other utterly in any test of force. The West, led by the United States, began the game of "defense" and "deterrence" by seeking to prolong the short-lived American atomic monopoly, by ringing the U.S.S.R. with bombing bases in the name of "containment," by threatening "massive retaliation" (meaning the thermonuclear massacre of millions of people), and by concocting a series of anti-Soviet alliances. The sequence began with the Truman Doctrine of March, 1947, inspired by Soviet threats to Greece and Turkey, and the Marshall Plan of 1947 f., designed to restore the economies of

Western Europe. The sequence proceeded with NATO (April 4, 1949), following the Communist coup of February in Czechoslovakia and the unsuccessful Soviet blockade, 1948–49, of West Berlin; United States and United Nations defense of South Korea in June, 1950 f., against invasion from Communist North Korea; and an American treaty of peace and alliance with Japan (September 8, 1951), postulating Japanese rearmament against Russia; alliance agreements with the Philippine Republic (August 30, 1951) and with Australia and New Zealand (September 1, 1951); a treaty of peace and alliance with West Germany (May 26, 1952), postulating German rearmament against Russia; SEATO (September 6, 1954), embracing the United States, Britain, France, Australia, New Zealand, Pakistan, Thailand, and the Philippines; the Baghdad Pact of November 22, 1955 (Britain, Turkey, Iran, Iraq, and Pakistan), renamed CENTO when Iraq withdrew in 1958; alliance with Chiang Kai-shek on Formosa (proclaimed an American "protectorate" in June, 1950), December 2, 1954; and a whole series of other products of American "pactomania," designed to confront the Communist bloc with avowed enemies around all its frontiers in the name of defense of "freedom"—though many of the members of the Grand Alliance of the "Free World" had no knowledge of the meaning of the term.

Communist response to challenge (or counter-challenge) assumed a simpler and less ambitious form. Soviet policy-makers in the late 1940s contented themselves with bilateral security pacts with the Communist-controlled regimes of the European satellites. Stalin's miscalculations lost Jugoslavia to the Communist bloc in 1948 through the expulsion of the Jugoslav Party from the Cominform or Communist Information Bureau, a loose association, as successor to the Comintern (dissolved in 1943), of European Communist Parties. (The Cominform was dissolved in 1956 in an effort, only partially successful, to achieve a *détente* with Tito.) When the Chinese Communists, led by Mao Tse-tung, Chou En-lai, and Chu Teh, conquered China in 1948–49, contrary to Stalin's advice and expectations, most Americans, including Dean Rusk, avowed that Russia had "taken over" China, than which nothing could have been farther from the truth. Making the best of an unanticipated and not altogether welcome contingency, the policy-makers of the U.S.S.R. concluded an alliance (February 14, 1950) with Red Peking, and subsequently gave up Soviet privileges in Manchuria and granted economic and technical aid to their giant ally. Not until May 14, 1955, did Moscow consolidate its ties with its European satellites into the multilateral alliance treaty of the Warsaw Pact.

The complex and confused relationships between the two Great Coalitions, increasingly complicated by the emergence of more and more new nations in Africa and Asia committed to "neutralism," we must leave to other chroniclers and commentators. The "score" admits of no precise calculation. Since all the world is governed with little wisdom, each side has gained more from the mistakes and stupidities of the other than from any successful pursuit of its own purposes.

Thus Western prestige was enhanced by Stalin's vain attempt to overthrow Tito; by the 1953 riots in East Germany; by Khrushchev's "de-Stalinization" campaign, which contributed to bewilderment and defections among Communists elsewhere and to the Polish "revolution" of 1956, acquiesced in by Moscow, and to the Hungarian rebellion of 1956, brutally repressed by Soviet troops— albeit in the latter instance the United States also suffered "loss of face" by virtue of encouragement to the "freedom fighters" via the Voice of America and Radio Free Europe, followed by total inability to give them any aid without risking a world war. By the same token, Soviet prestige was enhanced by the success of American "cloak-and-dagger" operators in overthrowing the Leftist government of Guatemala in 1954, thus reviving hatred of "Yankee imperialism" throughout Latin America; by the incredible ineptitude of the Eisenhower Administration in dealing with the U-2 incident and the ensuing fiasco of the Paris "Summit" in May of 1960; and by the even more incredible ineptitude of the Kennedy Administration in launching the abortive anti-Castro invasion of Cuba in April of 1961. Both lists could be multiplied almost indefinitely from the record of the 1950s and early 1960s—with appropriate attention to Lebanon, Egypt, Formosa, Laos, the Congo, and all other areas of conflict.

Interlude

The most striking feature of world politics in the mid-1960s was the disintegration of the Grand Alliances of the 1950s. In the West,

De Gaulle, pursuing a vision of French glory and a Europe of sovereignties from the Atlantic to the Urals (whatever this phrase might mean), reduced NATO to a negation. In the East, the "Communist bloc" dissolved in the face of nationalistic rivalries between the men of Moscow and the men of Peking (and of Warsaw, Budapest, Belgrade, Bucharest), all rationalized in terms of divergent interpretations of the Marxist-Leninist gospels.

In the face of ever-mounting hostility, Moscow refused to aid Peking to become a nuclear power, withdrew its technical and scientific advisors from China, abandoned its program of economic assistance, and, more in grief than in wrath, strove for reconciliation. Successive conferences were fruitless. A "Declaration of 1957" and a "Statement of 1960" were said to have been repudiated and betrayed by Khrushchev's "revisionism." He was charged by Peking (1962) with "adventurism" and "capitulationism." The political downfall of the flamboyant Soviet Premier in mid-October, 1964 (coinciding by happenstance with the test explosion of China's first A-bomb) in favor of the more prosaic leadership of Alexei Kosygin and Leonid Brezhnev effected no change in Sino-Soviet recriminations. Khrushchev's enforced retirement, insofar as it was influenced by considerations of foreign policy, was less motivated by denunciations from Peking than by his flirtations with Bonn, whose leaders were regarded by most Russians as "revanchists" and "militarists," bent upon undoing the verdict of 1945.

The Kosygin-Brezhnev regime fared no better in Peking than its predecessor. By 1966, Red China was refusing to send even "observers" to Congress XXIII of the C.P.S.U. (March 29–April 8) and denouncing the new Soviet power-holders for more "revisionism" and for "collusion" with "American imperialism" to divide up the world in base betrayal of "revolutionary proletarian internationalism."

In this context, other things being equal, Moscow and Washington might have found common cause against Red China, which in the American image of the world had replaced Red Russia as the Devil. But other things were not equal. American and Soviet interests in Cuba came into conflict. In 1961 the newly elected President Kennedy initially followed advice about Cuba from the "experts," that is, the Pentagon, the Joint Chiefs of Staff, the C.I.A., and the State Department. The result was the Bay of Pigs fiasco of April,

1961. At his June meeting with Khrushchev in Vienna, Kennedy felt "threatened." Another "Berlin crisis" was marked by a vast increase in American spending on armaments and by resumption of nuclear testing in the atmosphere (U.S.S.R., September 1, 1961; United States, March 1, 1962). Moscow countered by making Castro's Cuba a Soviet protectorate. By autumn of 1962 renewed threats of an American invasion of Cuba led Khrushchev to install intermediate range ballistic missiles, regarded as "defensive" in Havana and Moscow, and as "offensive" in Washington. By the final week of October the United States and the U.S.S.R. were on the brink of thermonuclear war. Kennedy had by now learned not to trust the "experts," most of whom urged an air strike against the bases. He ordered instead a naval "quarantine" and insisted the Soviet missiles be removed.

Khrushchev yielded in a complex bargain. Moscow agreed to remove the missiles and to cease pressure on West Berlin. Washington agreed not to invade Cuba and to withdraw Jupiter missiles from Turkey. (The latter decision had already been made on the ground that the Jupiters were "obsolete.") The bargain led in turn to a major Soviet-American *détente,* manifested in Kennedy's plea for peace and understanding of June 10, 1963, at the American University, the "hot-line" accord, the limited test-ban treaty of July 23, 1963 (which Paris and Peking refused to sign), and further cultural exchanges.

Dilemma

Had President Kennedy not been slain in Dallas, November 22, 1963, it is conceivable, albeit not demonstrable, that the Kremlin's pursuit of "peaceful coexistence" might have led to an enlargement of the *détente* and to informal collaboration between Moscow and Washington, as a novel form of Security by Coalition, to checkmate or "contain" Red China. This was not to be. Following his over-whelming electoral victory over Barry Goldwater in November, 1964, President Lyndon Baines Johnson adopted the Goldwater foreign policy and yielded to the pressures of the "military-industrial complex" against which President Eisenhower had warned in his Farewell Address of January 17, 1961. In the name of anti-

Communism, Washington had armed India and Pakistan—which used the arms against one another in the Kashmir War of August– September, 1965. At the UN, Washington and Moscow joined forces in pressing for a cease-fire. Soviet mediation led to a conference in Tashkent in January, 1966, whereby Karachi and New Delhi agreed to refrain from further hostilities.

Far graver from the perspective of Foreign Minister Andrei Gromyko was Johnson's decision, in the name of anti-Communism, to occupy the Dominican Republic (April, 1965) and to embark upon massive warfare against the National Liberation Front of South Vietnam. What De Gaulle described as an "idiotic" and "absurd" war was still under way, inconclusively, during 1967.

These American adventures, regarded throughout much of the world as manifestations of militarism and neo-colonialism, seemed to vindicate Peking's contention that "peaceful coexistence" with "American imperialism" was an impossibility. Faced with a grim impasse, the men of Moscow championed "wars of liberation," sent arms and other aid to Hanoi, and yet strove to avoid another open confrontation with the United States. Given the prospect of a Chinese-American clash, the Kremlin might honor the Sino-Soviet alliance treaty of February 14, 1950, and thus risk World War III; or, despite the treaty, once more seek Security by Balance; or, *in extremis,* contemplate the dangerous role of "Happy Third." Which option would be deemed to serve Soviet interests best was unclear on the eve of the fiftieth year after the October Revolution.

Let us now turn to a broader consideration of the basic assumptions about foreign policy and international relations entertained by the leaders of the C.P.S.U. These assumptions, not significantly modified by Congress XXIII in 1966, were embodied in the Third Program of the Party, adopted at Congress XXII in October, 1961. The comments that follow will be limited to issues of war and peace and world affairs. They may, I hope, throw light on the merits and defects of the way in which the rulers of this gigantic realm look upon their relations with the rest of mankind.

New Manifesto

The Third Program of the C.P.S.U. was published in its initial form in mid-summer of 1961.[3] Its analyses, conclusions, and prescriptions for the attainment of a transition in the U.S.S.R. from "socialism" to "communism" within the next twenty years are dealt with elsewhere in this volume. In its passages dealing with world affairs, as in those devoted to problems and prospects of the U.S.S.R. and of the "Socialist Bloc" as a whole, the Third Program is an amalgam, albeit not quite a synthesis, of three quite different and not altogether compatible elements. One comprises shrewd, realistic analyses of things as they are and hardheaded estimates of the probable shape of things to come. A second element consists of statements of aspiration regarding the future, expressive of wishes and hopes—which, by the test of time, may or may not coincide with probability. A third component looks backward, rather than forward, by way of quoting or paraphrasing formulations offered by Lenin almost half a century ago and by Marx and Engels a century or more ago—some of which are dated and few of which offer clear guidance for today and tomorrow. The Third Program simultaneously exemplifies Marxist method, sometimes employed with brilliant results, and Marxist dogma, sometimes restated in absolute or anachronistic terms. Before considering and evaluating the view of world politics set forth in the Program, it will be well to summarize major themes in the words of Premier Khrushchev in his several addresses to Congress XXII.

> The chief content of the period following the Twentieth Congress of the C.P.S.U. is the competition between the two world social systems—the socialist and capitalist systems. . . .
> If we view the whole globe as the scene of this competition, we see that socialism has been winning one position after another from the old world. In the first place, capitalism has been seriously cramped by socialism in a decisive sphere of human activity, that of material production. . . .

[3] See *Pravda* and *Izvestia* for July and August, 1961; *The New York Times* of August 1, 1961, full text; and *Program of the Communist Party of the Soviet Union, Draft* (New York: Crosscurrents Press, 1961). All quotes from the Third Program are from the Crosscurrents edition.

The industrial output of the socialist countries in 1960 was 6.8 times that of 1937, while the capitalist countries' was less than 2.5 times. The share of the socialist countries in world industrial production was 27 per cent in 1955, and in 1960 it had increased to roughly 36 per cent. . . . We are confident that socialism will be victorious in the competition with capitalism. We are confident that the victory will be won in peaceful competition and not through war. We have taken our stand and shall always take our stand for the peaceful coexistence of states with different social systems; we shall do everything to strengthen peace throughout the world. . . .

Mammon and Mars

Among naïve economic determinists, whether Marxist or non-Marxist, human motives are commonly reduced to a simple quest for material gain—by individuals, social classes, and sovereign States. Among naïve Marxists, war is attributed to "capitalism" and its alleged progeny, "militarism" and "imperialism." Lenin was never naïve. Yet he often espoused this formula, largely as a means of winning popular support for his cause through an oversimplified explanation of the world tragedy of 1914–18. The members of the Central Committee and the Presidium of the C.P.S.U. who drafted the Third Program, while obviously Marxists and therefore economic determinists, were also not naïve. They were concerned, as was Lenin, with the inescapable task of all political leaders—that is, winning friends and influencing people through schematic formulations and slogans. The Third Program, if compared with the quadrennial "Platforms" of the Democratic and Republican parties of the United States, is a model of sophistication and of rigorous intellectual analysis. Yet its language repeatedly implies or explicitly sets forth the old simplistic formula—so much so as to warrant a critical evaluation of assumptions and conclusions. For example:

> Imperialism is using technical progress chiefly for military purposes. It is turning the achievements of human genius against humanity. As long as imperialism exists, mankind cannot feel secure about its future. . . . State-monopoly capitalism stimulates militarism to an unheard-of degree. The imperialist countries maintain immense armed forces even in peacetime. Military expenditures devour an ever-growing portion of the state budgets. The imperialist countries are turning into militarist states run by the army and the police. Militarization pervades the life of bourgeois society.

The Party maintains that as long as imperialism survives, the threat of aggressive wars will remain. The CPSU regards the defense of the Socialist motherland, and the strengthening of the defense potential of the U.S.S.R., of the might of the Soviet armed forces, as a sacred duty of the Party and Soviet people as a whole, as a most important function of the Socialist state. The Soviet Union sees it as its internationalist duty to guarantee, together with the other Socialist countries, the reliable defense and security of the entire Socialist camp.

Constantly reiterated threats of war by American anti-Communist crusaders, coupled with massive preparations for atomic combat, leave the leaders of the U.S.S.R. with no choice in many of these matters. It is quite true, by any objective standard of judgment, that in the epoch of Cold War the menace of a hot World War III has emanated from the Washington of Truman, Eisenhower, and Kennedy rather than from the Moscow of Stalin, Malenkov, and Khrushchev.[4]

The broader issue of the "causes of war" in general is nonetheless worthy of consideration. It is arguable that the massive militarization of America since 1950, and particularly since the advent of the Kennedy and Johnson Administrations, with "war scares," measures of mobilization, and localized hot wars, is a phenomenon of a decadent "capitalism" whose leaders in business and politics can find no better way of "pump-priming" through public spending than the way of spending on preparations for war, rationalized as "defense," "prevention of war," and "deterrence" of enemy attack.[5]

All of this is irrelevant to the larger question of whether war, militarism, and imperialism are consequences of "capitalism." The

[4] Since this view is wholly contrary to prevailing American mythology, skeptical readers should consult D. F. Fleming's monumental and meticulously documented work, *The Cold War and Its Origins*, Vol. I, 1917–1950, Vol. II, 1950–1960 (London: George Allen & Unwin; New York: Doubleday, 1961). Dr. Fleming's masterly and definitive study can leave no reasonable reader in doubt regarding responsibility for initiating and perpetuating the cold war. Similar conclusions are reached in earlier journalistic efforts to tell the tale: for example, Kenneth Ingram, *History of the Cold War* (London: Darwen Finlayson, 1955); John Lukacs, *The History of the Cold War* (New York: Doubleday, 1961); Leo Perla, *Can We End the Cold War?* (New York: Macmillan, 1960). See also George F. Kennan's brilliant and scholarly study, *Russia and the West Under Lenin and Stalin* (Boston: Little, Brown, 1960).

[5] See Fred J. Cook, "Juggernaut: The Warfare State," in *The Nation* (October 28, 1961) and his subsequent expanded book, *The Warfare State* (New York: Macmillan, 1962).

record of history indicates that these destructive and exploitive practices of human beings are as old as civilization, long antedating the
advent of "capitalism" by any definition of the term. War dates
back to Neolithic times—perhaps to the Paleolithic era of human
fortunes—and was long considered the normal relationship of human groups when men began to practice agriculture, to devise written language, and to live in cities. "Militarism" and "imperialism"
are as old as Sumeria and the Hittites, Egypt and Assyria, Sparta
and Athens, Rome and Carthage, and the States of ancient India
and China—all of which were primitive or feudal, slave or serf,
societies wholly lacking in any arrangements for the production
and exchange of goods and services deserving to be called "capitalism."

The Communist fallacy of attributing war to the self-seeking
greed of "capitalists" has an American counterpart. Senator Gerald
P. Nye in 1934 conducted an investigation of the munitions industry
(the "merchants of death"), and came to the conclusion that the
United States had become involved in World War I by virtue of a
quest for profits by arms-makers and international bankers. The
"cure" for this evil was embodied in the successive "Neutrality Acts"
of 1935–39, forbidding Americans, under threat of heavy federal
penalties, to sell arms or lend money or send ships to foreign States
at war. The result was to help make the world "safe for aggression," since the embargo was applied impartially to Fascist aggres-
sors and victims of aggression alike—for example, Italy and Ethiopia
in 1935–36, Republicans and Fascists in Spain, 1936–39. This stul-
tifying misconception of the causes of war and of the realities of
world politics inevitably led to the result it was designed to avoid:
American involvement in World War II in 1941. This eventuality
could have been negated, and World War II prevented, only by
all-out aid to victims of Fascist aggression not in 1940–41, but in
the early 1930s. The only Great Power which (in vain) urged such
a course was the U.S.S.R.

Pressures for war and decisions for war are obviously related
to internal economic and social systems in the sense that military
adventures abroad have often been resorted to by power-holders
as a means of preventing class conflict at home and deflecting mass
dissatisfactions away from elite groups and onto foreign foes. It was
not Lenin but Cecil Rhodes who said in 1895: "If you want to

avoid civil war, you must become imperialists." It is nevertheless true that war as an age-old institution has invariably been a concomitant of power politics, which in turn is the inevitable product of international anarchy. When power is fragmented among separate sovereignties, with no common authority above them, each becomes the rival of others and seeks safety in arms. Nations, no less than individuals, compete with one another, often by force, for possession of positions and components of power when they live without any effective organization of law and order among them. And the power for which they strive, and frequently fight, is in the final analysis military power—on the time-honored and universal assumptions that security against enemies and realization of national purposes at the expense of others both require superiority in the arts of violence.

Urbis et Orbis

If the ultimate source of war resides in international anarchy, then the only ultimate assurance of peace lies in international government. The only great societies of the past which have enjoyed peace for long periods of time have been those ruled by Universal States or World Empires—for example, the Mediterranean world under the *Pax Romana* of ancient days and much of the Eurasian world under the *Pax Mongolica* of the Thirteenth, Fourteenth, and Fifteenth Centuries. Since the politics of the balance of power, now supplemented with weapons of mutual annihilation, precludes in our era any "conquest of the world" by any one Power capable of vanquishing all its rivals, world government is possible only through voluntary agreement—such as would be required to convert the United Nations into an entity competent to levy taxes and enact laws, or to bring into being a World Federation.

Communists have frequently denounced Federalist programs as schemes to promote American global hegemony. In fact the public and the policy-makers of the United States are no more willing to yield up any of their "sovereignty" to an international government than are their counterparts in the U.S.S.R. The Third Program, while rich in eloquent pleas for peace, nowhere takes cognizance of the need for enforceable world law under an effective world authority as the prerequisite of enduring peace. Its framers envisaged the problem in quite different terms:

> Socialism, in contrast to imperialism, advances a new type of international relations. The foreign policy of the Socialist countries, which is based on the principle of peace, the equality and self-determination of nations, and respect for the independence and sovereignty of all countries, as well as the fair, humane methods of Socialist diplomacy, are exerting a growing influence on the world situation. . . . The imperialist camp is making preparations for the worst crime against mankind—a world thermonuclear war that can bring unprecedented destruction to entire countries and wipe out entire nations. The problem of war and peace has become a life-and-death problem for hundreds of millions of people.
>
> The peoples must concentrate their efforts on curbing the imperialists in good time and preventing them from making use of lethal weapons. The main thing is to ward off a thermonuclear war, to prevent it from breaking out. This can be done by the present generation. . . . The victory of socialism throughout the world will do away completely with the social and national causes of all wars. To abolish war and establish everlasting peace on earth is a historical mission of communism.

This vision of a peaceful world postulates avoidance of war through the successful practice of the diplomacy of coexistence. Under such conditions, in which East-West competition is shifted away from rivalry in armaments toward emulation in economic progress and social welfare, it is assumed that the achievements of "Socialism" and ultimately of "Communism" will prove so impressive in the end that all mankind will see the light and embrace the new order, thus producing by mimesis a world community which will be one and indivisible, united by common ideology and by similar economic and social institutions. Such a world will be, it is contended, a world at peace.

All historical experience, including that of the "Socialist Camp" itself, renders this prognosis doubtful. "Capitalism" may indeed decline and disappear or, more probably, be transformed out of all recognition by the imperatives of the "Welfare State" and the "Warfare State." "Communism" may well score new triumphs and approach the goals of a classless society and the "withering away of the state" in its traditional form. But the world community is likely to remain, as always, a pluralistic congeries of diverse belief-systems and variegated institutional patterns, each reflecting local customs or meeting local needs. For all of the three billion members of mankind (whose numbers may well double by 1980) to cut their clothes of the same cloth is not only wholly improbable but, if realized, would be insufferably dull and wholly lacking in the stimuli to creativity which stem from differences in the ways of men.

Ideological and institutional uniformities, moreover, offer no assurance of peace. One world—even a Communist world—will still be a world of war in the absence of world law and government to keep the peace. This is a challenge which Communists have not confronted, either in the Third Program or elsewhere. One third of the world's people now live under Communist rule. But their rulers have thus far devised no workable common institutions for reconciling differences and keeping the peace among them, either on the Party level or the governmental level. As for the former, the Comintern expired in 1943 and the Cominform in 1956, to be succeeded by periodical international conferences of Party delegations. As for the latter, the Sino-Soviet alliance treaty of February 14, 1950, the Warsaw Pact of May 14, 1955, and the Comecom for economic cooperation bear no resemblance to an international federation of Communist-ruled States. None of these arrangements has prevented serious rifts and schisms within the "Socialist Camp" nor occasional recourse to armed violence as in East Germany, 1953, and in Hungary in 1956.

Communists have, to date, done no better than "capitalists" in meeting this crying need of all mankind for order in place of anarchy in international relations. The Third Program offers no blueprints, nor even any ideas, on the problem. World government in some form is both possible and imperative if the human race is to be saved from suicide during the remaining decades of the Twentieth Century. The only obstacles to its attainment are the ancient and obsolete superstitions of "sovereignty" and nationalism which continue to enthrall the minds of men—to their ruination if they cannot emancipate themselves from the ways of the past. Communists, dedicated to building a better world, dare not continue to evade this task if they are serious in their announced purposes. As of 1967 they have not faced the issue.

Peace by Balance

If we turn from long-range perspectives of possible world order to shorter-run prospects of averting World War III in the foreseeable future, we find that the Third Program of the C.P.S.U. offers reasoned and reasonable hopes of peace. The premises of such hopes and the conclusions drawn therefrom might well be put in a different vocabulary, as will be suggested below, with no change in the prognosis. In the current vocabulary of the Moscovite Marxists, the argument, here sampled, proceeds as follows:

> Peaceful coexistence implies renunciation of war as a means of settling international disputes, and their solution by negotiation; equality, mutual understanding and trust between countries; consideration of mutual interests; non-interference in internal affairs; recognition of the right of every people to solve all the problems of their country by themselves; strict respect for the sovereignty and territorial integrity of all countries; promotion of economic and cultural cooperation on the basis of complete equality and mutual benefit. . . .
>
> The Soviet Union has consistently pursued, and will continue to pursue, the policy of peaceful coexistence of states with different social systems.

In other passages of the Third Program the contention is advanced that the "Socialist Camp," supported by the "peace forces" in the Western countries, has now reached a point of power at which it can "deter" Western "warmongers" from embarking upon a course of madness. This view obviously has its mirror image in official United States and NATO views. Both views are new variants of what Sir Norman Angell in 1910 called *The Great Illusion,* a work which was translated into many languages, won for its author a Nobel Peace Prize, was read by millions of people, and produced no change whatever in the attitudes and policies of national publics and power-holders toward problems of power in world politics—with results ever more disastrous through half a century.

The Third Program nevertheless makes its point, despite dissent in Tirana and Peking. The point, phrased differently, is this: policy-makers of Great Powers never embark on war unless they are persuaded, however mistakenly, of military superiority over the prospective enemy and unless they have devised a plausible plan for victory. The Marxist rulers of Russia are cognizant, albeit obliquely, of these realities of *Realpolitik* in the 1960s. War is obsolete. Recourse to military violence in the relations among Great Powers will always in our time prove self-defeating and probably self-destructive. (Moscow's Marxists, to be sure, revert to the medieval distinction between "just" and "unjust" wars, with the former equated with "colonial wars of liberation," to which Moscow pledges its support.) War must therefore be avoided, the more so as the transition from "Socialism" to "Communism" in the U.S.S.R. presupposes peace. Neither, they believe, will the West seek war, thanks to the inability of American and Western European decision-makers to figure out any way to "win the war" under prevailing and prospective conditions. This belief is sound.

Horizon

The balance of power or "balance of terror" affords at best a precarious basis of peace. The prospects of disarmament by agreement are hopeless so long as Moscow insists on total disarmament before inspection and Washington insists on fool-proof inspection before disarmament. Within this context all so-called disarmament negotiations are either fraudulent or an exercise in self-deception.[6] Neither is any negotiated settlement of the Cold War probable, despite the hopes and prospects, all of which were wasted, of the early and middle 1950s. The militarization of the American economy—creating vast and powerful vested interests dependent for economic survival on a continuation of the arms race to the tune of periodical "war scares" and local wars to render politically palatable steady increases of the military budget—precludes any "negotiated settlement" of the East-West conflict during the foreseeable future apart from possible local accords, as in Berlin, Laos, Vietnam, the Congo, and other arenas of rivalry.

This prognosis, if it proves correct, will mean the frustration or postponement of many of the goals set forth in the Third Program of the C.P.S.U. Elementary considerations of security will

[6] See my "The Impasse of Disarmament" in *Current History* (November 1961).

require the U.S.S.R. to match massive American militarization, missile for missile and bomb for bomb. The economic consequence will be a constant diversion of resources in the Soviet economy away from "welfare" purposes and toward "warfare" purposes, with a resultant retardation of the transition from "Socialism" to "Communism." The political consequence may well be a slow erosion of the policies of Khrushchev, Kosygin, and Brezhnev, aiming at "peaceful coexistence," and a steady enhancement in the U.S.S.R. and other Communist-ruled lands of the influence of those who regard World War III as inevitable.

But it does not follow from these considerations that any such final catastrophe will necessarily come to pass. An endless arms race, to be sure, will mean a constant expansion of membership in the thermonuclear suicide club and a constant increase in the dangers of "accidental" war. On the other hand, there is no present basis for supposing that either side, whatever its scientific and technological breakthroughs may be, will acquire the means of annihilating the "enemy" without suffering annihilation in retaliation. Mankind, granted, is already half-mad. But given a minimum of rationality among policy-makers, no such psychotic decision is likely to be taken.

Short of such a disastrous outcome, how may we expect the struggle for power to develop in years to come? All recent signs and portents suggest that the American-led "Free World" will experience as many contradictions, failures, and frustrations as the "Socialist Camp." Frustration may breed aggression, as it has often done in the past. If much of mankind is to revert in the late 1960s to mass irrationality on the model of most Japanese, Italians, and Germans in the 1930s, then obviously there is no hope for the salvation of the race or of any of the values which human beings have cherished throughout much of history. But there is nothing inevitable in any such outcome. Frustration may promote a constructive reappraisal of ends and means in foreign policy on both sides, leading to an ultimate *modus vivendi*. The voices of reason may yet prevail. This is the hope of the present rulers in the U.S.S.R. Such also must be the hope of all of us in the West who prefer the survival to the extinction of *Homo Sapiens*.

VIII

The U.S.S.R. in World Affairs: Problems of a "Communist" Foreign Policy

by URI RA'ANAN

Ideology and "Raison d'État"

Confronted with the peculiar problems posed by the appearance and multiplication of communist states on the world arena, observers of the twentieth century have tended to forget that ideologically motivated societies by no means constitute a rare phenomenon in history. Indeed, ideologies, whether political or religious, do not survive for long *in vacuo;* inevitably, they seek to capture for themselves a host—a power base—in the form of a movement or party, a segment of society, and eventually, a whole nation. Such ideological conquests, however, should not be viewed as unilateral developments, but rather as subtle processes of symbiosis. Thus, after Constantine, the Roman Empire was, of course, profoundly influenced by the adoption of Christianity. At the same time, this transformation could hardly have occurred, nor could it have lasted, if Christianity had not adapted itself to the requirements of an official creed, meeting the needs of the state no less than the secular authorities furthered the goals of the church. In fact, the capture of a country by a "pure" or unreconstructed ideology, unable to embrace the vital requirements of *raison d'état,* cannot be envisaged except in mutually destructive terms. History is replete with ironic examples, demonstrating the inventiveness of the human mind when forced to square the apparently competing demands of political creed and of state interest.

The sixteenth- and seventeenth-century wars of religion constitute a classic example of an "ideological" age. Significantly, the Protestant struggle against the Counterreformation tended to become identified with the wars fought by the preeminent Protestant state, the Netherlands, against Catholic Habsburg Spain. Many Calvinists and some Lutherans came to regard a Dutch victory as a prerequisite for their own survival and the Dutch Princes of Orange were quick to presume that this entitled them to sacrifice foreign Protestants to the interests of Holland. With a small population and area, the Netherlands required the support of at least one major power against Catholic Spain and found such an ally—in the shape of another Catholic state, the France of Cardinal Richelieu. The French feared a Spanish victory in the Netherlands that might once again surround France with Habsburg territory to the north as well as to the south; therefore, Richelieu was perfectly willing to assist the Protestant Dutch state against his Spanish fellow Catholics. However, in trying to implement this policy, Richelieu was badly hampered by the fact that the French Protestants, the Huguenots, were in open revolt against his rule and that their fortress of La Rochelle could not be captured. The Cardinal regretfully informed his Dutch friends that he could not meaningfully help them against Spain as long as their French fellow Protestants were tying down his armies at the siege of La Rochelle. The Dutch leader, the Prince of Orange, decided that for the sake of the survival of his country—the very heart of the Protestant camp—other Protestants might be sacrificed and he offered Cardinal Richelieu the assistance of the Dutch fleet in subduing the French Protestants at La Rochelle! The logic of statesmanship seemed to have triumphed—but for the fact that the Dutch sailors were unable to comprehend the sophistries of their prince and mutinied rather than open fire upon fellow Protestants.

Richelieu is reported to have commented with a shrug that, unfortunately, the diplomats still stood alone in following the dictates of reason of state; their peoples would have to learn that crude sentiments of (religious or ideological) solidarity must not be taken too literally, but must be interpreted within the context of their country's interests.

In any case, the significant fact is that the House of Orange had obviously succeeded in synthesizing to its own satisfaction the requirements of Dutch power and survival and the ideological demands of international Protestantism, evolving the simple formula: Dutch interests = Protestant interests. Not having anything like a totalitarian grip upon Dutch society, however, the Prince of Orange was unable to impose this formulation upon his sailors, with whom unreconstructed ideology still took precedence over the needs of the state. The power of modern authoritarian regimes, on the other hand, has been sufficiently far-reaching not only to fuse the dictates of *raison d'état* with the requirements of ideology, but also to stifle dissenting views—at least within their own country. Nevertheless, there are obvious similarities between the actions of seventeenth-century princes, sacrificing coreligionists abroad in order to strengthen their own state, and the line taken by Lenin, Stalin, and Khrushchev alike toward fellow Communists outside the U.S.S.R.

Lenin maintained his alliance with Kemal Atatürk even when the latter suppressed the Turkish Communists, whose representative protested bitterly at the Fourth Congress of the Comintern in 1922. Lenin's associate, Karl Radek, stated bluntly at the time that the Soviet state required a continued understanding with the Turkish army, irrespective of Ankara's domestic policies, since Atatürk's successes had set Britain, France, and Italy at each other's throats, weakening the West as a whole. Stalin was quick to censure Tito during World War II, when the Yugoslav partisans took some overt steps toward setting up a communist regime in the liberated areas. Stalin warned Tito against antagonizing the exiled Yugoslav government in London, since such a development would cause tension between the Western Allies and the U.S.S.R. In other words, the prospects of a communist success in Yugoslavia must, if necessary, be sacrificed rather than jeopardize Western lend-lease supplies to Russia. Khrushchev in 1964 disregarded the protests of Khaled

Bagdash and other Mideastern Communists and proceeded to prod
the Egyptian Communists into merging with Nasser's Arab Socialist
Union and the Algerian Communist Party into dissolving itself and
joining with Ben Bella's F.L.N. Khrushchev made no bones about
the fact that he did not really expect his policy to advance the communist cause in the region but that he wanted to remove a cause
of friction with the one-party regimes concerned so as to cement a
block of anti-Western forces. For the sake of such an essentially
tactical gain he was prepared to destroy the organizational independence of the local communist parties, a doctrinal sin against
which Lenin had warned in his 1920 draft theses on the national
and colonial question. (There was a qualitative difference between
Lenin's silence concerning the suppression of Communists by his
Turkish allies and Khrushchev's initiative in attempting to dismantle
foreign communist parties—although both policies in fact relegated
international communism to the position of a mere handmaiden of
Soviet state interests. This "pragmatic," self-centered approach has
increasingly characterized Moscow's attitude toward the obligations
of "international proletarian solidarity"; in turn, the other communist parties have adopted a more autonomous, "polycentric"
stand, limiting the Soviet Union's ability to manipulate them for the
sake of purely Russian interests.)

It was the relationship with the Chinese Communists that perhaps best brought out the essentially state-centered concept guiding
the global policies of the C.P.S.U. leadership. It is true, of course,
that both in the 1920s and immediately after 1945 it was probably
Stalin's mistaken appraisal of the Chinese situation rather than
willful sabotage on his part to which the strange Soviet tactics in
China could be attributed. Even so, the question arises why the
local scene should have been judged always from the distant perspective of Moscow, rather than left to the judgment of the people
on the spot. (Comintern emissaries generally came to convey Comintern directives rather than to reappraise Moscow's evaluations.)
In any case, considering Stalin's known aversion to communist triumphs in distant places where Soviet power might be unable to
prevent the establishment of a rival communist center, it is a
suspicious coincidence that Stalin's mistakes always required sacrifices from the Chinese Communists. In the 1920s, for reasons
similar to those which moved Lenin to maintain his alliance with

Atatürk, Moscow regarded the Kuomintang leadership as a useful partner against anti-Soviet forces in the Far East; consequently, in the face of all evidence, Stalin insisted that the link with sections of the Kuomintang was still beneficial to the Chinese Communists and that the latter should not break away even when threatened with annihilation. In 1945 and for several years afterwards, Stalin assumed that Mao's appraisals were incorrect and that Chiang Kai-shek would succeed in controlling most of China. On the basis of this calculation, a Russo-Chinese treaty was signed, recognizing, to all intents, Chiang's rule over the rest of China, in return for Chinese territorial and economic concessions to the U.S.S.R. in Manchuria and the Northeast. Stalin did little subsequently, by way of aid to Mao, to make up for this gross abandonment of Chinese Communist interests. After Mao's final victory, and in spite of the requirements of ideological solidarity with a successful, "fraternal" revolutionary movement, Stalin was not prepared to treat the new China radically differently from the old—that is, he continued on the basis of circumspect state-to-state relations. Only some of the Russian territorial and economic acquisitions were given back to China—and only very grudgingly—while Soviet aid to Peking was extended on a highly commercial basis. As the Chinese later revealed, Stalin encouraged their entry into the Korean war so that the U.S.S.R. might safely stay in the background, while at the same time extorting high prices for Russian military aid given to the Chinese forces in Korea.

Khrushchev, in practice, left little doubt that Soviet economic, military, and scientific resources were not at the disposal of other communist states or parties, however dire their need. Peking soon discovered that no great economic sacrifices could be expected from the U.S.S.R. for the purpose of filling the insatiable maw of a huge and backward China; moreover, during a period of nuclear stalemate with the United States, Moscow would run no risks of an armed showdown with Washington simply in order to assist Mao's short-range objectives in the China Sea. Nor would "proletarian solidarity" persuade Khrushchev to share Russia's nuclear monopoly with another communist power that might be tempted to use such dangerous weapons for its own purposes. As for China's clash with India, Moscow's Afro-Asian policy since 1955 was based on good relations with the world's largest nonaligned state and, consequently,

Khrushchev was not prepared to annoy New Delhi in order to further Peking's dreams of hegemony over Asia.

Needless to say, there are other, very important aspects of the Sino-Soviet dispute, which are peculiar to quarrels between communist parties, being ideological in flavor and revolutionary in semantics, and which will be discussed in another context. However, the examples given here are sufficiently striking to raise the question how an avowedly ideological "internationalist" leadership can indulge in policies of such transparently egotistical, national (or state) character, without causing the total erosion of all ideological foundations of its power and authority. In dealing with this problem, it should be recalled that the Marxist classics were concerned very little with the nature of interstate relations after the outbreak of a socialist revolution, taking it for granted that socialism would start in the strongest, most advanced countries and would consequently dominate the world as a whole. Moreover, they also assumed that the antagonistic character of relations between nations was typical only of the presocialist world and that the revolution would completely transform such relationships, producing a new type of peaceful cohabitation across the globe. As a result, there were few ready Marxist prescriptions for international behavior on a planet containing only one, or some, communist states.

Lenin and, even more, Stalin, did concern themselves with such problems, but as interested parties; they worded their strategic formulations in so general a way as to be open to the widest possible interpretations, leaving themselves the maximum number of options for use in each individual case. Their tactical prescriptions were also highly ambiguous, even when they were not specifically limited to a very temporary situation in one particular place, and therefore, not easily applicable elsewhere. For instance, it was all very well to say that in colonial countries the comprador bourgeoisie was allied to the imperialists, while the national bourgeoisie was two-faced in character, being progressive at one stage and reactionary afterwards. What did this mean in practice and how did it help the Communists to decide which Chinese general might prove to be a useful ally and which one might open fire upon them? What usually happened in practice was that the ideological formulations provided useful labels *after the event;* the colonial leader who turned against them was called a typical member of the comprador bourgeoisie by the Communists, while the politician who continued tolerating them was named a representative of the national bourgeoisie and a living proof that the latter had not yet exhausted its progressive role.

Thus, while the earlier Marxist works provided little guidance for international action, the words of Lenin and Stalin abounded in vague generalities that could be twisted to mean all things to all men. Consequently, while a convinced Communist might often feel uneasily that a particular Soviet act in the international arena ran counter to the very spirit of Marxism-Leninism, it was usually difficult if not impossible to cite specific chapter and verse from the communist classics to prove that this was indeed the case. Moreover, Soviet leaders have traditionally barricaded themselves behind a wall of apt quotations from the same classics—suitable to the occasion if not always cited in their correct context.

In any case, foreign affairs and defense are as much the prerogative of the sovereign in the Soviet state as they were in the monarchies of the sixteenth and seventeenth centuries—except that the Soviet sovereign is the leadership of the C.P.S.U., which also happens to be the only authorized interpreter of communist ideology. (Certain limited fields of international relations have, in recent years, been opened to more objective analysis by young Soviet academicians, especially economists, who have also been given increasing access to contemporary sources from the West; on the whole, however, their work has remained confined to studies of the new nations of Afro-Asia and they have usually refrained from detailed commentaries upon Soviet actions and motives.) Thus a particular Soviet deed could be challenged on the grounds of unorthodoxy only from beyond the Soviet frontiers or by an antagonist within the Soviet elite who was trying to overthrow his rival. In the latter case, however, the challenger, if successful, was bound eventually to imitate his predecessor's foreign policy with its pragmatic pursuit of Soviet state interests. After all, a purely "communist" policy is hardly conceivable in a thermonuclear world that differs so basically from the conditions envisaged by the nineteenth-century fathers of the creed. Moreover, there is little cause for thinking that the broad masses of the Soviet people have nothing else to worry about but the ideological inconsistencies of their leaders. As far as the more intellectual strata of the population are concerned, or at least the younger people among them, the very word "ideology" has fallen into growing disrepute. Thus, there is no reason for believing that a pragmatic foreign policy runs counter to prevailing moods.

It should not, however, be deduced from these considerations that the U.S.S.R. is simply a state like any other and that its international posture is only marginally affected by the political preconceptions of the ruling elite. To start with, that elite has to explain and "justify" its self-perpetuating rule by constant reference to the unending external as well as domestic obligations which "history" (that is, the Marxist-Leninist interpretation of history) imposes upon the leaders of the "first socialist state." Although Stalin's successors abandoned his insistence upon an intensified "class struggle" within the frontiers of the U.S.S.R.—with its concomitant phenomenon of unrelenting terror—they have been all the more concerned to stress that they are still engaged in a gigantic international contest (even if that contest is now to be carried on by means short of total war). Such a dialectic concept of world affairs can, of course, be most easily propagated in the jargon of historical and dialectical materialism; perhaps the political leaders of the U.S.S.R. also have not yet entirely divested themselves of the belief that "Diamat" (dialectical materialism) does provide them with a suitable and "scientific" method of interpreting the global scene. The interaction of language and thought is one of the commonplaces of our age and it may be assumed that those who speak the peculiar tongue of Marxism-Leninism and use its vocabulary as a medium of communication with their subjects and with their associates abroad find that their view of events is inevitably colored by this fact. If, however, the actions of the rest of the world are generally viewed through the distorting glass of such an ideology, the U.S.S.R.'s environment is bound to be affected by this tendency. After all, regimes that are habitually described and treated as Moscow's antagonists in a vast historic struggle are likely to conform, to some extent at least, to the role that Soviet ideology has ascribed to them. In return, of course, such developments usually strengthen the belief of Soviet leaders in the essential correctness of their formulations concerning historical processes.

It would not, in any case, be practical for the Soviet political elite to cease expressing itself in ideological terms; this is not only a matter of upbringing, education, conditioning, and habits—it must also be remembered that the U.S.S.R. has by no means yet abandoned all hope of restoring, at least partially, its former position as center of a worldwide political organization. It is true that Lenin, Stalin, and their successors had repeatedly ridden roughshod over the aspirations of various local communist parties, but they did find the existence of a centralized and Soviet-controlled world communist movement to be a most useful adjunct to their foreign policy— a brake upon the actions and plans of their adversaries. While the formal dissolution of the Comintern in 1943 did not basically affect this situation, the dissolution of the Cominform in 1956 marked the beginning of a sharp decline of central authority over the other communist parties, both inside and outside the bloc. The traumatic effects of destalinization, the risings in eastern Europe, the Sino-Soviet conflict, and the growth of polycentrism everywhere undermined the prestige and standing of the C.P.S.U. and permitted foreign Communists not only to voice divergent views but to pursue different policies. Consequently, Moscow has tried repeatedly to restore at least some measure of coordination, if not to reassert its full hegemony; for this purpose, the U.S.S.R. has persistently attempted to initiate or utilize international communist gatherings, formal and informal, using every excuse from the call for proletarian solidarity to the cry of "aid for North Vietnam." These Soviet efforts have been due both to Moscow's global aspirations and to fear of being preempted by Peking. While in 1957 and 1960 such attempts at least still served to paper over the cracks in the cohesion of the communist camp, by 1961, 1965, and 1966 they could, at most, help to isolate the Chinese and a few of their satellites. However, even if Moscow failed to reestablish its leadership over the communist world as a whole, it could hardly do less than try to gather around it all those communist parties that were indifferent or hostile to Peking's pretensions. While pursuing such a policy, the Soviet leadership was unlikely to take steps that would undermine its own position, such as abandoning the claim to be a communist power or ceasing to pay lip service, at least, to communist ideology.

A state with ideological commitments is not a unique historical phenomenon, but, to some extent, the Soviet political elite differs qualitatively from earlier regimes of this kind since Marxism-Leninism has furnished it with an allegedly "scientific" blueprint of the workings of historical forces. (This blueprint even claims to contain both a plan for and a guarantee of final victory.) In fact, this "scientific" aspect of communism is none too relevant to the conduct of Soviet foreign policy, since it does not provide prescriptions for Soviet reactions to various situations; it merely claims to have established a standard measuring rod for sizing up other peoples' intentions and actions. Moreover, because communist doctrine ascribes decisive importance to the class struggle, Soviet analysts, in dealing with interstate conflicts, keep using terms that are not very meaningful outside the arena of domestic politics. Soviet commentators frequently speak as if they were referring to the relations between a foreign ruling class and its proletariat when, all the time, they are thinking of the attitude of that ruling class toward the U.S.S.R. and the West respectively. Thus, a relatively advanced, democratic, industrial state, in which the local Communists enjoy a fair amount of immunity, may be described as "reactionary" because its international posture is essentially anti-Soviet; on the other hand, a one-party dictatorship in a backward, semitribal society, which suppresses a handful of local Communists together with all other political opposition, may be called "progressive," simply because it is emotionally anti-Western. Clearly, therefore, it is the reality of the international balance that matters to Moscow, while the vocabulary employed by Soviet analysts still seems to imply that the question at issue is primarily socioeconomic or ideological.

It is by no means certain, however, that this double standard is necessarily the result of conscious manipulation. The Soviet political elite undoubtedly is conditioned to talk and, for that matter, to think, in doctrinal jargon and it may still be very hard for any one of the senior personalities in Moscow to view the outside world in different terms. The real question is whether the Soviet leaders are prepared, if necessary, to make any meaningful sacrifices, at the expense of their state and of themselves, in order to fulfill the international tasks set by their ideology. It is true that a few weeks after the October Revolution, Lenin did say that "if it were necessary for us to go under in order to assure the success of the German revolution, we should have to do it." It is highly significant, however, that even at that early date he went on to say "but when will it come? No one knows. And at the moment there is nothing so important as our revolution. It must be safeguarded against danger at any price."

The observer would have difficulty discovering other occasions, during the half-century that has passed since then, when Soviet leaders have seriously considered jeopardizing the reality of the U.S.S.R. for the sake of some enticing revolutionary opportunity elsewhere. Not even marginal Soviet interests have been exposed to risks for the sake of foreign communist parties. (The Soviet intervention in Hungary was intended to prevent the loss of the Soviet empire in eastern Europe—the rescue of Hungarian communism was only a by-product.) That does not mean, of course, that the U.S.S.R. has never suffered objective losses because of ideological considerations. But when this has occurred, it has usually been the result of errors committed because of ideological preconceptions and not the outcome of a conscious decision to make a sacrifice for the sake of ideological goals. Thus, a rigid class interpretation of history made Stalin insist, in the face of stark evidence, that Hitlerism was simply one more subdivision of capitalism and that its advent would, therefore, bring no radical changes to Germany. ("Hitler, Goebbels . . . are the chained dogs of the German bankers.") Consequently, Moscow failed completely to comprehend the whole dynamic aspect of Nazism or its basically irrational urges; this was one of the reasons why, even a decade later, Stalin was psychologically unprepared for the German attack upon the U.S.S.R.

While, therefore, Stalin's political vision was seriously limited by ideological blinkers, his ascendance to power undoubtedly brought the reins of Soviet affairs into the domineering hands of a self-consciously pragmatic and cold-blooded ruler, who despised the Comintern as a "grocery shop" and whose lieutenants said that "one Soviet tractor is worth more than ten good foreign communists." Earlier, in Lenin's day, Soviet leaders had certainly given no less attention to the objective needs of the state; nevertheless, there was some attempt, in the conduct of international affairs, to leave a little room for the requirements of ideology. The living illustration of this fact was the uneasy coexistence of the *Narkomindel* (Foreign Ministry)and the Comintern, which frequently pursued mutually contradictory policies. Thus, in the case of the Weimar Republic, the Soviet state was clearly interested in furthering an understanding, since the two countries could be considered fellow victims of the victorious Entente and a Russo-German rapprochement could completely change Moscow's unfavorable international position. These considerations finally brought about the Rapallo agreement in 1922. Yet during that period the Comintern apparatus encouraged the German Communists to attack some of the same German bourgeois, conservative, and military groups that constituted the mainstay of Germany's new pro-Russian course! This dichotomy was due, in part, to the fact that different segments of the top leadership were dealing with foreign affairs and with the Comintern respectively; thus, during the early days, the Soviet conduct of international policy could aspire to be monolithic neither in personnel nor in approach. Perhaps there was also a naïve attempt to have one's cake and to eat it, to safeguard the interests of the Soviet state without at the same time sacrificing major revolutionary opportunities elsewhere. Thus, the aspirations of the Turkish Communists could be written off, but those of the important German Communist Party could not.

With Stalin's victory over the various rival factions, however, all these ambiguities disappeared. Comintern personnel was totally subordinated to the C.P.S.U. leadership and, by the time of the Sixth Comintern Congress in 1928, the foreign communist parties were bluntly told that it was their internationalist duty to dedicate themselves completely to the support of the world's "one socialist state." This concept received its clearest illustration in the Spanish Civil War. Although a genuinely revolutionary situation prevailed, at least in Catalonia, Stalin cold-bloodedly used the Spanish Communist Party, the foreign Communists fighting in the International Brigades, and his own rather niggardly supplies of Soviet arms, ammunition, and military experts to the Republican government, to impose a "conservative" policy. His desire was not to frighten the West by the outright creation of a really revolutionary Spain, but rather, if possible, to embroil Leon Blum's France with the Axis Powers in a struggle for supremacy over the peninsula. If successful, such a policy could leave the U.S.S.R. in the enviable position of being able to sway the balance either way. Moscow could throw in its lot with France, if Hitler proved determined to proceed to a confrontation; alternatively, Stalin could impress the Germans sufficiently with his "long arm" to convince them of the need for an accommodation.

In the pursuit of this policy, Moscow turned its tap of supplies off and on to overthrow Spanish cabinets that did not prove sufficiently amenable to Soviet control. The U.S.S.R. never gave the Loyalists enough to win and they were finally thrown away like "squeezed lemons," when Stalin's purposes had been served. It might, of course, be objected that this particular instance of *raison d'état* at work also happens to be a typical illustration of "good bolshevik thinking," as prescribed in Lenin's day. Stalin simply acted as a real Bolshevik was supposed to act—unsentimentally, interested only in "objective reality." It is misleading, however, to reduce the problem of ideological motivations in Soviet foreign policy to such simple terms. While it is perfectly true that hard-headed tactics were prescribed for bolshevik leaders, they were, after all, supposed to be employed in the furtherance of a cause— the final victory of the international proletariat. A great deal of sophistry would be needed to show that this aim was really served by the cold-blooded manipulation and final abandonment of the Spanish revolutionary situation.

On the other hand, there are some instances where Soviet actions may originally have been due to power considerations, but where Soviet reactions can be explained largely in ideological terms. The Soviet-Yugoslav quarrel, for instance, probably was not a primarily ideological issue. After all, the conflict was finally precipitated by the question whether Soviet permission was required for rearrangements within the Soviet sphere of influence, such as the project for a confederation between east European communist states. In this context, Stalin's anger at Tito, the dependent who refused to behave like a satellite, was not qualitatively different from the resentment shown by the rulers of nineteenth-century Russia at the disappointing attitude of their client, Alexander Battenberg of Bulgaria. What was an entirely different phenomenon, however, was the consequent struggle between Stalinism and Titoism in eastern Europe. The realities of the power situation had forced Tito to adopt a new ideological posture that had obvious application to the rest of eastern Europe; it was this factor, more than the successful defiance of Yugoslavia alone, that enraged Stalin. An independent Yugoslavia outside the bloc was an unpleasant but bearable reality; on the other hand, a monolithic ideology clearly could not tolerate a growing Titoist movement within the other countries of the bloc.

Again, as has been shown, many of the primary issues over which the U.S.S.R. and China quarreled were far from ideological. Between 1957 and 1960, Moscow even revealed some willingness to compromise with Peking over a number of ideological definitions; what the Soviet leaders were not prepared to do was to sacrifice their economic resources to build up China, to risk an armed confrontation with the United States by extending a protective cover over Chinese adventures in the Pacific, or to assist China's ambition of becoming an independent nuclear power. On the other hand, these practical issues alone might not have produced the venom that has characterized the Sino-Soviet dispute, but for the fact that both powers have pretensions to global ideological leadership and have therefore considered themselves to be involved in a momentous struggle in which defeat would have disastrous consequences. Each leadership has also shown considerable sensitivity over the possibility that the other side might successfully show up its policies to be heretical—a development that could have serious domestic repercussions. The rulers of both countries hold power "legitimately" only insofar as they can show their direct doctrinal descent from the fathers of the creed; Stalin, Khrushchev, and the present Soviet leaders all tried to prove that they were the true inheritors of Lenin's legacy. To be convicted of heresy, therefore, might seriously undermine domestic authority—at least to the point of making it easier for rivals within the Party leadership to seize power. This is one of the reasons why Moscow and Peking have bombarded the Russian and Chinese publics, as well as the various "fraternal" parties, with ideologically phrased notes to prove where true orthodoxy may be found.

The relationship of ideology to policy is thus truly a complex matter. The inherent ambivalence of the Soviet approach to world affairs is rather neatly illustrated by Brezhnev's opening address to the Twenty-third Congress of the C.P.S.U. almost half a century after the October Revolution. Stating that "the Party's Central Committee has been conducting its foreign policy with an eye to the processes occurring in the capitalist world," Brezhnev presented what at first glance appeared to be a rigidly ideological analysis of these "processes." Adhering to the orthodox concept that this is the era of the "general crisis of world capitalism," he was careful to ascribe the "contradictions" within the Western camp to the usual factor of economic antagonism between the capitalisms of the United States and of its Western allies.

However, while paying lip service to the doctrine that the basic ailments of capitalism cannot be cured, Khrushchev's successor, in typically realistic fashion, did concede that "the rates of economic growth in the main capitalist countries have been higher since the war than between the two world wars." While speaking of the weakening of ties within the Western camp, Brezhnev did relate this phenomenon to the traditional motives of economic rivalry; then, however, he revealed his awareness that this development is, in fact, due to the new feeling of security in a strengthened West that no longer fears the Soviet threat.

> A process of disjunction has set in, in the imperialist bloc, impelled by contradictions among its members. The United States is no longer able to direct the latters' policy as sweepingly as before. It is a long time now since any serious politician, let alone the people, has given credence to the myth of a threat of Soviet aggression, which once helped to forge these blocs.

In other words, what really count in international affairs are not the "objective economic processes" of the Marxist classics, but the subjective mistakes of Stalin in adopting an unduly militant posture after the war.

Particularly striking are the logical gaps, not to say contradictions between Brezhnev's theoretical analysis of the general world scene and the practical conclusions that he draws from it. Brezhnev's thesis is that the United States is now embroiled in a renewed economic struggle with Italian, West German, British, and Japanese industry. Then, however, he proceeds to state that it is Moscow's relations with France that have improved most of all, emphasizing that this is due to "a coincidence of interests of both countries on a number of key international issues" and to "long-standing traditions of friendship between our peoples." The question must arise why Soviet relations have not improved most of all with the countries that are said to be embroiled in a new economic struggle with the United States. And if friendship with Paris is, in fact, due to such "old-fashioned" motives as a meeting of interests over foreign policy questions, then what is the point of placing so much emphasis on an economic analysis of world affairs—only to show that these economic factors are not decisive? Again, Brezhnev pays lip service to international communist solidarity and denounces Jakarta's treatment of the Indonesian Communists. He clearly shows that the U.S.S.R. does not, at this stage, intend to renounce its role as international guardian and protector of the various communist parties, even if it can no longer aspire to be the sole center of a worldwide, monolithic movement. Yet, in the same address, Brezhnev stresses that "the Soviet Union has always favored the development of friendly relations with Indonesia"; this is a clear hint that, platonic sympathy for the Communist Party of Indonesia's (P.K.I.) fate apart, Moscow does not intend to abandon its ties with Jakarta, having invested huge sums in economic and military aid to the Indonesian government. The simple, practical truth is, of course, that Moscow has not been altogether sorry to see the P.K.I. punished for its virulently anti-Soviet attitude during recent years; however, even had this not been the case, it is more than doubtful whether the U.S.S.R. would have been prepared to jeopardize its relations with an important country in Asia for the sake of a local communist party.

Brezhnev's survey brings out some of the subtle changes that the Soviet leadership has undergone. The earlier generation was, of course, always extremely capable of distinguishing between long-term ideological goals and the harsh necessities of the moment, as is evident from many of the examples cited before. However, their doctrinaire approach to the outside world and the resulting preconceptions distorted their evaluation of the international situation and led to occasional serious errors of policy. The present Soviet leaders seem to be increasingly well equipped to appraise reality in the world around them. Thus, there is real significance in the fact that, after making dutiful obeisances to the Marxist version of the situation, Brezhnev repeatedly proceeded to draw conclusions based upon entirely different criteria, which take account of such unexpected phenomena as the vitality of the capitalist system or the personality of Charles de Gaulle. Lenin and Stalin would, perhaps, have been just as realistic, but they might also have attempted to square the new factors with their ideology—or vice versa—and, in so doing, would have subtly distorted the picture. Their successors are content to pay homage to doctrine and then to leave it strictly alone and to go on to deal with the hard facts. Of course, it should not be assumed for one moment that Moscow's vision is now entirely uncolored by ideological preconceptions or that the jargon employed does not, of itself, reflect the outside world in strangely grotesque shapes. However, it does seem to be true that the present generation has relatively fewer mental obstacles to overcome in arriving at a realistic analysis.

Whether a further decline or a temporary comeback awaits ideology within the U.S.S.R., it seems likely that the value of international ideological bonds will steadily diminish. During the last five decades, needless to say, the Soviet state has used the international movement as an important tactical auxiliary; it is hardly necessary to mention the countless instances in which foreign communist parties were used as a brake upon the implementation of policy by noncommunist governments. This took many forms—subversion, espionage, "mass movements," "fronts," major disturbances, and even uprisings. However, Stalin's "long arm" has disappeared and, with it, not only Soviet control but even Soviet moral authority, which has been undermined by the disputes and revelations that have riven the communist world. In an increasingly "polycentric" age, communist parties abroad have not only started to act independently, to assert themselves within their own "spheres of influence," and to defy the U.S.S.R., but have even gone as far as attempting to teach the C.P.S.U. how to run its own affairs. The strictures of the western European communist parties upon Soviet management of the Sinyavsky-Daniel affair constitute perhaps the most striking example of this kind. Thus, international ideological ties have not only become less useful to Soviet foreign policy, but they are threatening the most jealously guarded preserve of the Soviet elite—its monopoly over the conduct of Soviet domestic affairs.

U.S.S.R. or Russia?

If the U.S.S.R. has generally diluted its ideological motivations with a suitable admixture of *raison d'état* and if the importance of ideology in international affairs has steadily declined, the question must arise whether the Soviet leaders are not simply continuing traditional Russian policies under another guise. It is only too tempting to jump to the facile conclusion that this is indeed so. After all, it is a simple geographic fact that the U.S.S.R. occupies roughly the same area as its czarist predecessor, has more or less the same neighbors, many of the same frontiers, some of the same geographic-military problems. It was inevitable, therefore, that any history of Soviet foreign policy should be replete with place names and issues familiar to the student of the czarist period, giving the impression that nothing had changed. Indeed, such a conclusion seems hard to avoid when the reader keeps encountering, again and again, the very same problems: the question of the Straits, Kars and Ardahan, the northern provinces of Iran, the creation of dependencies in the smaller Slavic and Balkan countries, eastern Galicia and the Polish frontier in general, the attempt to dominate the Baltic region, Finland, Bessarabia, the Chinese Eastern Railroad, Port Arthur, Sakhalin. Nevertheless, it would be a major mistake to see in the U.S.S.R. simply the old Russia "writ large."

The aims of czarist policy, when all is said and done, were merely territorial, in the narrow sense of the word. It is true, of course, that even czarist moves were not entirely devoid of "ideological" aspects: after the defeat of Napoleon in 1815, again in 1848, in 1863, and in the 1870s and 1880s, Russia undoubtedly did try to play the part of protector of conservatism—whether within the framework of the "Holy Alliance" (actually the Quadruple Alliance), the "Three Emperors' League," or on its own. Dynastic considerations also mattered—by causing the Romanovs to devote attention to remote and relatively unimportant areas, such as the Kingdom of Württemberg or the Grand Duchy of Oldenburg, simply because of a relationship with the Ruling House. However, by and large Russian foreign policy was devoted to the extension of the country's territorial frontiers, through the outright annexation of immediately adjacent areas or the creation of protectorates over kindred peoples (ethnically Slav or Orthodox in religion). Geopolitical considerations were certainly not absent, since it was logical for a country marked by large rivers to seek control over the coastal areas where these streams enter the sea. Moreover, as these maritime outlets are themselves icebound for part of the year, czarist aspirations called for the extension of Russia's coasts to include ice-free ports and for Russian domination over the narrows that give access to warm-water oceans.

It would hardly be adequate to think of Soviet foreign policy in such narrow and old-fashioned terms. If the point was made earlier that even an ideologically motivated society operates according to *raison d'état,* this does not at all mean that the U.S.S.R. behaves simply like any traditional state; it would be more correct to think of the Soviet Union as a political organism with a global horizon and worldwide aspirations, limited only by a healthy instinct of self-preservation. It has usually not been the annexation of this or that strip of adjacent territory that has been uppermost in the minds of Soviet leaders, but rather the problem how to manipulate the global balance in such a way as to ensure both the safety of the U.S.S.R. and eventual Soviet supremacy in a prolonged contest for direct or indirect control of the planet itself.

If, on the Soviet agenda, narrowly territorial aspirations have usually occupied a secondary place, there have, of course, also been very practical reasons for this. Thus, before the late 1930s, the U.S.S.R. was simply too weak to challenge the established territorial order, while, after the full onset of the cold war in 1947, first the United States atomic monopoly and then the thermonuclear stalemate rendered any attempt to change frontiers by force a prohibitively costly proposition. Moreover, when it was feasible to seize large areas with relative impunity, Stalin was only too quick to take advantage of this fact. This opportunity occurred during the short period of 1939–1946, when Hitler's destruction of the Versailles system had rendered conditions completely fluid and the post-World War II order had not yet caused a refreezing of the lines. The 1940 Berlin meeting between Molotov and Ribbentrop characterizes the spirit of those years since, on that occasion, the two men haggled about zones of interest and national objectives in the Baltic, Balkans, and the Middle East in a manner reminiscent of pre-1914 diplomacy. Later, after surviving the first impact of the German invasion of Russia, Stalin showed equally little inclination to make serious concessions to the embarrassed pleas of his new Western Allies, who found it hard to acquiesce in the Russian seizure of Poland's eastern territories, when it was precisely to safeguard Poland's territorial integrity that they had gone to war. By the end of the war, Stalin was pushing his frontiers not only into Europe and East Asia, but also southward, advancing claims against Turkish and Iranian territory and even demanding a share of former Italian possessions in the Mediterranean. In addition to the large areas annexed to the U.S.S.R. itself, the Soviet leaders had seized control of an empire of client states extending right into the heart of central Europe. In a very real sense, therefore, the U.S.S.R. had every reason to consider itself a territorially satisfied power after World War II.

However, granted that before 1939 and after 1946 territorial expansion would have entailed prohibitive risks for the U.S.S.R. and that, in any case, by 1946 Moscow had achieved almost all of Russia's historic aspirations, the fact still remains that the Soviet leaders have, on the whole, shown exceptionally little concern with boundary issues. In half a century of Soviet foreign policy, the 1939–1946 period constitutes a relatively brief interlude, in which Moscow opportunistically exploited unusual chances for pushing the Soviet frontiers outward with reasonable impunity. At most other times, the leaders of the U.S.S.R. have regarded territorial questions as secondary matters when compared with the historic contest for eventual control of the globe itself, in which they believe themselves to be engaged. In this struggle, they have considered it to be of far greater importance to achieve a decisive say in other countries through the imposition of regimes amenable to Soviet direction, than to annex a few more provinces to the U.S.S.R.

Even a communist victory was not worthwhile, as far as Moscow was concerned, if it occurred in a place in which it would be difficult to maintain Soviet control; this was one of the reasons for Stalin's tortuous path in Spain and he may have had similar misgivings about the Chinese Communists. In the immediate postwar period, when many of the new communist rulers in eastern Europe, such as the Rumanians and even the Yugoslavs, thought that their countries might join the U.S.S.R. as additional Soviet republics, it was Stalin who was unenthusiastic. He apparently did not feel that Soviet rule could successfully absorb large territories and populations with an economic, social, and cultural standard markedly superior to that of the rest of the U.S.S.R.; he seems to have feared that the result of such annexations might be to infect and suborn his own more docile population and thus to weaken his regime. He much preferred controlling the east European communist rulers indirectly, through ideological bonds, penetration of their secret police and intelligence services and of their armies, and by interposing hermetically sealed frontiers between the various communist countries in order to prevent the free mingling of their populations. Perhaps the most serious obstacles to the successful implementation of such a policy of indirect control were to be found in countries of which only certain parts had fallen under Soviet domination. In these partitioned states—such as Germany and Korea—the West either held enclaves within the Soviet zone, like West Berlin, or had reestablished independent republics that acted like magnets upon their fellow countrymen in the Soviet-controlled sectors. These were the very areas in which Stalin felt it necessary to "round off" his postwar conquests and where, therefore, as in the case of the Berlin blockade and the Korean war, he was prepared to take certain, very limited risks. (In Berlin he tried severe harassment and retreated when it failed; in Korea he acted when he thought the West had written the area off and, in any case, made sure that Soviet troops would not be directly involved.)

With these exceptions, Stalin was extremely careful not to attempt overt use of force in bringing about further territorial changes in the postwar period. Where action was taken to consolidate the Soviet empire, as in Czechoslovakia in 1948, this was done under the guise of "domestic" issues so as to ensure immunity against Western counter action. The Soviet invasion of Hungary in 1956 could not be disguised in this manner, in spite of efforts to present it as a response to a Hungarian "appeal"; however, this was not a quest for further territory, but rather a desperate attempt to prevent the total disintegration of Soviet control over eastern Europe.

Perhaps it would be correct to say that, while Soviet leaders have been very happy to seize foreign territories when this could be done safely and cheaply, they have not been prepared to run really serious risks for this purpose. In this attitude they have differed somewhat from their czarist predecessors, who undermined their own rule in disastrous wars, and more so from a regime like Hitler's, which constantly took the most appalling risks and finally destroyed the Reich in its search for *Lebensraum.*

However, it should by no means be assumed that a line of caution over territorial issues, together with a policy of indirection and gradualism in the global contest, is necessarily devoid of serious danger to world peace. Khrushchev, for instance, repeatedly indulged in gambling, not so much for the purpose of annexing new territories, but rather in the hope of pulling off a sleight of hand to sway the political and psychological balance in the "Third World" or the strategic balance between the powers. His actions in the Near East, 1955–1958, and, much more so, his Cuban adventure of 1962, belonged to this category. After revolutionizing the Near Eastern situation through his arms deal with Egypt, Khrushchev discovered during the consequent Suez-Sinai conflict that his action had left Soviet weapons and military-technical personnel in an exposed position. He therefore faced a serious dilemma: to risk possible involvement in fighting against Britain and France or to abandon the Egyptians and to evacuate Soviet personnel and many Soviet planes to a safer place. He chose the latter course, but then had to recoup his tarnished prestige, for which purpose he publicly threatened London, Paris, and Tel Aviv with his missiles. Admittedly he did so when there was already very little risk that he would be called upon to implement his threats; nevertheless, his was hardly a safe or reassuring policy, nor did Soviet Near Eastern pronouncements of the following year reveal a less adventurous mood.

The Cuban missile crisis of 1962 constituted a far more vivid example of the possible dangers of Khrushchev's policy of gambling without providing for his opponents' possible countermoves and without leaving himself with a safe and easy way of retreat that would not entail serious loss of prestige. It must be stressed, however, that Khrushchev's behavior was hardly in line with the bolshevik *modus operandi* as practiced by Lenin and Stalin (and apparently also by Khrushchev's successors), all of whom dealt cautiously and cold-bloodedly with world affairs and attempted to avoid unnecessary risks, while leaving themselves several tolerable options for each eventuality. (Of course, they were not immune to blunders, as in the case of Stalin's policy toward Hitler, but these were usually due to miscalculation rather than to rashness or adventurousness.)

The contrast between Stalin's and Khrushchev's tactics was partly due to obvious differences of temperament; it must, however, also be ascribed to Khrushchev's attempts to maneuver in an increasingly complex world, with which Moscow had not yet fully come to terms but which, nevertheless, seemed to be beckoning with opportunities. It was only in Khrushchev's day that the I.C.B.M.

finally lifted the U.S.S.R. from a situation of one-sided vulnerability to the position of a partner in a genuine nuclear stalemate. (Although the Near Eastern crisis preceded this event, Khrushchev must already have known at that time that such a development was imminent.) Needless to say, he was perfectly aware that this achievement did not restore full freedom of action to the U.S.S.R., and that he would have to continue eschewing direct armed confrontation with the West in order to avoid a holocaust. On the other hand, neither Khrushchev nor any other Soviet leader could resign himself to a completely static policy—thus freezing into immobility. The achievement of some form of victory in the global contest remained the Soviet long-term aim; Khrushchev apparently thought that this goal could be brought closer, even while the stalemate lasted, through a policy of bold sleight of hand in those areas which did not participate in Western defense arrangements and in which the West, sensitive to its own growing vulnerability, might be reluctant to take risks. However, he implemented this concept in characteristically precipitous and drastic fashion, thereby increasing his own risks, since he left the West little choice except to take countermeasures and, thus, to call his bluff (as in the case of Cuba).

Khrushchev's successors have not entirely abandoned his blueprint for action during the period of stalemate, but they have proceeded in an altogether more cautious and gradual manner. According to a recent authoritative definition (in *International Affairs,* the unofficial organ of the Soviet Foreign Ministry), the aim of Soviet international policy is:

> to ensure peaceful conditions for the building of Socialism and Communism, for consolidating the unity, friendship and fraternity of the Socialist countries, for supporting revolutionary liberation movements, developing solidarity and cooperation with the independent states in Asia, Africa and Latin America, for asserting the principles of peaceful coexistence with capitalist states.

Translated into plain language, this means: The consequences of the nuclear stalemate force the U.S.S.R. to continue avoiding any armed showdown with the West and this period must be utilized to overcome some of Russia's worst economic deficiencies, to consolidate the bloc politically, economically and militarily and to repair some of the ravages of the Sino-Soviet dispute. At the same time, Moscow can continue with covert moves to change the psychological and political balance in the "Third World," but always within a context that will appear as "domestic" rather than as outside interference. Thus, the U.S.S.R. can give limited or indirect support to "national liberation struggles" against colonial or pro-Western governments, while at the same time wooing independent rulers in the "Third World" who cherish radical or anti-Western sentiments and some of whom might turn out to be the Castros of the future. It is with this concept in mind, that Moscow advances the slogan "no export of revolution, no export of counterrevolution"; that is, no Soviet troops will be involved in the "Third World" (the Soviet blueprint does not require their presence in any case), provided the West will sit by and watch passively while events unfold in that part of the world.

The importance of this approach does not lie in the measure of its success—by and large the U.S.S.R. has suffered setbacks rather than achieving triumphs in the "Third World"—but rather in the psychological insight it affords into the outlook of the Soviet leadership. These are the complex, perhaps even sophisticated, policies of a great power with truly global interests and commitments, operating with an awareness that the world is not just divided into two but into many camps of various subtle shadings. Of course, the outlook of the old bolshevik leadership was also global—but only in the measure of its aspirations. Not that recent Soviet formulations leave any doubt about Moscow's continued belief in a deeply antagonistic world in which the West is the enemy who must be combated and overcome, however long it may take; it is the techniques of that struggle that have changed, becoming increasingly modern. Today's definitions of Soviet foreign policy stand in dramatic contrast to Trotsky's well-known statement on becoming the first Commissar for Foreign Affairs of the infant Soviet state, "I will issue a few revolutionary proclamations and then close up shop" and to Chicherin's explanation, "the basic feature of our foreign policy was the revolutionary offensive . . . it was directed over the heads of governments to the revolutionary proletariat of all the countries." Between these early "agitational" concepts and the present approach, there lie nearly five decades of change that have transformed not only the Soviet state but also the world around it. As for Czarist Russia, in terms of today's complexities it was not a global power at all and its rather narrow territorial interests and commitments can provide no meaningful guide to the behavior of the U.S.S.R. on the present scene.

For that matter, the modern framework of international affairs brings out some of the inadequacies of the traditional "balance of power" concept, within which the czars, Lenin, and Stalin alike operated. As an essentially weak power, Russia before World War II sought adroitly to play off the competing blocs of great powers against one another, in order both to prevent the creation of an overwhelming, hostile coalition and to keep open a number of alternative options for its own policy. Lenin, at the end of 1920, said frankly, "our foreign policy, while we are alone and the capitalist world is strong, consists of utilizing existing antagonisms." He went on to explain that such "antagonisms" existed not only between bourgeois governments and their proletarian opponents and between imperialist countries and their colonies, but between the members of the Western Entente and the former Central Powers and, within the Entente, between the United States and Japan and between the United States, Britain, and France. These were the differences within the "enemy camp" upon which the Soviet leaders intended to play and did play—as at Rapallo.

To some extent, the thermonuclear stalemate from about 1957 onwards reduced the advantages of such a policy. Before developing the I.C.B.M., the U.S.S.R. had been exposed to superior Western nuclear might, which the United States, from its adjacent bases, could easily bring to bear upon Soviet territory, while the Western Hemisphere was hardly vulnerable to Russia's air-striking power. During this period, the Soviet leaders had concentrated upon hampering the United States, should it attempt to exploit its supremacy; this was the reason why the "peace movement" was fostered by Moscow and why Khrushchev, prior to Suez, ardently wooed the junior members of the Western alliance, Britain and France. Once, however, both sides were in possession of reliable nuclear delivery systems, so that each could seriously injure the other, a policy of merely playing off one member of the Western camp against another became increasingly unrewarding. It was quite clear that the concentration of destructive force in the hands of the two superpowers, the United States and the U.S.S.R., was so overwhelming (and, in the case of the United States, less and less dependent upon overseas bases) that a successful attempt to detach a junior member from the Western alliance would not affect the military balance—although it might have political repercussions. Moreover, it became essential for the two giants to be in some form of contact, if only to make clear to each other the precise "rules of the game" which, alone, could prevent fatal miscalculation or error. The Cuban missile crisis showed how minutely each would have to be able to size up the other's considerations and intentions if a holocaust was to be prevented. Both would have to know exactly where the lines were "frozen," so that any infringement was likely to set off the gravest repercussions, and just where sufficient fluidity still prevailed for advances and retreats to be feasible. In addition, the two superpowers were beginning to discover that they shared certain interests, if only to a very limited extent, for instance in the prevention of further nuclear proliferation. This realization was later to find expression in the test-ban treaty and elsewhere. Because of all these considerations, it became increasingly urgent for the U.S.S.R., from 1957–1958 onward, to establish some meaningful, ongoing contact, not just with useful junior members of the other camp, but with the main "enemy" himself.

In the ideological context it was, of course, bound to be very difficult to explain away such a development. A rapprochement with secondary Western powers could always be justified on tactical grounds—as a way of weakening the mainstay of the "imperialist camp," the United States itself. A dialogue with the latter, however, could hardly be said to be serving this purpose. (There was no such problem with regard to the dealings between the Big Three during World War II, since then it was Germany that was the "main" enemy, so that ideologically it was unobjectionable for Stalin to be working with Roosevelt and Churchill.) It therefore became incumbent upon Khrushchev to put forward a new theory, according to which the ruling forces in the United States itself were split into the "sensible" and the "mad" forces—so that Moscow had to strengthen the former against the latter in order to foil plans for an enemy attack. This did not prove convincing to the Chinese rulers, who could not believe that the "spirit of Camp David," the Khrushchev-Eisenhower meetings and other such contacts, could betoken anything less than class treason; what they really suspected and feared was a secret division of the world between the two superpowers, leaving the third would-be great power, China, out in the cold.

Chinese misgivings had been triggered by Moscow's unwillingness to provide a nuclear shield for Peking's adventures in the China Sea —an ominous indication that the U.S.S.R. might be more concerned to avoid an armed showdown with the "class enemy" than to safeguard "socialist solidarity."

Actually, Moscow under Khrushchev and his successors has never really made up its mind how to deal with the United States. On the one hand, the Soviet leaders cannot resist the temptation to harass the United States and to play upon any divisions within the Western camp—such as those relating to de Gaulle and those between West Germany and her allies; on the other hand, the U.S.S.R. cannot avoid the conclusion that, basically, only an understanding with Washington itself is likely to mean very much. The "hot line" and other symbols of the requirements of a thermonuclear age have been brought into existence, but rarely into use. The Russians are not only embarrassed by Peking's strictures about U.S.S.R.-American relations, but also seem to be inhibited themselves by an atavistic aversion to any direct deal with the "main enemy." They are much more comfortable when applying the method of the indirect approach—such as "reading between the lines" and "negotiating back to back." (It is for these and similar reasons that Moscow is increasingly appreciating the usefulness of the existence of the U.N. and other multilateral meeting grounds.) At the same time, the U.S.S.R. regards this particular form of "peaceful coexistence" as fully compatible with its unswerving pursuit of a bitter and lengthy global struggle, by means short of actual war, to the point where the international political balance may be shifted irreversibly.

It is within this context that Moscow has continued its forward policy in the "Third World," although at a much slower pace than in Khrushchev's day. However, in this area too Soviet policy has been ambivalent. One aim of Moscow's tenuous alignment with Afro-Asian "national liberation movements," with radical anti-Western rulers, and with some of the local communist parties has been to tilt the regional balance against the United States, while fending off Peking's forays. Yet, at the same time, the U.S.S.R. has hoped to use these links, as well as its military and economic assistance, as a means of "leverage" upon its associates in the "Third World" so as to avert any unpleasant surprises in that part of the globe. The Soviet leaders have been far from enamored at the thought that "revolutionary" adventures might be started in the developing areas without their knowledge or consent and that this might present them with a dilemma. If, for instance, certain key areas were drawn into conflict and the U.S.S.R. permitted itself to become involved, it might well find itself in dangerous confrontation with the West; if Moscow refused to help its "fellow revolutionaries," it would suffer damaging loss of prestige. So far, there has been little indication that, with all their assistance, the Soviets have acquired real leverage or control over their proud, touchy, and unpredictable associates in the "Third World." Moreover, as long as the U.S.S.R. persists in its attempts to woo recalcitrant radical elements in that sector of the globe, it will find itself subject to pressures that will constantly divert Soviet international policy into detours. While that is the case, the adoption of any consistent Soviet line toward the West appears hardly feasible.

Thus, as the U.S.S.R. approaches the second half-century of its existence, its posture on the world scene is marked by ambiguities, paradoxes, and contradictions that remain unresolved. On many major issues, the Soviet leadership has displayed typical "state" mentality—as self-centered, cold-blooded, and logical as that of any seventeenth-century devotee of *raison d'état*. Yet the U.S.S.R. is still very far from conforming to the behavior patterns of a "traditional" state; its ideological childhood infection has left it with distorted vision and it perceives images that lead it to stumble along uncertain paths toward dimly seen goals. The same malady has fostered the growth of those aspects of its dynamic character which cause it to be not only fiercely competitive, but preternaturally suspicious and hostile. It has never entirely completed its adolescent transition from an international political movement, intending to monopolize the globe, to a mature state and society. However, in a precariously balanced thermonuclear world, it is at least possible to harness those factors in the mental makeup of the Soviet leadership that are totally rational and predictable—namely, the narrow, but "healthy," Soviet egotism, the urge to place the survival of the regime and state above all other aims. As for any possibility that the U.S.S.R. may advance beyond this stage and relinquish its view of the world as an arena of unending, if limited, conflict, it remains a truism that such a development will have to await far-reaching changes in the Soviet system itself.

IX

The "Socialist Commonwealth": An Appraisal

by R A N D O L P H L . B R A H A M

> In contrast to the laws of the capitalist
> system, which is characterized by antagonistic
> contradictions between classes, nations and
> states leading to armed conflicts, there are
> no objective causes in the nature of the
> socialist system for contradictions and
> conflicts between the peoples and states
> belonging to it.
>
> —STATEMENT OF EIGHTY-ONE COMMUNIST AND
> WORKERS' PARTIES, *Moscow, 1960.*

Introductory Survey

Less than fifty years after the bolshevik revolution was depicted by its leaders as the dawn of a new, ideal era in human history, the world communist movement is in general disarray. The vision of the harmonious world order based on the identity of the class interests of the proletariat gradually gave way to the acceptance of the supremacy of states and the realities of interstate relations.

Theoretically and ideologically the Marxists were unprepared for the possibility of international relations between "socialist" states within the context of a nation-state system. Confident of the scientific nature of Marxism as a theory of history, the Communists were convinced that once the proletarian revolution broke out—and this was expected to occur more or less simultaneously in the industrially most advanced countries—it would soon "have the whole world as its arena." Their preoccupation with social classes rather than the nation led them to disregard fatally the nationalist attachments and aspirations that in crucial historical periods proved far more important than economic class solidarity.

The Marxist vision concerning the emergence and evolution of the new international community was irreparably marred by both the non-Marxist way in which the Communists acquired power and the system of interstate relations they subsequently developed. Belying the theory of historical materialism, with its emphasis on economic determinism, they came to power by employing almost exclusively political-military techniques. Once they were in power and their dominant position was safely assured, they became increasingly concerned with the preservation of the status quo. Trapped by their ideological preconceptions, they rationalized their exclusive position in the new system by identifying the protection of the regime and the advancement of national interests with the basic tenets of Marxism-Leninism.

At first, the illusion of the future world communist system was nourished by the identification of the bolshevik revolution as a concrete step in that direction and the portrayal of the U.S.S.R. (formally established about five years later) as its genuine prototype. Referred to as the only true fatherland of the international proletariat, the U.S.S.R. clung to this image throughout the period it enjoyed the exclusive position of being the only "socialist" country. The world communist movement prior to World War II consisted only of a worldwide array of subservient legal or outlawed parties operating under the general guidance and control of the Soviet-dominated Comintern.

However, with the emergence of a series of socialist states after the war (most of them created with the direct assistance of the

U.S.S.R.) the exclusive position of the Soviet Union as the leader of the socialist camp assuring institutional and ideological uniformity was gradually questioned, then openly challenged.

During the transitional period of 1945–1948, when the eastern European countries were systematically transformed into "people's democracies," and during the Stalinist era, the preeminence of the Soviet Union was assured by its neocolonial policies and by the fact that the leadership of these countries was entrusted primarily to the Moscow-trained *apparatchiki* who, in the absence of an independent domestic power base, were totally dependent on the U.S.S.R. In the wake of the cataclysmic changes effectuated by the Soviet-Yugoslav dispute of 1948 and the revolutionary upheavals following Khrushchev's denigration of Stalin, however, the old underground and Kremlin-appointed leaders were slowly replaced by domestically trained young *apparatchiki*. These, now enjoying an independent power base through the monolithic control of their respective political and military-police apparatuses, became increasingly self-centered, bolstering their position by policies appealing to the traditional nationalism of the peoples they ruled. Reminiscent of the "domesticism" and autarky practiced during the Stalinist era, they became ever more blatantly concerned with the economic development of their own countries and decreasingly interested in the objectives of the world communist movement per se.

With the exacerbation of the Sino-Soviet dispute, their area of maneuverability expanded. The original disagreements over conflicting economic interests gradually gave rise to conflicts over clashing ideological ambitions and national-territorial aspirations. With varying emphasis they seem to be ever more attracted to the principles of national independence, sovereignty, and mutual respect for territorial integrity. As was the case with the Second International, which was destroyed in 1914 when the leaders of the national social-democratic parties rallied behind their respective flags rather than follow the ideological dictates of international class solidarity, it appears that the forces of nationalism are merging once again victorious over those of internationalism.

These polycentric developments notwithstanding, however, it would be quixotic to assume that the "socialist commonwealth of nations" is about to disintegrate or that any of its members, no matter how vocal their opposition to the leadership of the U.S.S.R., are ready or willing to extricate themselves fully from either the economic or the military alliance in the near future. For aside from the realities of geography and Soviet power there is an identity of interests—national and political—that unites these countries, if not necessarily in the classic Marxist-Leninist sense then in the traditional spirit of alliances.

Although enjoying an independent power base, the communist leaders of eastern Europe are still indirectly in power because of the immediate adjacency of the U.S.S.R., as shown in the case of Hungary. Moreover, while they may differ on strategy and tactics and interpret the tenets of Marxism-Leninism to suit their specific interests, they subscribe to the same ideology and strive toward the attainment of the same long-range objectives. Finally, as is especially the case of Czechoslovakia and Poland, they are bound to the U.S.S.R. for the protection of their territorial integrity against possible German revanchism.

It is this general picture of the "socialist commonwealth" that this essay aims to bring into focus in light of the Marxist vision of the future communist society.

The Marxist Vision

Convinced that historical materialism, with its emphasis on economic determinism, constituted the master key unlocking the mysteries of societal evolution, the Marxist classics paid very little attention to the national question. Their preoccupation with the class and the class struggle as reflecting the development in the material forces of production made them oblivious of the possibility of interstate relations in the post-capitalist phase of historical evolution. They believed that the antagonistic contradictions between classes, nations, and states were characteristic only of the exploiting systems, above all capitalism. With the destruction of the system of private ownership over the basic modes of production and the consequent elimination of exploitation of man by man, they expected that all contradictions and conflicts between nations would also vanish. The Marxist apocalyptic vision entailed a replacement of the nation-state system by a supranational community—the world communist system—guided by the victorious working class composed of the new, omnicompetent "socialist" man. In *The Communist Manifesto* (1848), this process was envisioned as beginning already in the decaying phase of capitalism:

> National differences and antagonisms between peoples are vanishing gradually from day to day, owing to the development of the bourgeoisie, to freedom of commerce, to the world market, to uniformity in the mode of production and in the conditions of life corresponding thereto.
> The supremacy of the proletariat will cause them to vanish still faster. . . .
> In proportion as the exploitation of one individual by another is put an end to, the exploitation of one nation by another will also be put an end to. In proportion as the antagonism between classes within the nation vanishes, the hostility of one nation to another will come to an end.

Believing that the proletarian revolution would take place more or less simultaneously in the industrially and technologically most advanced countries powerful enough to dominate the rest of the world, the Marxist classics assumed that once the economic basis for national conflicts had been removed the states would gradually "wither away" yielding to a new, harmonious world community of peoples. The end of the nation-state system would bring about the merger of national states, the fusion of nations, and the end of governments within the states.

The Road to Utopia: The Bolshevik Revolution, The Comintern, and the Formation of the U.S.S.R.

In contradistinction to classical Marxism, which is viewed primarily as a critique of industrial capitalism, Leninism is to a large extent depicted as a critique of imperialism—the highest stage of monopoly-finance capitalism. An outgrowth of industrial capitalism that is portrayed as having enjoyed a relatively smooth evolution based on "free competition," capitalism in the era of imperialism, the Leninists argued, experienced a spasmodic development characterized by increasingly exacerbating contradictions on a worldwide scale.

Identifying Russia as one of the capitalist, albeit industrially still undeveloped, countries constituting one of the antagonistic camps of imperialism, the Leninists insisted that it was the responsibility of the Russian proletariat (that is, the party of professional revolutionaries) not only to the oppressed peoples of Russia but also to those of the entire world to "split the chain at its weakest link." They were convinced that once the proletarian revolution broke out anywhere, even in a basically backward country like Russia, its echoes would soon reverberate and engulf the entire industrially advanced world into a general conflagration, bringing with it the inevitable triumph of the working class. The Leninists had no scruples about the revolution first breaking out in the basically feudal, agriculturally backward, and highly illiterate Russia devoid of a sizable industrial proletariat, for they were convinced that under the leadership of a disciplined party it was possible in the age of imperialism to telescope two revolutions—the antifeudal bourgeois and the antibourgeois socialist—into one.

Taking advantage of the military and economic ills confronting Russia in 1917, the Leninists, guided by the dictates of political realism rather than the precepts of Marxist orthodoxy, compensated for the absence of a mature proletariat by appealing to the *private ownership* instincts of the landless peasantry and the *national* aspirations of the oppressed nationalities. It is perhaps unfair to assume that after acquiring power, the Bolsheviks became exclusively concerned with the solidification of their position and the "building of socialism in [only] one country." Realists as they were, the Bolsheviks were also motivated by the fervor of idealism and believed that their *coup d'état* of November 7, 1917, constituted the first step toward the creation of a harmonious world order. The ultimate objective of the Revolution, according to Trotsky's statement before the Second Congress of Soviets (November 8, 1917), was "the union of the oppressed everywhere."

Identifying the failures of the Second International with the "narrow-mindedness, opportunism and revolutionary inefficiency" of socialist leaders who transformed the workers' parties into "obedient agents of the bourgeoisie," the Leninists proceeded with what they envisioned as the second concrete step toward the creation of the Soviet world state—the organization of a new International Association of Workers, the Third Communist International (Comintern). On March 5, 1919, in a speech before the First Comintern Congress, Lenin declared that the foundation of the Comintern was "the forerunner of the International Republic of Soviets, of the international victory of Communism."

This theme pervaded the subsequent six congresses of the Comintern. The ultimate aim—World Communism—was reiterated in every major document, including the statutes and programs adopted at the Second and Sixth Comintern Congresses. The Comintern itself was designated as the "World Communist Party" whose primary mission was to assure "the transition from the world dictatorship of imperialism to the world dictatorship of the proletariat" and bring about the establishment of a "World Union of Socialist Soviet Republics, for the complete destruction of classes and the realization of socialism, the first stage of Communist society."

The formal establishment of the U.S.S.R. at the end of 1922 was envisioned not only as still another concrete step toward the achievement of World Communism, but also as the prototype of the future World Soviet Socialist Republics. The Declaration of Union that Stalin read before the First Congress of Soviets of the U.S.S.R. (December 30, 1922), and which was subsequently incorporated into the Soviet constitution of 1924, envisioned the gradual expansion of the U.S.S.R. into a world communist system by stipulating that "admission to the union is open to all Socialist Soviet Republics, both those . . . in existence and those which will arise in the future."

Because of its class content and internal structure, the new Soviet state was depicted not only as superior to Western bourgeois states, but also as the "highest form of democracy" represented by the dictatorship of the proletariat. It was portrayed by the program adopted by the Sixth Comintern Congress as the prototype of federative unions of proletarian republics which would eventually grow into the "World Union of Soviet Socialist Republics uniting the whole of mankind under the hegemony of the international proletariat organized as a state."

The Primacy of the U.S.S.R.

The prognostications of Lenin concerning the imminence of the world revolution failing to materialize—the communist parties of

the industrially more advanced Western countries actually becoming less influential as the working class, motivated by what Lenin
had called a "trade union mentality," strove to acquire an ever
greater share in the capitalist pie—the Soviet leaders became increasingly ethnocentric. Abandoning many of the substantive goals
that motivated them before and during the Revolution, they became ever more preoccupied with the maintenance and expansion
of Soviet (that is, Party and/or personal) power. The ideological
requirements of the world revolution were gradually replaced by
empirical policies calculated to advance the national interests of the
U.S.S.R. struggling for survival in a world based on the nation-state
system. Trotsky's "permanent revolution" was subordinated to "socialism in one country," that is, the primacy of the Soviet state.

The ideological-theoretical rationale for the violation of Marxist
revolutionary doctrine was offered by Stalin. Motivated, *inter alia,*
by the desire to demonstrate the "legitimacy" of his ever greater
powers in terms of his mastery of the tenets of Marxism-Leninism,
Stalin reviewed the logic of the primacy of the Soviet state in a series
of lectures at Sverdlov University (April 1924). In a masterly display of doctrinal opportunism, he "demonstrated" not only that the
strengthening of the Soviet state was in accord with Marxist-
Leninist doctrine, but also that it was a necessary prerequisite for
the speedy destruction of imperialism:

> The goal is to consolidate the dictatorship of the proletariat
> in one country, using it as a base for the overthrow of imperialism
> in all countries. . . . The very development of world revolution
> . . . will be more rapid and more thorough, the more thoroughly
> Socialism fortifies itself in the first victorious country, the faster this
> country is transformed into a base for the further unfolding of world
> revolution, into a lever for the further disintegration of imperialism.

The subordination of the aim of world revolution to the national
interests of the Soviet Union brought about the transformation of
the Comintern into an agency of the Soviet Foreign Office. The
Comintern became increasingly concerned with the justification of
Soviet foreign-policy moves, often to the great discomfiture of the
communist parties the world over. In the pursuit of policies based
on the power interests of the Soviet state, though rationalized in
Marxist ideological terms, the leaders of the U.S.S.R. established
and developed diplomatic relations with foreign states, frequently

at the expense of local communist movements. They embraced a series of regimes (from, for example, Kemalist Turkey in the 1920s to Nasser's Egypt in the 1950s) that not only outlawed, but literally decimated the communist parties operating in their respective countries. In was in this vein, too, that the Soviet Union guided the German and Chinese communist parties to disaster in the 1920s.

Nevertheless, by identifying the U.S.S.R. as the "exclusive fatherland of the international proletariat," the 1928 Comintern program sanctified the Soviet leaders' assertion that the first and foremost duty of the workers of the world was to further the state interests of the first "socialist motherland." The U.S.S.R. was depicted not only as the prototype and nucleus of the world communist society to come, but also as its prime mover—the powerful base of the world revolutionary movement. The definition of a true revolutionary was offered by Stalin in his formulation of the concept of "proletarian internationalism" in 1927:

> He is an internationalist who unreservedly, unhesitatingly and unconditionally is prepared to defend the USSR, because the USSR is the base of the world revolutionary movement, and it is impossible to defend, to advance this revolutionary movement without defending the USSR. Whoever thinks of defending the world revolutionary movement without, and against, the USSR, goes against revolution, and must slide to the camp of the enemy of the revolution.

Dedicated communist revolutionaries, consequently, were expected to see no contradiction in subordinating and often sacrificing themselves for the advancement of Soviet interests, for they had to "realize" that a strong U.S.S.R. was the *sine qua non* for the ultimate success of communism the world over. Whatever was good for the U.S.S.R. was *ipso facto* good for the international proletariat.

It was in this context that the communist parties of the world were called upon to defend the mutual-assistance and nonaggression pacts of the U.S.S.R. signed in the 1930s with a number of bourgeois and fascist-reactionary states.

The triumph of Nazism in the wake of Stalin's disastrous directives to the German Communist Party induced a tactical change in Soviet foreign policy. The rising might of the Third Reich made imperative a Soviet drive for collective security. The U.S.S.R. joined the League of Nations (September 18, 1934) while the members of the future Axis Alliance withdrew, and called for the establishment of a "united front" of all "progressive" forces opposed to fascism.

The propagation of the new Soviet line was again entrusted primarily to the Comintern. To deter attention from this basically tactical shift and maintain the illusion that the Third Communist International was not merely a tool of the Soviet government, the Seventh (and last) World Congress was placed under the leadership of Georgi Dimitrov, the Bulgarian Comintern agent of "Reichstag Fire Trial" fame. Condemning fascism as "the most reactionary and most ferocious type of imperialist capitalism," Dimitrov called upon the comrades (August 2, 1935) to adopt a new "flexible" line involving the unification of all truly patriotic forces against the common enemy. Referring to Lenin's *"Left-Wing" Communism,* he emphasized the necessity of adapting the strategies and tactics of the communist parties to the specific conditions of the time and place in which they operated. The "united front" policy was not conceived to repudiate, but merely to postpone, the ultimate goal— the acquisition of power and the establishment of a dictatorship of the proletariat.

It was Dimitrov's task to reformulate the principles of "proletarian internationalism" by synchronizing them with those of "genuine nationalism" as required by the new "united front" policy. In his drive to harness the forces of nationalism and graft its symbols onto those of "proletarian internationalism," Dimitrov insisted that while Communists were the "irreconcilable opponents" of bourgeois, chauvinist nationalism, they were not the supporters of "national nihilism." Redefining the bolshevik tenets on the national question, he went on to demonstrate—in partial contrast to Stalin's teachings of the 1920s—that the class struggle can acquire national characteristics, which are in complete harmony with the requirements of "proletarian internationalism":

> Comrades, proletarian internationalism must, so to speak, "acclimatize itself" in each country in order to sink deep roots in its native land. *National forms* of the proletarian class struggle and of the labor movement in the individual countries are in no contradiction to proletarian internationalism; on the contrary, it is precisely in these forms that the *international interests* of the proletariat can be successfully defended.

The victory of the working class in the capitalist countries, Dimitrov hastened to add, cannot be assured within an isolated national framework; it can be secured *only in closest alliance* with the victorious proletariat of the Soviet Union." Such a victory would bring about the flourishing of a truly national culture as reflected by the experience of the U.S.S.R., which is *national in form and socialist in content.*

The failure of the "united front" strategy, by which the U.S.S.R. had hoped to play the role of *Tertius Gaudens* while the Western "imperialists" devoured each other, coupled with the shortsightedness of France and Great Britain, who seemed more fearful of the long-range menace of bolshevism than the immediate threat of Nazism, forced the Soviet leaders to reappraise the priority requirements of the Soviet Union. The new tactics called for a rapprochement with the Third Reich—the archenemy—which, for imperialistic reasons of its own, was willing to pay a high price for the temporary neutrality of Russia, for a respite that would enable Hitler to satisfy his ambitions in the West. Litvinov's replacement by Molotov paved the way for the signing of the diplomatic masterpiece, the Nazi-Soviet Non-Aggression and Neutrality Pact (August 23, 1939), whose secret protocol provided for the division of eastern Europe into Russian and German spheres of influences.

Identified as still another step in the long-range strategy of world revolution, the communist parties of the world were called upon to defend the Pact and campaign against intervention in the "capitalist war." They saluted the territorial expansion of the U.S.S.R. through the forced annexation of the Baltic states, eastern Poland, Bessarabia, and northern Bukovina, to say nothing about the military campaign against Finland, as "an outstanding example of a genuine solution of the national question, making possible the peaceful and fraternal collaboration of numerous peoples within a multinational socialist state."

The Nazi invasion of the U.S.S.R. on June 22, 1941, brought about another radical shift in tactics. Abandoning their earlier "isolationist" position, the Communists assumed a nationalistic posture and, in accordance with the policy directives of the Kremlin, now called upon all "patriotic" forces to rally behind the defense of "liberty and democracy." While pursuing their own ultimate interests, they emerged into the forefront of the resistance movements and bore the brunt of the underground war against the Nazi occupants.

Under the impact of the "Great Patriotic War," the gradual increase in the prestige and preeminence of the Soviet Union in the world communist movement was paralleled by the steady emergence of the Great Russians as *primus inter pares* among the nationalities of the U.S.S.R. In mobilizing the energies of the nation in the war against the Nazis, Stalin appealed to Great Russian nationalism urging the peoples to come to the rescue of the Russian, not "socialist," motherland. He invoked the "manly images" of the great Russian national heroes like Alexander Nevskii, Dmitri Pozharskii, Alexander Suvorov, and Mikhail Kutuzov, rather than the revolutionary images of Marx, Engels, or even Lenin.

The new, communist-style "Russification" trend continued into the postwar period. In raising a toast at a Kremlin reception in honor of Red Army officers celebrating the victorious end of the war in Europe (May 24, 1945), Stalin singled out the Russians as "the most outstanding nation of all of the nations which reside in the Soviet Union. . . ." He continued:

> It deserves general recognition in the war as the leading force in the Soviet Union among all the peoples of our country. . . . It is the leading people, because it has a clear mind, firm character, and endurance.

While the Soviet leaders continue, however distortedly, to strictly uphold the "socialist content" of the official Marxist-Leninist formula, the term "national in form" has to a marked extent come to denote "Russian" in practice. Although never officially recognized, Russian has become the dominant means of communication in the state and party apparatuses and its mastery is increasingly considered as desirable, nay necessary, for advancement in all spheres of life. The xenophobia and chauvinism of the postwar period can be partially explained as the reaction of the Soviet leaders to the hostility and separatist tendencies manifested by some of the nationalities, especially the Ukrainians, during the war.

The influence and power of Russia were greatly enhanced by the outcome of the war. The penetration of the Red Army into the heart of Europe and the concurrent emergence of the U.S.S.R. as one of the two superpowers of the world revived the illusion, temporarily at least, that the cause of the international proletariat was further advanced toward the establishment of the harmonious world order of communism. The illusion was nurtured by the rationalization of the direct involvement of the Soviet Union in the transformation of the eastern European states into "people's democracies" and their subsequent inclusion in what came to be referred to in the West as the "Soviet bloc."

The Soviet Bloc

The objectives of the U.S.S.R. in eastern Europe were basically the same as the ones that motivated Soviet policy since the bolshevik acquisition and consolidation of power—the advancement of national interests rationalized in terms of their identity with the cause of "socialism." In the immediate post-armistice period, these objectives were successfully pursued not only because of the preponderant position of the Red Army in both the formerly enemy and technically allied states, but also because of the auspicious political climate created by the outcome of the war in eastern Europe. The upper classes were compromised by their direct or indirect collaboration with the Nazis, property relations were upset by wartime devastation and aryanization programs, and, above all, the Communists, camouflaging their ultimate intentions, advocated the adoption of measures with which no true liberal could quarrel. Embracing the flames of nationalism, they claimed to be working, *inter alia,* for the revitalization of national life, the punishment of war criminals, the restoration of liberties, the establishment of democratic representative systems of government, and the institution of meaningful agrarian reforms, which were long overdue in this part of the world.

The drive toward the acquisition and consolidation of power was pursued in several well-differentiated stages with minor policy variations to fit specific local conditions. During the first phase (1944–1945 to 1947–1948), the local communist leaderships, composed to a large extent of Comintern agents who returned to their former homelands in the wake of the Red Army, condoned, for tactical reasons, the establishment of representative coalition governments. In the absence of an independent power base of their own (with the exception of Yugoslavia and Albania), they acted under the protective umbrella of the Soviet occupation authorities. While they allowed the participation of traditional democratic elements in the management of public affairs, the Communists gradually infiltrated the key levers of power for purposes of establishing what they called "friendly and truly democratic" regimes. Although the façade of the external forms of parliamentary democracy continued to be neatly preserved, opposition became increasingly nominal. Using the so-called National Democratic Fronts as a cover, the Communists first infiltrated and then took over control of the parties composing them. Once the levers of power were safely assured, the Communists gradually transformed themselves from a ruling minority into a dominating majority. In appearance they continued to press only for the achievement of strictly democratic aims but in reality they were laying the foundation for the "socialist transformation" of their respective societies.

The role of the Soviet Union in the revolutionary changes in eastern Europe was at first minimized. In line with the then prevailing theory of people's democracy (I. P. Trainin, A. Leontiev, E. S. Varga, *et al.*), emphasis was placed on the dissimilarities between the "new democracies" and Soviet democracy. While the new system of "people's republics" was considered superior to Western bourgeois democracies, it was not to be confused with the Soviet dictatorship of the proletariat. This was made especially clear by Dimitrov in speaking about the future of his country (September 1946):

> Bulgaria will not be a Soviet republic but a people's republic in which the functions of government will be performed by an enormous majority of the people—workers, peasants, craftsmen, and the people's intelligentsia. In this republic there will be no dictatorship of any kind.

Having "legitimized" their power through elections they staged and won in the by now well-known manner, the Communists adopted a new line with regard to their internal and external relations. Internally, they no longer found it necessary to preserve the outward manifestations of parliamentary democracy and dropped even the pretense of collaborating with nonproletarian elements. Externally, the identification with, and emulation of, the Soviet Union were officially asserted. The theory of "people's democracy" was revised (N. P. Farberov, B. S. Mankowsky, J. Révai, *et al.*), demonstrating that the "people's republic" was a type of dictatorship of the proletariat differing only in form but not in essence from the Soviet model. The decisive role of the Soviet Union in bringing about the establishment and preservation of the new regimes was no longer denied. In fact, one was never permitted to forget that these regimes were based on cooperation and friendship with the Soviet Union and that any tendency to weaken the ties with the U.S.S.R. would be considered as inimical to the "best interests of the people."

New constitutions and Party statutes were adopted to reflect the new realities. While the earlier documents had failed to mention the contributions of the U.S.S.R. or the Red Army, the new Party and state documents fully acknowledged them. The Rumanian constitution of 1952, for example, referred to the U.S.S.R. and the Red Army five times. It depicted the Soviet Union as the liberator of the country whose "selfless and brotherly support . . . ensure the independence, State sovereignty, development and flourishing of the Rumanian People's Republic."

From the theoretical-ideological point of view, the setting up of these new communist regimes in eastern Europe was not considered as an end in itself but rather as a means for the achievement of the final objective—the establishment of a World Union of Soviet Socialist Republics. The Yugoslav Communists, for example, having crushed all opposition in the course of their partisan activities and established a "people's republic" almost immediately after the war, looked upon their Party and state as potential component units of the Soviet Party and state. According to a June 5, 1945, dispatch of the Soviet Minister in Belgrade, Kardelj is quoted as having said:

> We would like the Soviet Union to look at us as representatives of one of the future Soviet Republics, and not as representatives of another country, capable of independently solving questions. . . . [They] consider the Communist Party of Yugoslavia as being a part of the All-Union Communist Party, that is to say, that our relationship . . . [should emphasize] that Yugoslavia in the future would be admitted a constituent part of the USSR.

It is interesting to note that the overtures of the Yugoslav communist leaders, who at this time were more "dogmatic" than their Soviet counterparts, were not very enthusiastically received by Stalin. In this early postwar period prior to the conclusion of the peace treaties, the Soviet leaders were still sensitive to the possible reaction of the Western Allies whose aid was needed not only for the possible economic rehabilitation but also for the political normalization of the area. They probably also feared that the outright absorption of the "people's democracies" as constituent units of the U.S.S.R. might cause a cultural split within the "socialist homeland" since the standards of the eastern European countries—backward as they were from the Western point of view—were superior to those prevailing in the Union Republics. Finally, this proposal of the Yugoslavs, like the subsequent ones advanced by Tito and Dimitrov for the establishment of a Balkan Union that would gradually be expanded into a federation or confederation including the central and eastern European states, went counter to Stalin's grand neocolonial design for the area.

For tactical reasons, the leaders of the U.S.S.R. were very cautious at first in dealing with the problems raised by the envisioned establishment of a Soviet-dominated though integrated communist community of formerly independent nation-states. They condoned the development of an increasingly visible institutional and ideological diversity in order to provide the flexibility required by the Kremlin-appointed or supported leaders to consolidate their power.

The trend toward the integration of this extremely polyglot area was originally welcomed not only by most ritualistic liberals but also by some rabid anti-Communists. Unaware of the Soviet grand design and perhaps also misguided by the Marxist universalism of class interests, they saw in it a blessing in disguise. Socialism was envisioned as the common denominator that would do away with the historical animosities that plagued the many ethnic and national groups inhabiting this troublesome part of the world.

The conclusion of the peace treaties and the concurrent decline of Western interest in eastern Europe, coupled with the realization that the people's democratic leaders were becoming increasingly infected by what Brzezinski has called the disease of "domesticism" —the conscious and unconscious preoccupation with the building of communism at home at the expense of the broader considerations of Soviet-defined international goals—signaled the replacement of the Soviet policy of diversity with that of uniformity.

Aware that he now had to deal with established parties and official governments rather than with revolutionary movements,

Stalin came to heed Tito's earlier advice and decided on the establishment of a new communist international organization to replace the Comintern, which had been formally "dissolved" in May 1943 as a gesture of friendship and goodwill toward the Western Allies.

The founding of the Communist Information Bureau, or Cominform, in September 1947, marks the beginning of the Stalinist phase of communist interstate relations. Depicting the postwar world as divided into two antagonistic camps—one dominated by imperialist America and the other guided by the peace-loving U.S.S.R.—Andrei Zhdanov, one of the Soviet representatives at the Szklarska Poreba (Poland) Conference, warned that some of the comrades misunderstood "the dissolution of the Comintern to imply the elimination of all ties, of all contact between the fraternal Communist Parties."

In line with this implied ominous warning, the Conference resolved that the Information Bureau be entrusted with "the organization of interchange of experience and, if need be, coordination of the activities of the Communist Parties on the basis of mutual agreement."

As the self-proclaimed leader of the "camp of peace and socialism," Stalin launched a drastic campaign for the total subordination of the east European states. The docile satraps were ordered to lay the "foundation of socialism" in their respective countries through the assertion of the dictatorship of the proletariat, the exacerbation of the class struggle through the elimination of the last vestiges of bourgeois-landlord influence and the purging of the "opportunist, unreliable" elements in the communist parties, the launching of collectivization drives, and the development of industry on the basis of Soviet-style Five Year Plans.

In line with his policies of *divide et impera,* Stalin encouraged the self-contained autarchic development of the eastern European countries to assure both Soviet control and maximum exploitation. Instead of the advancement of the world communist order through peaceful and voluntary integration, the people's democracies were isolated from each other and feudally subordinated to the U.S.S.R. Under the guidance of Stalin, they were forced to march along parallel tracks theoretically toward the building of socialism but in reality toward the duplication of the structure of Soviet totalitarianism.

The subordination of the satellites was assured by both formal and informal ties. Formally, the people's democracies were bound to each other and separately to the U.S.S.R. by a series of bilateral —not multilateral—state agreements under which lip service was paid to the concepts of sovereignty and national independence. Although these treaties were basically meaningless, serving primarily to camouflage Soviet neocolonialism, they were held up for emulation as examples of the new type of friendly and cooperative relations among states dedicated to the building of socialism.

While less conspicuous, the informal ties were more real. The top government and Party leaders of the eastern European states were directly or indirectly selected by and responsible to Stalin; the agencies of government, including the ministries, police, the secret police, and the armed forces, like the Party organs, were either infiltrated by agents of the corresponding Soviet organs and organizations or were openly headed by Soviet citizens. As political initiative normally rested with Stalin or the C.P.S.U., the satellite leaders acted, generally speaking, either by anticipating Stalin's wishes or by clearing their policy decisions with the corresponding Soviet representatives.

The total subjugation of the formerly independent states of eastern Europe notwithstanding, the primacy of the U.S.S.R. was doctrinally defended by the traditional identification of Soviet national interests with the aspirations of the international proletariat. It was in this light that at the Nineteenth C.P.S.U. Congress (1952) Malenkov, then Stalin's heir apparent, referred to the relations of the U.S.S.R. with the people's democracies as setting "an example of entirely new relations among states, relations never yet encountered in history."

Ironically, the establishment of the Cominform, which was calculated to assure institutional and ideological unity under the aegis of the Soviet Union, led to the first major breach in the socialist camp with ominous implications for the future development of the world communist movement.

Stalin's efforts to impose total conformity on the eastern European countries through the establishment of a clearly defined institutional and doctrinal hierarchy conflicted with the interests of the Yugoslav leaders whose ambition was to play a *coordinate* rather than a *subordinate* role in the new International. Stalin, on the other hand, rationalizing the identity of Soviet interests with the cause of socialism the world over, insisted on the exclusiveness of the Kremlin as the one and only undisputed source of ideology and power within the camp. Underestimating or perhaps ignoring the fact that, in contradistinction to the communist leaders in the other Soviet-dominated countries, the Yugoslavs enjoyed an independent power base of their own, Stalin inadvertently drove them back to "domesticism," which they now gradually transformed into "national communism." In a note to Stalin on April 13, 1948, Tito insisted that "no matter how much each of us loves the land of socialism, the USSR, he can, in no case, love his country less."

The attitude of the Titoists reinforced Stalin's views originally formulated during the previous two decades, when he refused to come to the assistance of communist movements not directly under the command of the Kremlin or of leaders whose policies and aspirations tended to conflict with the immediate or long-range interests of the U.S.S.R. He now realized that not only revolutionary movements and leaders struggling to acquire power, but also communist parties in power, even though duplicating Soviet practices, must be subdued if their loyalty to the U.S.S.R. was to be assured.

The expulsion of Yugoslavia from the Cominform in 1948 and the subsequent evolution of two concurrent sources of dogma brought about not only the eventual destruction of the monolithic character of the world communist movement—Titoism providing the precedent for the Polish-Hungarian and later the Chinese-Albanian and Rumanian rebellions—but also weakened, if not totally destroyed, the faith of many Communists in the infallibility of Marxism. The basic assumptions of Marxism that the solidarity of the international proletariat would transcend the loyalty of individual proletarians and communist parties to their respective nations and governments, first repudiated by history in 1914–1918, suffered another setback. The Titoist crisis, like the subsequent Sino-Soviet and other disputes, revealed that communist-controlled "socialist" countries could *not* eliminate or control the "objective causes" that lead to "contradictions and conflicts between peoples and states."

The monolithic unity of the Soviet bloc was maintained during the lifetime of Stalin by a reign of terror, which in the name of anti-Titoism and proletarian internationalism silenced or eliminated all actual and potential proponents of national communism and genuine Marxist internationalism and, as was the case during the 1936–1938 purges in the Soviet Union, many champions of Stalinism. The test of a "true internationalist" and of a "devotee to the cause of socialism" again became absolute loyalty to Stalin and the U.S.S.R. The drive against Titoism was coupled with the campaign against cosmopolitanism and Zionism leading to the gradual aryanization of the governmental and political apparatuses and the concurrent destruction of Yiddish culture.

The simmering dissatisfactions and restiveness of the subjugated peoples of central and eastern Europe exploded into the open soon after the death of Stalin in 1953. The new leaders of the Soviet Union, while waging a desperate struggle for power, realized that sweeping changes were necessary in Soviet-eastern European relations if the unity of the socialist camp was to be maintained. The policies they subsequently adopted led to the gradual transformation of the one-man ruled monolithic Soviet bloc into a Soviet-guided "socialist commonwealth."

The "Socialist Commonwealth"

The death of Stalin and the subsequent erosion of the iron interparty discipline that characterized his era brought about dramatic if not immediately discernible changes in both domestic and communist interstate relations. The potential dangers of the post-Stalin interregnum were overcome—to the surprise of many Kremlinologists—with relative ease. To assuage the restiveness of the people, the communist leaders adopted, among other things, a "New Course" policy which was pursued with minor variations to fit local conditions in all the Soviet-controlled countries. Although the essence of communist rule was not altered—the parties remained as firmly in control as before—the new winds of change eased considerably the lot of the people. Aside from economic innovations, including the gradual abolition of the system of forced grain deliveries and the abandonment of irrational development projects like the building of the Danube-Black Sea canal, the instruments of terror were toned down, many of the internment camps were abolished, and the judiciary systems were separated from the secret police.

In the sphere of socialist interstate relations, the heirs of Stalin, especially Khrushchev, made a desperate effort to improve the image of the U.S.S.R. The Soviet-controlled joint stock companies—the symbols of Stalinist exploitation—were dissolved and the ambitions of the eastern European communist leaders concerning the industrialization of their respective countries were openly encouraged. Positive as these changes were, however, the new leaders of the Soviet Union soon realized the necessity of filling the vacuum left by Stalin's death in the informal ties that linked the people's democracies to the U.S.S.R. Khrushchev became increasingly preoccupied with the idea of striking a balance between unity and diversity that would ensure both Soviet predominance and allow the eastern European leaders to develop more viable systems of their own. The objective was to establish a conceptual framework sufficiently flexible to provide the organizational structure within which the goals of World Communism could be pursued under the direction of the Soviet Union.

In the drive toward the eventual establishment of what came to be referred to with ever increasing frequency as a "commonwealth of socialist nations" (*Sodruzhestvo Sotsialisticheskikh Stran*), the luring of Titoist Yugoslavia back into the communist camp was given one of the highest priorities. The decision to this effect was made sometime in the fall of 1954 and represented one of the first major victories of Khrushchev in his struggle against the "Stalinists." It was based on the assumption that unless Yugoslavia was drawn back into the camp, the other "people's republics" might be tempted to emulate it.

The Soviet and satellite press gradually changed its tone concerning Yugoslavia, preparing the ground for Khrushchev's visit to Belgrade in May–June 1955. The joint Soviet-Yugoslav declaration of June 2, 1955, like the subsequent denigration of Stalin (February 1956) and the dissolution of the Cominform (April 1956), largely in deference to Yugoslav sensitivities, prepared the ground for the official Soviet-Yugoslav Party Agreement of June 20, 1956. The Agreement incorporated some of the key elements of Titoism including the affirmation that "the roads and conditions of socialist development are different in different countries . . . and . . . any tendency to impose one's own views in determining the roads and forms of socialist development is alien to both sides."

The Soviet leaders did not, of course, expect nor envision the possibility that the "secret speech" and the Agreement might be "misinterpreted" or "abused" by the communist rulers of eastern Europe, hitherto loyal, unswerving allies. Their intention was to expand further and solidify the new Soviet-led "commonwealth" on a more streamlined basis, rather than to provide an opportunity for the eventual evolution of a new pantheistic secular creed sanctified in the name of "polycentrism."

But with the authority of Stalin destroyed, the doctrinal supremacy of Moscow embarrassed and challenged, and many of the claims of Soviet experience exposed as "crimes," the communist leaders of eastern Europe, now in firm possession of an independent power base of their own, demanded an opportunity to build "communism" in their respective countries in accordance with the principles of the Soviet-Yugoslav Agreement and in cooperation with the U.S.S.R.

The demands of the Poles, echoed by the Hungarians, set in motion a chain reaction of centrifugal forces that came to a climax in October–November 1956. Seeking vainly to keep the mounting crisis under control, the Soviet leaders issued an "October Declaration" (October 30, 1956) outlining the basic assumptions of the new "commonwealth":

> United by the common ideal of building a socialist society and by the principles of proletarianism, the countries of the great *commonwealth of socialist nations* can build their relations only on the basis of complete equality, respect for territorial integrity, national independence and sovereignty and noninterference in each other's internal affairs. This does not preclude, but on the contrary, presupposes close fraternal cooperation and mutual understanding among the countries of the *socialist commonwealth* in the economic, political and cultural fields.

Four days later Soviet tanks rumbled down the streets of Budapest, not only suppressing the Hungarian revolt but also destroying the hopes for genuine "national communism" and "socialist independence," exposing at the same time the realities of Soviet neocolonialism.

The horrors of the suppression and the massacre of fellow comrades notwithstanding, the intervention by the Red Army was defended as another proof of the fraternal assistance rendered by the U.S.S.R. to other socialist countries and of the fulfillment of its responsibilities to the international proletariat. In writing in the

March 22, 1957, issue of *Krasnaya Svezda,* the Soviet army organ, Colonel G. Fedorov stated:

> Trained by the Communist Party, the armed forces of the USSR live up to their international duty. This was demonstrated by the aid they gave to the working people of Hungary in suppressing the counterrevolutionary rebellion organized by international imperialism. The armed forces of the USSR performed their international class duty with honor.

In the wake of the Polish-Hungarian events of 1956, Yugoslavia once again was identified, temporarily at least, as the *bête noire* of the communist world. With the return of stability the Soviets manifested an increasing tendency toward the revitalization of the Stalinist content of "proletarian internationalism." The leading role of the Soviet Union in the socialist camp was openly acknowledged in the November 1957 Declaration of Communist and Workers' Parties of Socialist Countries, which the Yugoslavs refused to sign. Shortly thereafter the Yugoslavs published their own Draft Program (March 13, 1958) identifying themselves as the true standard-bearers of Marxism-Leninism. They attacked the Soviet conception of the two-camp world and deplored the impact of the "bureaucratic-etatistic tendencies" in the Soviet Union on the world communist movement. In criticizing the program of the League of Yugoslav Communists, *Kommunist,* the theoretical organ of the C.P.S.U., on the other hand, accused the Yugoslavs of harboring petty-bourgeois nationalist feelings and failing to understand the true interests of the international proletariat. *Kommunist* insisted that for the Yugoslavs "proletarian internationalism is reduced *exclusively* to the principles of equality and noninterference in another's internal affairs, while the necessity of strengthening unity and cooperation among the socialist countries and Marxist-Leninist parties is buried in oblivion." "Under certain conditions," the journal continued, "proletarian internationalism demands the subordination of the interests of the proletarian struggle in one country to the interests of the struggle on a world-wide scale," that is, to the interests of the U.S.S.R.

The fluctuation of Soviet-Yugoslav relations became gradually intertwined with the increasingly apparent Sino-Soviet dispute. After a brief but surprise-laden experiment with the "hundred flowers" theory, the Chinese launched an equally disastrous "great leap forward" drive calculated to overtake the U.S.S.R. in the attainment of Full Communism and establish themselves as *the true* representatives of Marxism-Leninism. While the bellicose posture of the Chinese reflected to a large extent their domestic requirements, the gradually evolving internecine dispute acquired the coloration of a gigantic struggle between two world powers pursuing conflicting national goals.

The main ideological differences came to the fore over the issue of destalinization and revisionism. They were further escalated at a series of international gatherings, including the Bucharest Party meeting of June and the Moscow conference of eighty-one parties of November 1960. The point of no return was reached at the Twenty-second C.P.S.U. Congress (October 1961), when Khrushchev excommunicated Albania from the bloc, elevating the differences from the ideological to the political plane.

For a while these differences were couched in esoteric language —the Chinese attacking Yugoslavia when they meant the U.S.S.R., and the Soviet leaders, in turn, condemning Albania when they had China in mind. With the publication of the by now famous Chinese open letter of June 14, 1963, however, the dispute became not only fully identified but also ever more exacerbated, extending from the political-ideological realm into the economic, geographic, and military spheres as well. A little over eleven years after the signing of the thirty-year "Friendship, Alliance, and Mutual Assistance Treaty" (February 14, 1950), the last Soviet technicians were withdrawn from China. The refusal of the U.S.S.R. to help China become a nuclear power, the gradual decline of Sino-Soviet trade from $2,055 million in 1959 to $370 million in 1964, the evolving and flourishing "Camp David spirit" in Soviet-American relations culminating in the test-ban treaty, and the subsequent alignment of "socialist" Russia with "bourgeois" India against "the people's democratic" China —an event unprecedented in the history of the world proletariat— contributed not only to the placement of the two behemoths of "socialism" on a collision course, but also to the irrevocable splitting of the world communist movement.

Accusing the Soviet leaders (of both the Khrushchev and post-Khrushchev era) of having "degenerated into a group of renegades from Marxism-Leninism" and having become "sinister accomplices of United States imperialism" for the encirclement of China—Foreign Minister Chen Yi actually declaring on July 10, 1966, that

Soviet troops were being deployed "along the Chinese border in coordination with the United States" for this purpose—the Chinese leaders adopted an irrevocably belligerent attitude. In order to "safeguard China's national sovereignty," they announced (April 1966) sweeping new rules governing foreign (mainly Soviet) ships sailing the Amur, the Sungari, the Argun, and related waterways, which link China with her northern neighbors.

Making an all-out attempt to snatch control of international communism from the U.S.S.R., the Chinese openly encouraged the formation of rival communist parties, declared their readiness to assume the leadership of the "world countryside"—meaning Asia, Africa, and Latin America—against the "world city"—the United States and western Europe—and latently encouraged Afro-Asian racial pressures against both the NATO and the Warsaw Pact nations. Emphasizing the irreconcilable antagonism between "true Marxism-Leninism" on the one hand, and Soviet revisionism and American imperialism on the other, the Chinese asserted that the major task confronting the "Marxist-Leninist parties" was to draw a clear line of demarcation both politically and organizationally between themselves and the revisionists:

> The antagonism between Marxism-Leninism and . . . revisionism is a class antagonism between the proletariat and the bourgeoisie; it is the antagonism between socialism and the capitalist road and between the line of opposing imperialism and that of surrendering to it. It is an irreconcilable antagonism.

With the line of demarcation clearly drawn, the battle against the dual enemy—revisionism and imperialism—was to be waged in a unified manner. According to the Chinese-Albanian statement of May 14, 1966, "the fight against imperialism headed by the United States and its lackeys and the fight against modern revisionism, with the leading group of the Soviet Communist Party at its center, are two inseparable tasks."

The struggle acquired momentum in August 1966, when a faction of the Chinese Communist Party leadership headed by Mao Tse-tung, Chairman of the Central Committee, and Lin Piao, Minister of National Defense and new heir apparent, launched a concerted drive against those who have embraced the "Soviet, capitalist-revisionist" road within China. They unleashed a massive campaign in the guise of a "great proletarian cultural revolution" against the supporters of Liu Shao-ch'i, the Head of State, and Teng Hsiao-p'ing, the Party Secretary General, which shook Chinese society to its foundation. Spearheaded by hastily mobilized, frenzied secondary school and college students—organized into Red Guards and armed with a new Communist gospel, the *Quotations From Chairman Mao Tse-tung*—the "cultural revolution" has increasingly acquired an anti-Soviet coloration climaxed in a long siege of the Soviet Embassy in Peking. According to Dr. Martyn Lazarev, a Soviet specialist in international law, "the steps taken against the Soviet Embassy in Peking [were] unprecedented in the fifty years of the Soviet state. The personnel of the Soviet Embassy [in Berlin] evacuated from Hitlerite Germany after the outbreak of World War II were in better condition than those created for Soviet representatives in Peking."

The Soviet leaders have launched a counteroffensive of their own against the Chinese "dogmatists" calling for the overthrow of Mao as a "renegade" and a return of China to the "socialist community." Towards this end the Soviet Union has consistently called for the convening of an international conference of the world's communist parties, a call that was repeated by its delegates and supporters at each and every Party Conference held in the people's and socialist republics. These efforts culminated in the fiasco of the Karlovy Vary Conference of April 24–26, 1967, which was boycotted not only by most communist parties, but also by such parties in power as that of Rumania, not to speak of those of Albania, China, and Yugoslavia.

The disarray in the once monolithic communist camp expanded tremendously the area of maneuverability of the eastern European leaders. The people's and socialist democracies gradually began to display a hitherto inconceivable posture of "independence" and economic nationalism. To the surprise of observers on both sides of the iron curtain, the greatest advantage of the battle between the colossi was taken by the once most servile of the Soviet satellites—Rumania. While retaining the essential features of monolithic party control, the Rumanian leaders—now mostly home-trained, nonintellectual figures of Rumanian ethnic origin and Greek Orthodox religious background—adopted a series of measures that appealed to the nationalistic instincts of the people they ruled. They stiffened their resistance to Soviet leadership in economic matters, manifested an ostentatious neutrality in the Sino-Soviet dispute and a conspicuous rapprochement with Albania, expanded their trade and cultural relations with the West, and adopted a series of spectacular de-Russification measures.

Paralleling to some extent the historical experience of Yugoslavia, the Rumanian "revolt" began with a refusal to sacrifice national economic goals of industrialization for the sake of enhancing the overall productive efficiency of the socialist bloc. At first strictly economic in nature, the revolt gradually acquired some political overtones that became increasingly disquieting to the Soviet leaders. The Rumanians began to question, then openly to challenge, Soviet supremacy in the two formal institutional organizations binding the people's and socialist democracies together, namely the Comecon and the Warsaw Pact.

While the Comecon or Cema (Council for Mutual Economic Assistance) was originally formed in 1949 as the Soviet answer to the Marshall Plan, it remained a dormant, basically paper organization until the late 1950s when Khrushchev revived it as the socialist world's challenge to the Common Market. Khrushchev's grandiose plan called for the multilateral integration and specialization of the Comecon countries' economies. The plan was favorably received by the industrially more advanced people's republics, especially Czechoslovakia and East Germany, which at the time were the most loyal followers of the Soviet leadership, but was vehemently opposed by the Rumanians, who argued that under the plan their country would remain primarily a supplier of raw materials, with an industry geared solely to the manufacture of petrochemical, lumber, food, and light industrial products.

Although the Rumanians agreed at the Moscow summit Comecon Conference of June 6–7, 1962, to support and abide by the "principles of international socialist division of labor," they subsequently made it clear that they expected these principles to be applied in accordance with the provisions of the Moscow declarations and/or statements of 1956, 1957, and 1960, namely "complete equality, respect for territorial integrity, national independence and sovereignty and noninterference in each other's internal affairs." The intransigence of the Rumanians led to the convening of another Moscow interparty conference (July 24–26, 1963), which shelved Khrushchev's plan and made possible the victory of bilateralism over multilateralism and of "national" industrialization over multi-lateral integration and specialization.

With the Comecon battle clearly won, the Rumanians proceeded more boldly to assert their right to "independence" in other spheres as well. On April 27, 1964, they issued a startling statement in which they attacked both the past and current policies of the U.S.S.R. and China and vigorously defended their right to protect the "national independence and sovereignty" of Rumania against any "superstate or extrastate" organizations. Justifying their dedication to the building of "socialism" in accordance with the conditions prevailing in their own country, they insisted on the equality of all parties. The 1964 statement declared:

> There are not and cannot be any "no-alternative" patterns and recipes [in the Communist world]. . . . No one can decide what is and what is not correct for other countries and parties. . . . There cannot be a "parent" party and a "son" party. . . . None is "superior" and none "subordinate" and none has a privileged position or can impose its line and opinions on other parties.

Rumania's predilection for ostentatious national independence gradually engulfed the Warsaw Pact as well. The Warsaw Treaty Organization (W.T.O.) was formally established on May 14, 1955, under the Treaty of Friendship, Cooperation, and Mutual Assistance, as the U.S.S.R.'s answer to NATO and its admission of the Federal Republic of Germany as a member. Although the treaty provided for a Unified Command of the armed forces of the signatory states, W.T.O. remained basically a Soviet-controlled body staffed and led by Soviet officers. It serves to a large extent as a cover for the "legalization" of the limitation of sovereignty imposed on its eastern European members and for the stationing of Soviet troops in East Germany, Hungary, and Poland.

When at the Twenty-third C.P.S.U. Party Congress (March 1966) Brezhnev hinted at the necessity of further strengthening the Warsaw Pact, the Rumanians reacted in an unusually belligerent manner. In a speech of May 7, 1966, marking the forty-fifth anniversary of the Rumanian Communist Party, Nicolae Ceauşescu declared that the "existence of blocs as well as the sending of troops to other countries is an anachronism incompatible with the independence and national sovereignty of peoples and normal relations among states." Paralleling President de Gaulle's policy toward the

Western military alliance, he emphasized implicitly that the Soviet policy of integration was tantamount to domination. The Rumanian Secretary General went further than any communist leader, including the Yugoslavs, in complaining about Soviet meddling in the internal affairs of other states under the aegis of the Comintern. In a scathing attack of past Soviet policy, he declared that the Soviet leaders, including Lenin, were responsible directly or indirectly for the blackest periods of Rumanian history in this century. Specifically, he accused the Soviet leaders, *inter alia,* of appointing non-Rumanians to positions of leadership in the Rumanian Party, of forcing the acquiescence of Rumanian Communists to Soviet claims to Bessarabia, and of throwing Rumania into German hands and onto the German side in World War II by ordering the Rumanian comrades to end their anti-Nazi activities in accord with the letter and spirit of the Nazi-Soviet Pact of 1939.

With respect to Soviet claims to loyalty in the name of proletarian internationalism, Ceauşescu vigorously defended the role and contribution of the "socialist fatherland" to the building of socialism and communism. Revising a basic tenet of Marxism-Leninism, he emphasized in the vein of Stalin's theory of the state that the "nation will undoubtedly continue for a long time to come to be the basis for our society's development throughout the entire period of building Socialism and Communism." Denouncing the attempts to declare the "socialist fatherland" incompatible with "socialist internationalism" as being "profoundly unjust and profoundly unscientific," he declared:

> The steady strengthening of each Socialist nation not only does not conflict with the interests of Socialist internationalism, but on the contrary corresponds fully to the interests of the cause of the workers' class, of the working people throughout the world, and of the general fight for the victory of Socialism and peace in the world.

This was a clear-cut challenge to the traditional identification of Soviet interests with the cause of socialism. It implied that the interests of the international proletariat were no longer intertwined exclusively with the interests of the U.S.S.R., but with the building of communism in each "socialist fatherland" apart.

With respect to Moscow's efforts to tighten up the Warsaw Pact and to make its members' armies more of a cohesive, integrated military force under Soviet command, the Rumanians demanded

that the command of the alliance be rotated among its members—
Bulgaria, Czechoslovakia, East Germany, Hungary, Poland, Rumania, the U.S.S.R., and nominally Albania—and that the use of
nuclear arms from the territory of a member state be subject to the
country's consent.

The countervailing pressure tactics of the Rumanians bore fruit
at the Bucharest meeting of the Warsaw Pact nations of July 1966.
While the two verbose declarations that emanated from the meeting
showed a ritualistic unanimous stand on the Vietnam issue—condemning American imperialist aggression and offering all help to
North Vietnam, including volunteers, "if requested"—they could
not hide the fact that the Rumanians again emerged victorious in
the sense that the W.T.O. was left unchanged. Having thus assured
continued independent control over their military forces, the Rumanian leaders went along with the Soviet line in declaring that the
dissolution of the Warsaw Pact must be preceded by the dissolution
of the "aggressive" NATO Pact.

As laudable as the Rumanian leaders' drive to assert their sovereignty and national independence is from the short-range point of
view and in its immediate impact on the Soviet empire in eastern
Europe, it may possibly prove negative in its long-range effects.
For in their attempt to enhance their popularity and buttress their
position by the twin approach of domestic de-Russification and
external desatellitization, the Rumanian communist leaders rekin-
dled the flames of nationalism—a source of potential danger in this
polyglot area of the world.

The revival of nationalism under the aegis of "national communism" or "socialist patriotism"—currently clearly discernible in
all the socialist and people's democracies—must be viewed with
guarded optimism as a mixed blessing at best. For, indeed, east
European nationalism, which has not in the past been distinguished
as a force tempered by the liberal spirit of tolerance and social
pluralism, is a two-, nay three-edged sword. It is a positive, cohesive
force in the sense that it provides a basis for the gradual weakening
and eventual termination of Soviet neocolonial domination in the
area. In fact, in many instances the manifestations of nationalism are
visibly focused on Russia. Tito's resistance in 1948, like that of
Gomulka in 1956, was as clearly anti-Russian in tone as was the
outraged explosion of nationalism in Hungary in October–November

1956. The Rumanian brand of nationalism, too, is to a large extent fed by opposition to Russia. Identifying themselves as the champions of the national interest and inheritors of the national past, the Rumanian leaders adopted a series of spectacular de-Russification measures and issued numerous statements with thinly disguised anti-Russian implications. They lost no opportunity, for example, to remind the Soviets about the unjust seizure of Bessarabia and northern Bukovina in 1940 under the provisions of the secret clauses of the Hitler-Stalin Pact. Preserving a residual claim to these territories, they even published some obscure statements by Marx condemning Russia's original incorporation of Bessarabia in 1810. Alluding to Moscow's attempt to create a new population balance in the Moldavian Soviet Socialist Republic by the forced transfer of thousands of Rumanians to Soviet Asia and their replacement with Great Russians, Ceauşescu openly deplored the "ruin" and "destruction" that characterized Soviet rule in the former Rumanian territories.

But east European nationalism is also a deeply divisive force, for its thrusts are frequently directed against a neighboring country. The basic Marxist assumptions notwithstanding, socialism and proletarian internationalism could not overcome the latent but clearly discernible historical disputes that plagued Rumanian-Hungarian relations over Transylvania, Hungarian-Czechoslovak relations over Slovakia, or Yugoslav-Bulgarian relations over Macedonia. In this respect, nationalism actually fragments east European opposition to Russia, enabling the Kremlin to perpetuate its influence through the time-tested device of *divide et impera*.

Finally, east European nationalism is a potentially destructive force since it is often manifested in a chauvinism directed against the coinhabiting national and ethnic minorities. This problem is especially acute in the multinational states like Yugoslavia, Czechoslovakia, and Rumania. The animosities that characterized Czech-Slovak, Rumanian-Hungarian, or Serbian-Croatian relations before the war—in the "bourgeois era"—are unfortunately still present in the "socialist era" in spite of the genuine efforts of the responsible leaders in these lands to overcome them. The "Jewish question," a major issue in most east European countries before the war, is no longer an important factor, the Nazis having "solved" it in the by now well-known manner. Although the remnant Jewish communities suffered in the wake of the concerted campaign against

Zionism and cosmopolitanism during both the Stalin and post-Stalin eras, anti-Semitism as such is officially outlawed in all the socialist and people's democracies. Nevertheless its effects are still discernible in the sense of the almost total aryanization of the governmental and party apparatuses and the restrictions imposed in some of these countries on the cultural-religious activities of the Jews, privileges not denied to other national and ethnic groups.

Positive as the contemporary manifestations of east European nationalism are, it would be foolhardy and dangerous to identify them as concrete steps toward the embracement of the West or the abandonment of the U.S.S.R. Although the east European countries have succeeded in asserting a greater degree of independence through the skillful exploitation of the opportunities offered, *inter alia,* by the Sino-Soviet dispute, they remain closely linked to the U.S.S.R. in many ways—*geographically,* by a common border; *militarily,* through the Warsaw Pact; *economically,* by Comecon and a network of bilateral and intrabloc arrangements. Moreover, these links are not exclusively a reflection of the realities of geography and Soviet power. The leaders of eastern Europe are closely linked to the U.S.S.R. by common bonds of ideology and long-range objectives and by the mutuality of national interests, especially with respect to possible German revanchism. But above all there is the implicit realization of the dual lesson of the Hungarian revolution: the readiness of Russia to crush both "bourgeois" and "socialist" elements alike in cases affecting her vital national interests, and the inability of a people's democratic regime to stay in power for long without the actual or potential support of the U.S.S.R.

Selected Bibliography

This bibliography was prepared on the basis of suggestions made by the contributing authors.

History

CURTISS, JOHN SHELDON. *The Russian Revolutions of 1917*. Princeton: Anvil (Van Nostrand), 1957.

DMYTRYSHYN, BASIL. *USSR: A Concise History*. New York: Scribner's, 1965.

DURANTY, WALTER. *Stalin and Co*. New York: Sloane, 1949.

FLORINSKY, MICHAEL T. *Russia: A History and an Interpretation*, 2 vols. New York: Macmillan, 1955.

KISCH, EGON ERWIN. *Changing Asia*. New York: Knopf, 1935.

MOSELY, PHILIP E. *The Soviet Union, 1922–1962*. New York: Praeger, 1962.

PRATT, H. and H. MOORE. *Russia: A Short History*. New York: John Day, 1947.

RANSOME, A. *Russia in 1919*. New York. Huebsch, 1919.

RESHETAR, JOHN S., JR. *A Concise History of the Communist Party of the Soviet Union*. New York: Praeger, 1960.

SCHAPIRO, LEONARD. *The Communist Party of the Soviet Union*. New York: Random House, 1965.

WEBB, S. and B. WEBB. *Soviet Communism*, 2 vols. New York: Scribner's, 1936.

WERTH, ALEXANDER. *Russia at War, 1941–1945*. New York: Dutton, 1964.

WOLFE, BERTRAM D. *Three Who Made a Revolution*. New York: Dial Press, 1948.

Theory, Government, and Politics

BARGHOORN, FREDERICK C. *Politics in the U.S.S.R.* Boston: Little, Brown, 1966.

BAUER, RAYMOND A., ALEX INKELES, and CLYDE KLUCKHOHN. *How the Soviet System Works*. New York: Vintage, 1961.

BRZEZINSKI, ZBIGNIEW and SAMUEL HUNTINGTON. *Political Power: U.S.A./U.S.S.R.* New York: Viking, 1963.

DANIELS, ROBERT V. *The Nature of Communism*. New York: Random House, 1962.

ENGELS, FRIEDRICH. *Anti-Duehring*. New York: International Publishers, 1966.

FAINSOD, MERLE. *How Russia Is Ruled*. Cambridge: Harvard University Press, 1963.

GRIPP, RICHARD C. *Patterns of Soviet Politics*. Homewood, Ill.: Dorsey Press, 1963.

LEONHARD, WOLFGANG. *The Kremlin Since Stalin*. New York: Praeger, 1962.

MARX, KARL. *Value, Price and Profit*. New York: International Publishers, 1952.

MEYER, ALFRED G. *The Soviet Political System*. New York: Random House, 1965.

MILLS, C. WRIGHT. *The Marxists*. New York: Dell, 1962.

MOORE, BARRINGTON, JR. *Soviet Politics: The Dilemma of Power*. Cambridge: Harvard University Press, 1950.

———. *Terror and Progress: U.S.S.R.* Cambridge: Harvard University Press, 1954.

SCHENK, FRITZ. "Enkel der Revolution," *SBZ Archiv*, East Berlin, No. 23, December 1966.

SCOTT, DEREK J. R. *Russian Political Institutions*. New York: Praeger, 1961.

SELSAM, HOWARD, and H. MARTEL. *Reader in Marxist Philosophy*. New York: New World, 1963.

SOLODOVNIKOV, A. "Ideology and the Crisis of Imperialism, Speaking Different Languages," *International Affairs*, Moscow, Nos. 10 and 11, 1963.

STALIN, JOSEPH V. *Problems of Leninism*. New York: International Publishers, 1934.

ULAM, ADAM. *The New Face of Soviet Totalitarianism*. Cambridge: Harvard University Press, 1963.

Economics

CAMPBELL, ROBERT W. *Soviet Economic Power*, 2d ed. New York: Houghton, Mifflin, 1966.

CARR, E. H. *The Soviet Impact on the Western World*. New York: Macmillan, 1947.

GERSCHENKRON, ALEXANDER. *Economic Backwardness in Historical Perspective*. Cambridge: Harvard University Press, 1962.

GRANICK, DAVID. *The Red Executive*. New York: Doubleday, 1954.

KHROMUSHIN, G. "The Anti-Soviet Nature of the Theory of 'Growing Similarity,'" *Kommunist*, Moscow, No. 11, July 24, 1965.

LABOR RESEARCH ASSOCIATION. *Labor Fact Book 17*. New York: New World, 1965.

LENIN, V. I. *New Economic Policy* (*Selected Works*, Vol. IX). New York: International Publishers, 1957.

LEWIS, ANTHONY. "The World Through Galbraith's Eyes," *New York Times Magazine*, New York, December 18, 1966.

NOVE, ALEC. *The Soviet Economy*. New York: Praeger, 1961.

SCHWARTZ, HARRY. *Russia's Soviet Economy,* 2d ed. New York: Prentice-Hall, 1954.

————. *The Soviet Economy Since Stalin.* Philadelphia: Lippincott, 1965.

SPULBER, NICOLAS. *The Soviet Economy.* New York: Norton, 1962.

WILES, PETER. *The Political Economy of Communism.* Cambridge: Harvard University Press, 1962.

————. "Will Capitalism and Communism Spontaneously Converge?" *Encounter,* London, June 1963.

Scientific, Social and Cultural

ALEXANDROVA, VERA. *A History of Soviet Literature.* New York: Doubleday, 1963.

BEREDAY, GEORGE Z. F., WILLIAM BRICKMAN and G. READ (eds.). *The Changing Soviet School.* New York: Houghton, Mifflin, 1960.

BEREDAY, GEORGE Z. F. and JEAN PENNAR (eds.). *The Politics of Soviet Education.* New York: Praeger, 1960.

BOWERS, FAUBION. *Broadway, U.S.S.R.: Ballet, Theatre and Entertainment in Russia Today.* Camden, N. J.: Thomas Nelson, 1959.

BRAVERMAN, H. *The Future of Russia.* New York: Grosset & Dunlap, 1965.

DE WITT, NICHOLAS. *Education and Professional Employment in the U.S.S.R.* Washington: National Science Foundation, 1961.

DUNN, S. P. and E. DUNN. *The Peasants of Central Russia.* New York: Holt, Rinehart & Winston, 1967.

FIELD, MARK G. *Doctor and Patient in Soviet Russia.* Cambridge: Harvard University Press, 1957.

GRAY, CAMILLA. *The Great Experiment: Russian Art, 1863–1922.* New York: Abrams, 1962.

HAYWARD, MAX and LEOPOLD LABEDZ (eds.). *Literature and Revolution in Soviet Russia, 1917–62.* New York: Oxford University Press, 1963.

HOUGHTON, NORRIS. *Return Engagement: A Postscript to "Moscow Rehearsals."* New York: Holt, Rinehart, & Winston, 1952.

LEYDA, JAY. *Kino: A History of the Russian and Soviet Film.* New York: Macmillan, 1960.

LONDON, IVAN D. "Towards a Realistic Appraisal of Soviet Science," *Bulletin of the Atomic Scientists,* Somerville, N. J., Vol. 13, No. 5, May, 1957.

MACE, DAVID and VERA MACE. *The Soviet Family.* New York: Doubleday, 1963.

MAKARENKO, ANTON S. *The Road to Life.* Moscow: Foreign Languages Publishing House, 1955.

MANDEL, WILLIAM M. *Russia Re-examined,* 2d rev. ed. New York: Hill and Wang, 1967.

RABINOWITCH, EUGENE. "Soviet Science: A Survey," *Problems of Communism,* Washington, Vol. 7, No. 2, March-April, 1958.

STALIN, JOSEPH. *Marxism and the National and Colonial Question.* New York: International Publishers, 1934.

U. S. SOCIAL SECURITY ADMINISTRATION. *A Report on Social Security Pro-*

grams in the Soviet Union. Washington: U. S. Department of Health, Education and Welfare, 1960.

YEVTUSHENKO, YEVGENY. *Bratsk Station and Other New Poems.* New York: Anchor, 1967.

Foreign Policy and International Communism

ASPATURIAN, VERNON V. "The Administration and Execution of Soviet Foreign Policy," *Foreign Policy in World Politics,* Roy C. Macridis (ed.). New York: Prentice-Hall, 1958.

BELOFF, MAX. *Foreign Policy of Soviet Russia, 1929–1941,* 2 vols. New York: Oxford University Press, 1947, 1949.

BORKENAU, FRANZ. *European Communism.* New York: Harper, 1953.

BROMKE, ADAM (ed.). *The Communist States at the Crossroads: Between Moscow and Peking.* New York: Praeger, 1965.

BRZEZINSKI, ZBIGNIEW K. *The Soviet Bloc,* 3rd ed. Cambridge: Harvard University Press, 1967.

CONQUEST, ROBERT. *Power and Policy in the U.S.S.R.* New York: St. Martin's, 1961.

DALLIN, ALEXANDER (ed.). *Soviet Conduct in World Affairs.* New York: Columbia University Press, 1960.

DALLIN, DAVID J. *Soviet Foreign Policy After Stalin.* Philadelphia: Lippincott, 1961.

DONNELLY, DESMOND. *Struggle for the World: The Cold War, 1917–1965.* New York: St. Martin's Press, 1965.

FISCHER, LOUIS. *The Soviets in World Affairs, 1917–1929,* 2 vols. Princeton: Princeton University Press, 1951.

FLEMING, D. F. *The Cold War and Its Origins,* Vol. I, 1917–1950, Vol. II, 1950–1960. New York: Doubleday, 1961.

FULBRIGHT, J. WILLIAM. *The Arrogance of Power.* New York: Random House, 1967.

GOODMAN, ELLIOT R. *The Soviet Design for a World State.* New York: Columbia University Press, 1960.

GRIFFITH, WILLIAM E. *The Sino-Soviet Rift.* Cambridge: M.I.T. Press, 1964.

HAMMOND, THOMAS. *Soviet Foreign Relations and World Communism. Selected Annotated Bibliography.* Princeton: Princeton University Press, 1965.

HORELICK, ARNOLD L. and MYRON RUSH. *Strategic Power and Soviet Foreign Policy.* Chicago: Chicago University Press, 1966.

KENNAN, GEORGE F. *Russia and the West Under Lenin and Stalin.* Boston: Little, Brown, 1961.

LABEDZ, LEOPOLD (ed). *International Communism After Khrushchev.* Cambridge: M.I.T. Press, 1965.

LOWENTHAL, RICHARD. *World Communism: The Disintegration of a Secular Faith.* New York: Oxford University Press, 1964.

MACKINTOSH, J. M. *Strategy and Tactics of Soviet Foreign Policy.* New York: Oxford University Press, 1963.

MILLS, C. WRIGHT. *The Causes of World War Three*. New York: Simon & Schuster, 1958.

MORRAY, JOSEPH P. *From Yalta to Disarmament*. New York: Monthly Review Press, 1961.

RUBINSTEIN, ALVIN Z. *The Foreign Policy of the Soviet Union*. New York: Random House, 1960.

SCHUMAN, FREDERICK L. *The Commonwealth of Man*. New York: Knopf, 1952.

SHULMAN, MARSHALL D. *Stalin's Foreign Policy Reappraised*. Cambridge: Harvard University Press, 1963.

Index

CONTRIBUTORS

RANDOLPH L. BRAHAM, Associate Professor of Political Science at The City College of The City University of New York, is author and editor of 12 books, including *Soviet Politics and Government* and *Documents on Major European Governments.* A specialist on Central Eastern Europe, he has undertaken a number of missions for the U.S. Office of Education and published numerous articles on various aspects of the people's and socialist democracies in leading journals and encyclopedias. Professor Braham has also taught at Fairleigh Dickinson University, Hofstra University, and Hunter College.

SAMUEL HENDEL, Professor of Political Science and Chairman of the Russian Area Studies Graduate Program at The City College of The City University of New York, is the author of *Charles Evans Hughes and the Supreme Court,* editor of *The Soviet Crucible,* and co-editor (with Hillman M. Bishop) of *Basic Issues of American Democracy.* Recipient of a Ford Faculty Fellowship and of a grant from the Inter-University Committee on Travel Grants, he has visited the U.S.S.R. three times. He has held visiting professorships in the graduate faculty of Columbia University and at Claremont Graduate School.

WILLIAM M. MANDEL, a specialist on the U.S.S.R. and translator of Soviet social science works into English, is the author of *The Soviet Far East and Central Asia; A Guide to the Soviet Union; Russia Re-Examined;* and numerous articles. One of the first post-doctoral Fellows in a Slavic Studies program at the Hoover Institution at Stanford University and a former Research Associate of the American Russian Institute of New York, he has taught contemporary Soviet social thought at the Free University of Berkeley, and is currently teaching in the Sociology Department, San Francisco State College. He has made four visits to the U.S.S.R. over a span of 35 years, including one stay of a year's duration.

ALFRED G. MEYER, Professor of Political Science, University of Michigan, is author of *The Incompatible Allies* (with Gustav Hilger); *Marxism: The Unity of Theory and Practice*; *Leninism*; *Communism*; and *The Soviet Political System.* He earned his Master's and Doctor's degrees at Harvard University. A former Assistant Director of the Russian Research Center, Harvard, and Director of the Research Program on the History of the C.P.S.U., Columbia University, Professor Meyer also taught at Harvard, the University of Washington, Michigan State University, Hunter College, and the Free University of Berlin.

WRIGHT MILLER, author and lecturer, has lived in the U.S.S.R. for some three years and traveled there extensively both privately and as a member of the British Embassy. He is the author of *Russians As People; The U.S.S.R.;* and *Russia: A Personal Anthology.* A former assistant of the BBC European Service with special Russian duties and former editor of *British Ally* (a British Government weekly published in the U.S.S.R.), Mr. Miller has also contributed articles and reviews to various collective works and scholarly journals.

URI RA'ANAN is Professor of International Politics at The Fletcher School of Law and Diplomacy, Tufts University, and Visiting Professor of Political Science at the Massachusetts Institute of Technology. He is also a Research Associate of the Center for International Studies of M.I.T. and an Associate of the Russian Research Center at Harvard. A graduate of Oxford University, he is author and co-author of a number of books and numerous articles on political science, international relations and diplomatic history.

FREDERICK L. SCHUMAN, Woodrow Wilson Professor of Government at Williams College, is the author of numerous works, including *The Cold War: Retrospect and Prospect*; *Government in the Soviet Union*; *Russia Since 1917*; *Soviet Politics*; and *International Politics*. His articles have appeared in scholarly and popular journals, yearbooks, and symposium volumes. Professor Schuman has also taught at the University of Chicago, Harvard, Cornell, Columbia, and California.

PETER WILES, Professor of Russian Social and Economic Studies, London University, is author of *Price, Cost and Output* and *Political Economy of Communism*. A former Fellow of All Souls College and New College, Oxford, he also served as Professor of Economics at Brandeis University and as Visiting Professor of Economics at The City College of The City University of New York.

BERTRAM D. WOLFE, author, lecturer, and teacher, is a specialist on the U.S.S.R. He has visited and lived in the Soviet Union and personally knew leading figures of the Bolshevik Revolution, including Bukharin, Molotov, Trotsky, and Stalin. Professor Wolfe is Senior Research Associate at Stanford University's Hoover Institution on War, Revolution, and Peace. Author of *Three Who Made a Revolution; Khrushchev and Stalin's Ghost*; *Communist Totalitarianism*; *Marxism: Ambiguous Heritage*; *Marxism: One Hundred Years in the Life of a Doctrine*; and *The Bridge and the Abyss: The Troubled Friendship of Maxim Gorky and V. I. Lenin,* he has also contributed numerous articles to scholarly and popular journals.

A Note on the Type

The text of this book was set on the Linotype in a face called *Times Roman*, designed by Stanley Morison for *The Times* (London), and first introduced by that newspaper in 1932.

Among typographers and designers of the twentieth century, Stanley Morison has been a strong forming influence, as typographical advisor to the English Monotype Corporation, as director of two distinguished English publishing houses, and as a writer of sensibility, erudition, and keen practical sense.